From Court to Capital

From Court to Capital

A Tentative Interpretation of the Origins of the Japanese Urban Tradition

Paul Wheatley & Thomas See

The University of Chicago
Chicago and London

PAUL WHEATLEY is the Irving B. Harris Professor in the Department of Geography and in the Committee on Social Thought of the University of Chicago.

THOMAS SEE is a visiting instructor in the Department of History of the University of Chicago.

The University of Chicago Press, Chicago 60637
The University of Chicago Press, Ltd., London
© 1978 by The University of Chicago
All rights reserved. Published 1978
Printed in the United States of America
82 81 80 79 78   987654321

Library of Congress Cataloging in Publication Data

Wheatley, Paul.
    From court to capital.

    Bibliography: p.
    Includes index.
    1. Cities and towns--Japan--History. 2. Urbaniza-
tion--Japan--History. 3. Japan--Capitol. 4. Sociology, Urban. I. See, Thomas, joint author. II. Title.
HT147.J3W44   301.36'3'0952   76-25637
ISBN 0-226-89430-4

知可良倍知

宇知比佐受宮弊能保留等多羅
知斯夜波波何手波奈例常斯良
奴国乃意久迦袁百重山越弖須
疑由伎伊都斯可母京師乎美武
等意母比都都迦多良比遠礼騰

To go up to the Palace (*miya*)
That radiates the brilliance of the sun lineage,
I parted from the hands of my mother
    Who had cared for me tenderly,
And, crossing many a mountain range,
I journeyed through the innermost recesses
    Of far distant lands,
Always talking about it and wondering
    When shall I see the City (*misato*)?

        [*Man'yōshū* 5, 886; attributed
          to Ōtomo Kumagori, A.D. 731]

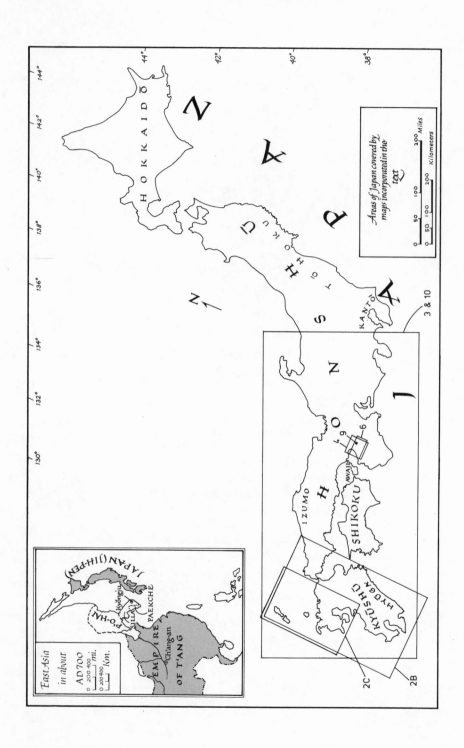

Contents

List of Figures

Preface

This study was motivated by a desire to learn more about the process that has been termed secondary urban generation. Most investigators of urban origins have pursued one of two lines of inquiry. Either they have sought to document and advance a rationale for the founding of cities under the aegis of already established centers of power and authority, or they have been concerned to elicit the processes and mechanisms subsumed under the term "primary urban generation," by which is meant the spontaneous rise of cities in a manner essentially independent of external influences from equally or more advanced cultures. Much less attention has been directed to those territories where the process, although internally generated rather than externally imposed, has been significantly influenced by the diffusion of culture traits from already urbanized regions.

Japan was one such realm of secondary urban generation that appeared especially likely to repay investigation. In the first place, its urban tradition was known to have been strongly influenced by developments on the East Asian mainland. Second, the earlier phases of the urbanization process were at least partially recoverable, thanks to the existence of three mutually complementary bodies of evidence. These were (1) a by no means negligible corpus of archeological materials accumulated over the past century; (2) an indigenous literary tradition, which, although severely archetyped and distorted, could yet be made to yield, if not always precise happenings, at least some of the cultural values that informed early Japanese society; and (3) a series of Chinese annalistic accounts of southern Japan that purported, not entirely without reason, to be both objective and contemporary.

We are not the first to have inquired into the origins of the Japanese city, nor have we drawn on hitherto unutilized sources; but we believe that our approach to the problem of urban genesis and our interpretation of the evidence differ significantly from those of our predecessors in the field. The measure of that difference will be apparent to anyone who cares to read either the specialized works of professional urbanists such as Kiuchi Shinzō and Yazaki Takeo or the more general studies of settlement history by scholars such as Fujioka Kenjirō, Kishiro Shūichi, Kita Teikichi, Murayama Shūichi, Ōi Jūjirō, Ōshima

Nobujirō, Satō Kijorō, and Yonekura Jirō, all of whom at one time or another have discussed the specifically Japanese manifestations of the transition from folk to urban society. On the other hand, our conceptualization of that transition and our method of resolving the problems it poses, although derived predominantly from recent Western scholarship, have a good deal in common with the approach adopted by certain contemporary students of the origin of the Japanese state. Our thinking on these matters has been especially strongly influenced by the writings of Egami Namio, Suzuki Takeo, Inoue Mitsusada, Mizuno Yū, and Gari Ledyard.

In several respects this is not an altogether propitious time at which to undertake an investigation of urban genesis in Japan. Since the end of World War II the traditional interpretation of early Japanese history, which had become sacrosanct as early as the end of the seventh century A.D. and which arguably reached its apogee in the work of Motoori Norinaga in the eighteenth, has become progressively less acceptable as a record of events. Once the cloak of sanctity that formerly invested the emperor and all that concerned him had been stripped away by the debacle of 1945, the traditional account of the origin of the Japanese state was seen for what it really was, an ideational framework contrived to validate the supremacy of the Yamato lineage and, through that lineage, the rights and prerogatives of the only imperial dynasty ever to have ruled over Japan. While this reevaluation has opened the way for a totally new interpretation of early Japanese history, there is at present only limited agreement as to the precise form that the new exposition should take. The result is that we have been unable to fit our interpretation of urban origins into an assured and tested framework of social and political history; instead we have been forced to accommodate it to a flux of competing formulations none of which as yet commands anything approaching total assent. This ambivalence about the social organization (in the broad sense) of Archaic and Ancient Japan assumes especial importance in view of our relational conception of urbanism as a patterning of the social process in its totality, with the corollary that urban genesis is to be conceived as a transformation of levels of sociocultural integration. It follows that our interpretation of Japanese urban origins can be only provisional, being no more securely founded than the theories of society on which it is based.

In what follows we have had to assume some familiarity on the part of the reader with early Japanese history. However, we have provided a broad outline of events, more or less as an *aide-mémoire* for those who need it; but this outline, like our conclusions, is subject to the general uncertainty that currently pervades the study of the earlier periods of Japanese history. The most we can claim is that, in presenting our own interpretation of urban origins in Japan, we have tried to give due weight to contrary opinions. Dogmatism is inappropriate at this stage in the investigation of urban genesis anywhere in the world, but it would be especially ill advised in the case of Japan.

As our title implies, this study is restricted specifically to what we judge to have been the formative phase of the urbanization process in Japan, that is, the period roughly from the beginning of the Christian era to the establishment of Heijō-kyō early in the eighth century. By this point in time not only had social differentiation attained a degree of complexity that in our terms qualified indisputably as urban, but the built form of the city had been cast in a continental mold that in subsequent ages would come to be regarded as classically Japanese. This is clearly the prescriptive point at which to halt our investigation. We have made no attempt to deal comprehensively with Heijō as representing a particular genre of built form, as epitomizing a culturally distinctive way of life, or as constituting the functional center of control in Nara society; adequate treatment of any one of these aspects would deserve a monograph to itself. What we hope we have provided is just enough information to enable the reader to appreciate the style of life and the form of city which resulted from the initial phases of the urbanization process which it has been our primary purpose to elucidate.

A very high proportion of the sources and expositions consulted in the preparation of this volume are cited only once and have no continuing relevance to the work as a whole; we have therefore dispensed with a formal bibliography. The reader who wishes to follow up any particular aspect of the subject can draw upon the *Notes and References*. These also serve as a repository for a good deal of illustrative and elaborative material relegated from the text in order to render the somewhat complicated narrative as readable as possible. Full bibliographic citations are furnished on first mention in each chapter; abbreviated titles appear thereafter. In similar fashion, appropriate scripts have been provided for certain Japanese and Chinese names and terms on their first occurrence in each chapter. Japanese words, with a few exceptions noted in the text, have been transcribed into English according to the modification of the Hepburn system used in the 1942 edition of *Kenkyusha's New Japanese-English Dictionary*, edited by Takenobu Yoshitaro (Harvard University Press). In dealing with technicalities of style arising from peculiarities of the Japanese language, we have, generally speaking, followed the practices recommended by Herschel Webb in *Research in Japanese sources: A guide* (Columbia University Press, 1965).

Finally, we wish to acknowledge with gratitude our indebtedness to the (to us) anonymous referees who provided trenchant commentaries on our work, to Mrs. T. H. Tsien whose elegant calligraphy graces our text, to Mr. John Hanner who executed the maps and diagrams, and to the Center for Far Eastern Studies at the University of Chicago which contributed to the cost of production of the illustrations.

From Court to Capital

1 The Nature of the Inquiry

Definitions dictate conclusions, and the answer to the question When and where did urban life originate? is inevitably determined to a large extent by the manner in which the concept of urbanity is explicated. For this reason it is a matter of great importance that the city[1] cannot be posited unambiguously as a first-order object of study, that is, as an entity functioning simultaneously as a unitary system at its own particular scale and as a component in a more inclusive system at a higher scale.[2] The nub of the problem is simply that the permanent built forms inhabited by dense aggregations of population which are all but universally recognized as theaters for the acting-out of a distinctive manner of life characterized as urban do not necessarily, or even predominantly, function as unitary systems. Nor is their organizational efficacy, except in a few highly unusual cases, restricted to their own confines. Rather, they are what Brian Robson has referred to as sets of low-scale objects each so jumbled that definition of its operational extent in terms of a single functional area is virtually impossible.[3]

In attempting to resolve this problem of operational definition it is necessary to distinguish between two components of the general concept of urbanism, namely, *urbanization* and the *urban process*. Whereas the former can be interpreted as denoting the rate of change in the proportion of urban dwellers to total population, which in practice means a change in the number and size of cities,[4] the urban process is here to be understood as a complex nexus of functionally interrelated, parallel-trending changes by means of which increasing numbers of people in society at large become involved in some way in the affairs of the city. Whether or not they live within its physical purlieus, they come under the influence, and more often then not the control, of its institutions. This means that an urbanized society subsumes both a spatially urban and a spatially rural component. On the one hand there is the city dweller proper, the resident within the urban enclave; and on the other there is the urbanized countryman, who lives in terms of the city but not in it, who is bound to the city (or perhaps more accurately to the institutions of state located within the city)

3

in an asymmetrical structural relationship that requires him to produce in one
form or another a fund of rent, and who is often referred to as a peasant *sensu
stricto*.[5] But it is only within the walls or other boundary of the city that
there is a measure of congruence between urbanization and the urban process as
these concepts are defined here.[6] Or, phrased differently, urbanized society in
its totality is to be contrasted not with that of the surrounding countryside but
with pre- or non-urbanized society.

An important implication of this perspective on the city is that, from the
point of view of the student of urban genesis, the urban process can be regarded
as the systemic transformation of one qualitatively distinct level of sociocultural integration into another with a higher degree of complexity, which in turn
enhances its potentialities for adaptation.[7] In broadly cultural terms the generalized integrative patterns involved in this transmutation of a folk into an
urbanized society are those of relatively egalitarian, ascriptive, kin-based
societies at the simpler level and stratified, politically structured, territorially defined societies as the more complex resultants of the process. In equally
broad ecological terms they are levels, respectively, of reciprocally integrated
developed village-farming efficiency and of redistributive integration about an
administrative and ceremonial center that is distinguished from other settlements
of the time by the presence of an assemblage of public ceremonial structures.[8]

The transformation between these particular levels of integration can be
effected by means of two distinct and, for all analytical and most practical purposes, unrelated processes, namely, *urban imposition* and *urban generation*.
Whereas the first of these processes reflects an extension of symbolic and organizational patterns developed in one territory into another, the latter signifies
a progressive differentiation of autonomous institutional spheres and the emergence of specialized collectivities and roles as a response to societal pressures
generated internally within a specific region.[9]

Urban imposition constitutes a mode of urban diffusion that is virtually
inseparable from the expansion of empire, and it is usually accompanied by the
establishment of an administrative organization designed to sustain the value
system of the colonial power, the imposition of the legal definitions of property

current in the colonists' homeland, and the introduction into the dependent territory of certain sectors of the metropolitan economy. To that extent it can be regarded as a mode of systems interaction, in particular of compound systems interaction.[10] By this it is meant that three modes of interaction are involved simultaneously — or are at least potentially involved. In the first mode, each system, although itself comprising a complex compound set of relationships,[11] acts and responds as a unit. This type of interaction might represent reasonably accurately, for example, the operation of political linkages at government level between the colonizing power and its dependent territory, though Parsons and Shils, by referring to social collectivities as actors, would seem to extend its applicability to analysis of a very much wider range of social relationships.[12] In the second mode of interaction it is the components of the discrete systems (rather than the systems themselves) that act directly on each other in a manner that would seem to represent fairly accurately the most widely held conception of the social system. The third mode of interaction, which is probably less common in the colonial experience than the two preceding processes, operates when one system acts as a unit on one or more of the constituent components of another system. A representative example might be the founding by the central government of the metropolitan power (symbolizing one system in its entirety) of a fortified city (a component of the second system) for frontier defense in a colony. A cursory review of the admittedly obscure and ambivalent evidence available for the study of urban genesis in ancient Japan indicates that, though the imposition of authority patterns from the Korean peninsula almost certainly played some part in the process, the three modes of interaction described above, either singly or in combination, were not the primary agents bringing about the transformation from folk to urban society.

Urban generation, the only alternative to urban imposition as a means of effecting a transformation of this sort, is a mode of processual change subsumed within the more inclusive field of social differentiation and stratification. If urban imposition is viewed as a case of systems interaction, then urban generation is to be regarded as a form of systemic evolution. At one extreme of the spectrum of systemic changes encompassed by this term are those situations in which cities have arisen when some particular conjunction of internal forces has induced spontaneous readjustments in institutional forms and relationships. In such circumstances the transition *ideally* may be conceived as the structural transformation of a closed system, though it needs no emphasis that, in the real world, social systems are seldom, if ever, of the closed type. Even ancient Sumer, the region with an undisputed claim to historical priority in the initiation of the process of urbanization, was by no means immune to external influences during and immediately preceding the emergence of its earliest urban forms. In fact, what entitles an evolving society at an appropriate level of complexity to be characterized as an instance of primary urban generation is not its degree of systemic closure so much as the fact that none of the external cultures able to influence its development is significantly more complex than the particular society under consideration.[13] Although opinions may vary as to precisely which communities at one time or another have generated urban forms in this manner, there is a virtual consensus among scholars in the field that the Middle East was the first region to experience this quantum transformation of society. There might be a divergence of views, though, as to whether Mesopotamia and Egypt should be treated as separate manifestations of a single process or as discrete regions. Other realms of primary urban generation on which there would be very substantial scholarly agreement are the Indus Valley, the North China plain, Middle America (where again there might be a division of opinion as to whether two realms or one have been involved), the central Andes, and — the realm on which there would probably be least agreement — the Yoruba territories of southwestern Nigeria.

On the peripheries of these core regions of primary urban generation, particularly in those sectors where political jurisdiction has lagged behind cultural imperialism, cities have often arisen as a result of a secondary diffusion of cultural traits that has stimulated the evolution of society toward an urban level of integration. In such circumstances the process has still been one of urban generation rather than of imposition, but it has been a generational process stimulated by the diffusion of cultural traits from already urbanized regions. It must be emphasized that it has been the diffusion of individual traits that

has effected this transformation, not, as is true of urban imposition, the transference of the total set of functionally interrelated institutions that constitutes the city. In other words, it is not the artifact of the city itself that
has been diffused but particular institutional components of an urbanized society.[14] It was with an a priori conception of Japan as a realm of secondary urban
generation that we began this study, and succeeding chapters will reveal the
extent to which our preconceptions were confirmed when tested against the evidence.

The operational view of urbanism as a level of sociocultural integration
that we have advanced in the preceding paragraphs (as opposed to the more commonly essayed attempt to represent the city as something approaching a first-
order object of study) implies that the city in the narrow material sense of the
built form cannot properly be isolated as a functional operating unit from the
totality of the society of which it is simultaneously both mirror and image, both
creator and created, elixir and excipient, cause and effect. This is, of course,
only another way of saying that the city is not merely an aggregation of population of critical size and density but also an organizing principle, an agent of
regional integration, in short, a creator of effective space.[15] There is, however, a significant exception to this generalization during the initial phase of
urban imposition. When it is first established, the colonial city is essentially
a subsystem of the metropolitan urban system that happens to have been transferred to a dependent territory. Its links with its environing territory are by
definition rudimentary, so that the influence of its institutions necessarily
ceases at the city wall. Only with the passage of time does a combined process
of political absorption and cultural diffusion, often with assistance from the
socially consolidatory mechanism of the market, induce a mutual interdependence
between city and country. From that phase of development onwards, generated city
and imposed city are structurally homologous, though significant ethnic and other
distinctions within their populations may persist for many generations.

The emphasis that we have accorded the city as an organizing principle, and
the concomitant relational view of urbanism as a hierarchical patterning of society in its totality, have important implications for the study of urban genesis,

particularly insofar as primary and secondary urban generation are concerned.
The creation of effective space through the continuous interaction of social
process and built form, wherever and whenever it has occurred, has necessitated
the restructuring of the functional subsystems of society, afforded opportunities
for the concentration of power, wealth, and prestige, and initiated the evolution
of an urban-orientated Great Tradition. At the same time, the engrossing of
power and authority by institutions located within the city has ensured that
relations between subsidiary settlements, hitherto managed directly by the participants, are now mediated, notionally if not always physically, through the
focally situated city. In other words, the generated city in its earlier phases
was a city-state, with the clear implication that city and state were coeval and,
indeed, constituted different-scale manifestations of the same processes.
Although the institutions of power and authority were usually located physically
in the built form of the city, their organizational capacities extended far
beyond the physical limits of that form; and it is debatable whether in the study
of urban genesis it is at present more profitable to focus the inquiry on the
area of functional interaction in its totality or to concentrate on the
restricted sociopolitical core within which the organizing institutions were
aggregated: in short, whether the limited system (the city) or the extended system (the state) is the more manageable category of investigation.[16] In the following chapters we have opted for the former, though almost every paragraph will
attest to the close functional interdependence of the two systems.

URBAN GENERATION AS ECOLOGICAL TRANSFORMATION

The Ecological Complex

In a previously published work entitled *The Pivot of the Four Quarters*[17] one of
the present authors attempted to interpret the process of urban genesis in terms
of Duncan and Schnore's theory of the ecological complex,[18] a formulation which
itself owes a good deal to Durkheim's *De la division du travail social.*[19] The
functionally interrelated basic components of this complex are environment, population, technology, and social organization, with the last conceived as "an
adaptation to the unavoidable circumstance that individuals are interdependent

and that the collectivity of individuals must cope with concrete environmental
conditions."[20] On this view the study of urban generation involves, in Duncan
and Schnore's words, "the precise technological, demographic, and environmental
conditions under which various urban forms of organizations may be expected to
appear and — once established — to develop at given rates."[21] In other words,
in the complex sequence of interdependent processual changes that eventuated in
the emergence of the ceremonial and administrative center, it is social organization that is to be regarded as the dependent variable. From this it follows that
the central thrust in any attempt to reach an understanding of the process of
urban generation must be directed toward isolating those factors which, generally
throughout all realms of primary urban generation or specifically in prescribed
instances, are capable of inducing social differentiation.[22] As a classificatory
concept, differentiation

> describes the ways through which the main social functions or the major
> institutional spheres of society become dissociated from one another,
> attached to specialized collectivities and roles, and organized in rel-
> atively specific and autonomous symbolic and organizational frameworks
> within the confines of the same institutionalized system.
>   Specialization is manifest first when each of the major institu-
> tional spheres develops, through the activities of people placed in
> strategic roles within it, its own organizational units and complexes,
> and its specific criteria of action. The latter tend to be more con-
> gruent with the basic orientations of a given sphere, facilitating the
> development of its potentialities — technological innovation, cultural
> and religious creativity, expansion of political power or participa-
> tion, or development of complex personality structure.
>   Secondly, different levels or stages of differentiation denote the
> degree to which major social and cultural activities, as well as cer-
> tain basic resources — manpower, economic resources, commitments —
> have been disembedded or freed from kinship, territorial and other
> ascriptive units. On the one hand, these "free-floating" resources
> pose new problems of integration, while on the other they may become
> the basis for a more differentiated social order which is, potentially
> at least, better adapted to deal with a more variegated environment.[23]

In the *Pivot* an attempt was made to document the disjunctive processes of
this sort that were involved in the formation of the earliest urban forms, primarily on the North China plain but also in the other main realms of urban generation. Given the enormous disparities and deficiencies in the evidence available for the several regions, the analysis was inevitably deficient in both
breadth of coverage and depth of analysis. More fundamentally, however, the ecological approach incorporated a particular functionalist bias of a type better
adapted to the analysis of distributional than of structural change. It was

usually more readily able, for example, to explicate a change in the proportion
of the total labor force engaged in craft activities than it was to provide
explanatory insights into the transmutations from patriarchalism to patrimonialism, chiefdom to state, or village to city. Generally speaking, it was more
likely to throw light on the elaboration of an existing partial structure (a type
of subgroup, a role, a social norm, a cultural value) than on the appearance or
elimination of such a structure. This, of course, is only one manifestation of a
difficulty inherent in virtually all functional analysis, namely, that most
changes exert a stronger and more immediate effect on subgroups than on the total
system, but in the *Pivot* it imparted to the analysis a static quality somewhat at
variance with the professed aim of the book to investigate a structural transformation between levels of sociocultural integration. Nor was the ecological
approach as developed in the *Pivot* especially helpful in explaining why the
transformation occurred only in certain of the rather numerous regions that had
seemingly attained the level of integration requisite for take-off into urbanism.
Was there an unsuspected component or relationship in the simpler (preurban)
integrative systems of those regions where urban generation did take place (as
opposed to those where it did not) that rendered the process inevitable? Or was
it initiated by a presently undiscerned triggering mechanism, and, if so, did it
operate from only one threshold of integration or from a range of thresholds? To
these and similar types of questions the *Pivot* provided at best only qualified
answers. Although it did afford some understanding of the kinds and degrees of
structural differentiation (or fusion) of the functional subsystems of society at
successive levels of integration[24] — the tendency to fuse pattern-maintenance
and adaptive (so-called economic) functions at the folk level of integration,
integrative and adaptive functions at the level of the ceremonial-administrative
center, and goal-attainment and adaptive functions during the expansionist phase
of incipient empire — it is probably true to say that the analysis ultimately
foundered on the stubborn certitude that social needs do not automatically induce
the emergence of responsive social mechanisms, nor does a functional explanation
of a partial structure constitute a sufficient explanation of its existence. In
the old Aristotelian phraseology, to assume that the functions of a partial

structure are the causes of its existence is to explain by final rather than
efficient causes, a logical solecism against which Homans and Schneider have
warned us in more recent time.[25]

The Flannery Model

Since the *Pivot* was written, Kent Flannery has carried the argument forward by
suggesting how and when the process of state (and, concomitantly, on our definition urban) generation may have been initiated, in short, how the transforma-
tional triggering mechanism may have worked.[26] His argument, in abbreviated
form, is as follows. If human society is postulated as a class of living system
on the model proposed by J. G. Miller,[27] then the state can be regarded as a system whose well-nigh incredible complexity can be comprehended in terms of two
concepts: *segregation*, by which is denoted the degree of internal differentiation and specialization of its subsystems, and *centralization*, by which is meant
the intensities and strengths of the linkages between the various subsystems and
the highest-order controls operating in a particular society. The investigation
of state/urban origins then resolves itself into an attempt to elicit the principles of operation of the diverse processes subsumed under these two terms.
Flannery further discriminates among the *processes* themselves, the *mechanisms* by
which they operate, and the *socioenvironmental stresses* which select for those
mechanisms. These are shrewdly conceived distinctions; for, whereas both processes and mechanisms are viewed as universal in their application, the socioenvironmental stresses are specific to particular regions and societies and thus provide a tool with which to probe the elusive problem of why urban generation
should have occurred in so few of the regions technologically equipped to support
it. The socioenvironmental conditions envisaged by Flannery include both components of the ecological complex that formed the basis of analysis in the *Pivot*
and an array of extracultural factors, such as the managerial imperatives of various adaptive activities, which in the earlier work were adduced as factors
influencing the dependent variable.

The model of the ecotype adopted by Flannery as a framework for his analysis
is specified as

11

a series of subsystems arranged hierarchically, from lowest and most specific to highest and most general. Each subsystem is regulated by a control apparatus whose job is to keep all the variables in the subsystem within appropriate goal ranges — ranges which maintain homeostasis and do not threaten the survival of the system . . . On all levels, the social control apparatus compares output values not merely with subsistence goals but with ideological values, the demands of deities and ancestral spirits, ethical and religious propositions — the human population's "cognized model" of the way the world is put together. The highest, most abstract, and most unchanging of these propositions lie in the highest-order (or "governmental") controls, which deal in policy more often than commands.[28]

Within the limits of this hierarchy of subsystems, the controls exercised by higher-order institutions extend to the output of lower-order institutions but not to the variables that they regulate, although in the event that a lower-order control fails to keep its subordinate variables within their appropriate ranges, the control apparatus at the next-higher level may be activated. In terms of the Theory of Integrative Levels, the hierarchy of subsystems exemplifies the law that, for an organization at any given level, its mechanism is to be investigated at the level below and its purpose at the level above.[29] Or, phrased differently: A comprehensive evaluation of any organizational structure must be conducted at three levels: its own, where the mechanics of its operation are most directly apparent; the one below, which is the analytical level at which attention is transferred from the whole to the parts; and the one above, at which the organization under consideration becomes part of some more complex system. This inclusion in the field of analysis of the highest of the three levels implies some concern with purpose, not purpose with the teleological import ridiculed by Ben Franklin (see note 25) but, rather, purpose conceived as vectors built into organizations and manifesting themselves in the manner in which higher levels furnish direction to lower.[30]

Adopting Slobodkin's formulation that the stress induced by variables transgressing their assigned goal ranges can bring about *either* the disruption of a system *or* its progressive evolution,[31] Flannery proposes that the processes of segregation and centralization are brought about by the operation of two evolutionary mechanisms, which he terms, respectively, *promotion* and *linearization*.[32] Promotion occurs when an institution rises from its original place in the control hierarchy to a position at a higher level. During this translation, either a new

entity is born through the amplification and elaboration of a particular role
within a preexisting institution, or an already developed institution becomes
less system-serving (special-purpose) and more self-serving (general-purpose).
Both occurrences are characteristic of evolutionary advance, primarily through
their contributions to the process of segregation. Linearization, by contrast,
makes its main contribution to the process of centralization. It is said to
occur when lower-order controls are permanently (or at least repeatedly) bypassed
by higher-order controls, a situation likely to arise when a lower-order institution fails for some critical period adequately to retain its variables within
appropriate goal ranges.

In addition to these two functional mechanisms, the model also incorporates
three dysfunctional mechanisms — or systemic pathologies, as Rappaport calls
them[33] — each of which can subject a system to additional stress and possibly,
through the development of positive-feedback loops, to increased segregation and
centralization. The first of these pathologies is *usurpation*, defined as "the
elevation of the purpose of one's own subsystem to a position of pre-eminence in
a more inclusive system."[34] It is induced by the proclivity of promoted institutions to serve their own interests rather than those of society at large. The
second pathology is *meddling*, the direct subjection to a higher-order control of
the variables properly regulated by lower-order controls.[35] It occurs when linearization impairs the effectiveness of the controls that insulate one subsystem
from perturbations in another. The third pathology is *hypercoherence*, which may
be regarded as an excessive degree of centralization. It is a potentially unsta-
ble condition, said to exist when institutions or subsystems are deprived of the
autonomy proper to their status in the total system. As Flannery puts it, ". . .
one by one, they are coupled more closely to each other and/or to the central
hierarchical control until, like an old-fashioned string of Christmas tree lights
set in linear sequence, change in one does in fact affect all the others too
directly and rapidly."[36] Possibly the most common way in which hypercoherence
occurs is through uncontrolled meddling. Needless to say, for any system to
function effectively, it must achieve a level of integration appropriate to its
operational needs; so the central problem inherent in an attempt to diagnose

13

hypercoherence is that of recognizing the signs denoting an excessive deficiency in institutional autonomy.

In the succeeding chapters of this report the origin of urban forms in Japan will be explicated within the broad ecological framework adapted in the *Pivot* but with the crucial refinements of the Flannery model adduced, whenever possible, to account for specificities of time and place. The discrimination which this model requires between mechanisms and processes, which are universal, and socioenvironmental selection pressures, which are local, not only casts the problem of the so-called prime movers in a new light but also focuses attention on systemic relationships between variables rather than on the variables themselves or on simple matter and energy exchanges.[37] In this type of interpretation socioenvironmental conditions and managerial imperatives are less direct mechanisms of cultural evolution than selectors for one of those mechanisms — or indeed for one of the pathologies. Population increases or organized warfare, for example, in any particular instance are to be regarded not so much as prime movers but rather as socioenvironmental settings exerting potentially strong pressures for linearization and meddling, the end results of which are likely to be increased centralization. But linearization and meddling could both have been selected for by any one or more of a whole range of alternative socioenvironmental factors. A further implication of the model is the importance for evolutionary advance of shifts in the hierarchical organization of decision-making procedures, from which it follows that information-processing and ritual activities are likely to play a prominent part in any reasonably comprehensive interpretation of urban genesis. From this point of view, in fact, the city can be regarded as a multichanneled instrument for the facilitation of human communication. The secular aspects of the enormously complex flows of messages that constitute the communications network of even the smallest city have already been studied by Richard Meier,[38] but the role of religious ritual as a regulatory mechanism deserves a few additional words of explanation.

Ritual as a Regulatory Mechanism

In the *Pivot* it was argued that, although religion was not to be considered a prime mover in urban generation, it did merit special consideration as a validatory and control mechanism.[39] Several reviewers were critical of this interpretation, which was, in truth, but poorly construed and its implications inadequately elucidated.[40] However, a recent paper by Roy Rappaport[41] has provided a framework within which to elaborate on this theme.

Rappaport defines ritual as "conventional acts of display through which one or more participants transmit information concerning their physiological, psychological, or sociological states either to themselves or to one or more of their participants."[42] It is, therefore, an important component in the communications network of a society, transmitting information through both its content and its occurrence. Through its content it can convey information relative to social and political arrangements, and, as a public accounting device, it can divulge the states of systemic variables not otherwise discernible. Through its occurrence it can transmit a binary signal capable both of reducing the ambiguity inherent in continuous, analogic information and of facilitating the transduction of information between unlike systems. Specifically religious ritual, in addition to fulfilling these functions, always incorporates a reference, explicit or implicit, to the sacred, a quality which Rappaport takes to signify the "unquestionable truthfulness imputed by the faithful to unverifiable [but equally unfalsifiable] propositions."[43] Although statements strictly of this type have no material referents, which is of course why they are capable of neither verification nor falsification, they may extend their sanctity to propositions that do have such referents through association either in rituals or, more commonly, in discursive structures, such as theology. And the propositions sanctified in this way may be of direct importance to the regulation of society. In other words, sanctification diffuses outward from purely religious contexts to certify the truthfulness not only of ultimate sacred propositions but also of statements concerning all the subsystems, both functional and structural, that make up society.

As Rappaport points out, human social organization is genetically underspecified.[44] The particular control mechanism operating in a specific situation is generally only one of a number that could maintain an appropriate degree of systemic coherence; and man, who is endowed with an adaptability that enables him to

learn a whole range of social conventions, is quite capable of recognizing the
essential arbitrariness of the set of conventions under which he does in fact at
any time live. What sanctity can, and does, do is prescribe the options that the
integrity of the particular social organization permits or demands. In Rappaport's apt phrase, sanctification transforms the arbitrary into the necessary.
Indeed, it often goes farther than that and castigates recalcitrance as sacri-
lege.[45] In short, it reinforces the conventions that regulate society. This is
an especially important function if, as Rappaport suggests, higher-order controls
(defined in terms of the greater inclusiveness attributed to them) are of a
higher logical type, so that "Gödel's theorem, or something like it, may operate
between controls on different levels."[46] As the output reference values of a
regulatory mechanism derive not from the operation of that mechanism itself but
from one at a level above (cf. the Theory of Integrative Levels cited on p. 12,
above, and the accompanying note 29), the reference value of a lower-order control has to be deduced from the "cognized model"[47] of a higher-order control.
It is, therefore, clearly desirable that the purposes of higher-order systems
should be diffused through, and, as it were, internalized by, lower-order systems
so as to subvert possible attempts by social groups to "promote" (in the technical sense defined on p. 12) their own interests to positions of dominance in
higher-level systems. In Rappaport's forthright language, "Sanctity helps to
keep subsystems in their places."[48] Within levels of organization, moreover,
sanctification of conventions is a potentially efficacious instrument for conflict resolution, for it defines the requirements of society as the ultimate
needs of the individual. Or, as the *Pivot* concluded, "[The great ceremonial cen-
ters] functioned as instruments for the dissemination through all levels of society of beliefs which, in turn, enabled the wielders of political power to justify
their goals in terms of the basic values of that society, and to present the
realization of class-directed aims as the implementation of collectively desirable policies."[49]

The function of rituals in the process of social change is also worthy of
comment, especially since this volume is concerned primarily with a particular
manifestation of one of the most important social transformations in the history

of the world. From the present point of view, the process that we shall attempt to document in the following chapters can be conceived as the transmutation of a congeries of communities in which sanctity was a functional equivalent of political power to a society in which authority commanded little power but claimed great sanctity, and, finally, at the close of our analysis, to a polity in which power and sanctity were mutually reinforcing. Given the fact that technological development commonly invests authority with increasingly powerful instruments of coercion, it is not surprising that the processual change outlined here should have correlated fairly closely with advances in technology. Generally speaking, the more sophisticated the technological base, the more powerful the locus of authority and the less need it has for sanctity. But at this point in the progression with which we are here specifically concerned the relationship between sanctity and power was transformed. Whereas in the earlier phases of the process authority had been validated by its association with the sacred, authority now manipulated sanctity as an instrument for the acquisition and retention of power. Whereas regulation by means of religious ritual had formerly permitted the control of sizable populations in the absence of focused power, now the wielders of power had discovered how to employ sanctity to validate the use of force. In the heyday of the Yamato court, to say nothing of later periods of Japanese history, it is only too evident that the Japanese rulers had mastered the art of cloaking power in a garb of sanctity.

2 The Rise of the Ceremonial Center
(Prior to the Fifth Century A.D.)

The climacteric transformation of society that eventuated in the emergence of the Japanese city was apparently initiated during the first four centuries of the Christian era. As literacy is itself a common, though by no means necessary, by-product of such processual change, it is not surprising that the earlier phases of the transformation were not chronicled factually and directly in indigenous writings. Indeed, the only contemporary literary evidence relating to the period is that incorporated in certain Chinese dynastic histories. This can be complemented by a not inconsiderable array of archeological finds from the soil of Japan itself, including a few extant inscriptions. Third, two chronicles compiled in Japan early in the eighth century preserve archetyped versions of the country's past, selected for the purpose of validating the authority of the ruling house. Both works include genealogies of ancient rulers, which, regrettably, become consonant with the information in the Chinese histories only in the fifth century A.D. Indeed, the implications of these three main corpora of evidence for the emergence of the Japanese city and state are not always easily reconcilable, and for that reason they are here evaluated separately before being combined into what can at best be an only partial account of the process of urban genesis.

THE CHINESE EVIDENCE

The earliest descriptions, as opposed to bare mentions, of the Japanese islands are to be found in two Chinese standard histories, that of the Later Han dynasty (*Hou-Han Shu* 後漢書)[1] and that of the Three Kingdoms (*San-Kuo Chih* 三國志).[2] Although the Han dynasty (A.D. 25-220) preceded the period of the Three Kingdoms (220-280), its official history was compiled later than that of the Three Kingdoms. In the former work the so-called Biographical sections (列傳), in which the accounts of Japan are incorporated, were prepared by Fan Yeh 范曄 in the second quarter of the fifth century. When Fan was executed for having committed a state offense, his work was suppressed and was not formally made available until it was printed in the decade 994-1004. The *San-Kuo Chih*, by contrast, was completed as a private venture by Ch'en Shou 陳壽 not later than 289, was furnished, on imperial order, with a commentary by P‘ei Sung-chih 裴松之 early in the fifth century, and was presented to the throne in 429. The work was ultimately printed between 1000 and 1002. It recounts the histories of the three states that divided China among themselves on the dissolution of the Han, namely, Wei 魏 (220-266), Shu 蜀 (221-264), and Wu 吳 (222-280). The Wei section of the work alone incorporates a short concluding chapter on foreign peoples, including groups in Japan.

Because the relevant parts of the *Hou-Han Shu* were completed a century and a half after those of the *San-Kuo Chih* and because the phrasing of passages relating to Japan is often similar, if not identical, in the two works, it has often been assumed that the Han account was derived from Ch‘en Shou's history of the Wei.[3] It is true that Fan Yeh, writing toward the middle of the fifth century, was almost certainly cognizant of a work that had been presented to the throne a few years earlier; but it is equally evident that he made some effort to select, from whatever records were to hand, materials relating specifically to the Han dynasty and to exclude those of subsequent periods. That records other than the *San-Kuo Chih* were available is attested by Fan Yeh's use of certain materials not included in that work, but the manner of their preservation and the conditions of their use are today unknown. It is not impossible that similarities in the two texts arose not simply because one author plagiarized the other but rather because both relied for their information on a third source or collection of sources.[4] We cannot be certain of the care with which the texts of Fan Yeh and Ch‘en Shou were transmitted by successive copyists until they were finally printed at the beginning of the second millennium, but suffice it to say that other texts with similar histories did often retain a high degree of accuracy.

A third Chinese work which appears to have contained references to Japan in early times was the *Wei Lüeh* 魏略, generally attributed to Yü Huan 魚豢, who was more or less contemporary with Ch‘en Shou. The text of this compilation is no longer extant, but quotations from it have been preserved in at least half a dozen later works[5] and have occasionally been adduced by scholars in support of particular points of interpretation. For the sake of completeness, mention must also be made of the *Chin Shu* 晉書, compiled by Fang Hsüan-ling 房玄齡 and

others in 635 and dealing with the period 265–419, but its account of Japan adds
nothing at all to the information contained in the *Hou-Han Shu* and the *San-Kuo
Chih*. The presumed relations between the *Hou-Han Shu*, the *San-Kuo Chih* (*Wei
Chih*), the *Wei Lüeh*, and later Chinese histories containing accounts of Japan are
depicted graphically in figure 1.[6]

The Testimony of the *Hou-Han Shu* (chüan 115, fols. 16 verso - 19 recto)[7]
The inhabitants of Japan known to Fan Yeh — certainly by report only — were
referred to simply as *·*Jwi̯e* 倭.[8] They allegedly comprised upwards of a hundred
entities characterized as *kuo* 國.[9] In Chinese history this term has had a broad
connotation, ranging from a vague implication of "country" through the somewhat
more specific concepts of "nation," "state," or "kingdom" to the relatively precise signification of "capital" and even "dynasty." Generally speaking, the
chroniclers of Han times seem not to have used it in connection with societies
totally without some manifestations of hereditary inequalities and territorially
defined institutions. The term is noticeably absent, for example, in Ssŭ-ma
Ch'ien's 司馬遷 account in the *Shih Chi* 史記 of the Southwestern Tribes
西南夷, some of whom are described specifically as "lacking regular [sc. per-
manent] settlements and chieftains 毋常處毋君長,"[10] but a few folios later
in the same work *kuo* is conjoined with *Śi̯en-dʻuok 身毒 (= Sindhu), the name
currently used for India.[11] Similarly, *kuo* was seldom, if ever, adduced in connection with the Lặc (*Lâk 雒) tribes of the Tong-king delta,[12] but was applied
to numerous polities in southern Indochina at least as early as the middle of the
third century A.D.[13] and — what is perhaps more relevant to the present study —
to the agricultural communities of southern Korea at the very time the Chinese
were first becoming aware of the existence of the Japanese islands. In the present instance, the term is probably best rendered by some neutral phrase, such as
"territorial grouping."

Between 108 B.C., when Emperor Wu had extended Chinese political control
almost to the threshold of the Japanese culture realm by incorporating into the
Han empire the semi-Sinicized Korean kingdom of Chosŏn, more than thirty of these
groups had entered into communication with the Chinese government. Presumably it

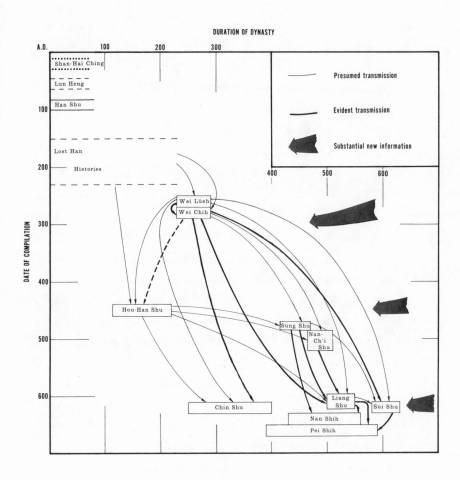

Fig. 1. The apparent derivation of early Chinese accounts of Japan.

was from the records of this intercourse that the Chinese historians obtained their information about the people of the Japanese islands. During the Han this knowledge was far from extensive, and much of the ethnographic detail that was transmitted is not particularly relevant to our immediate purpose. What is significant for the present study, however, is the report that the divers groups all acknowledged (稱) a hereditary ruler (王), and that this ruler of Great *·Jwiẹ (Modern Standard Chinese = Wo; Mod. Jap. = Wa)其大倭王dwelt in the territory (*kuo* 國) of *Ịa-ma-dʻậi (MSC = Ya-ma-tʻai)邪馬臺.[14] The remark that litigation was infrequent (少爭訟) and the citing of designated punishments for the transgression of specified rules of conduct would appear to imply, if not the beginnings of positive law, at least the existence of a formalized corpus of judgments on the pattern of the dooms of Teutonic, or the *themistes* of Homeric, chieftains.

According to the *Hou-Han Shu*, the *·Jwiẹ lived in walled or palisaded settlements on mountainous islands situated in the ocean to the southeast of Han (*γân 韓), the name by which contemporary Chinese referred to the congeries of tribes in the southern half of the Korean peninsula.[15] That the country referred to was Japan is beyond doubt, but the precise region within the archipelago is unspecified beyond the obvious implication that only the more southerly islands could have been regarded as lying to the southeast of Korea.[16] The location of *Ịa-ma-dʻậi is a problem that, despite more than a millennium of discussion, has still not been resolved.[17] On the available Han evidence alone it is clearly not soluble, but we shall return to the matter in a subsequent section in the light of additional information.

A thousand *li* across the sea to the east of *Ịa-ma-dʻậi was the *kuo* of *Kịu-nuo 拘奴 ,[18] inhabited by another group of *·Jwiẹ who were not, at least in the later decades of the Han, subject to the ruler mentioned above.

From among the instances of intercourse between the *·Jwiẹ and Chinese authorities that had taken place either in the imperial capital at *Lâk-ịang 洛陽 (Modern Standard Chinese = Lo-yang) or at the commandery city of *Lâk-lâng 樂浪(MSC = Lo-lang) in what is now North Korea, Fan Yeh selected only two for explicit mention. The first occurred in the second year of the Chien-wu

Chung-yüan 建武中元 period (A.D. 57), when the *·Jwiẹ of *Nuo 奴 — one of
the hundred or so groups mentioned above — sent to the Chinese court a tribute-
bearing envoy who styled himself by a term that the Chinese record-keepers rendered as *dʻâi-piụ 大夫. It would seem that this individual had persuaded the
Chinese that he was an official of some substance in the *Nuo community,[19] which
was allegedly located on the extreme southern boundary of the *·Jwiẹ territories.
In any case, the emperor formally bestowed on him a seal. The second diplomatic
exchange recorded by Fan Yeh took place in the first year of the Yung-chʻu 永
初 period (A.D. 107), when the ruler of *·Jwiẹ presented 160 war captives (生
口) and requested an imperial audience.

One of the more interesting passages in the *Hou-Han Shu* relates that during
the reigns of Huan Ti 桓帝(A.D. 147-168) and Ling Ti 靈帝(A.D. 168-189) the
*·Jwiẹ territories were in turmoil. For a period there was no supreme ruler 無
主. Then a woman whom the Chinese referred to as *Piĕt-mjiẹ-χuo 卑彌呼 managed,
by serving in the way of the lower and higher spirits, to inveigle the people by
supernatural means into establishing her as their ruler 事鬼神道能以妖惑衆
於是共立為王. A natural inference that the Chinese were here trying to
describe some Ural-Altaic form of shamanistic practice is strongly reinforced by
a series of supplementary comments.[20] Although of mature years, *Piĕt-mjiẹ-χuo
remained, significantly, unmarried. She lived in seclusion, seldom seen by the
populace 少有見者, but was served by a thousand female attendants. A single
male transmitted her instructions and pronouncements 傳辭語(presumably meaning
that he interpreted her utterances made while in a state of *kami*-possession), and
provided her with food and drink. Her dwelling 宮室 was furnished with towers
and defenses and was protected by armed guards, possibly tribute males (*toneri*
舍人) similar to those who served the Yamato court in later times.

The skeletal description afforded by the *Hou-Han Shu* is an inadequate basis
on which to formulate conclusions about *·Jwiẹ society in the first two centuries
of the Christian era. It is evident, however, that it manifested inequalities in
rank which, at the highest level at least, were hereditary. It is not unlikely
that heredity also played a part in differentiation at lower levels which — a
point not previously mentioned — were discriminated by facial and body markings 皆黥

面文身以其文有左右大小別尊卑之差. At the summit of the rank hierarchy was the ruler of *Ia-ma-d'ậi, who appears to have exercised the functions of a paramount chief, an office which clearly existed independently of the person who occupied it and which therefore exercised a true authority. In other words, though it was a private prerogative of the chief, it was exercised on behalf of the group as a whole. During the time of *Pi̯ět-mji̯e-χuo the paramount chief exploited, in a characteristically shamanistic manner, her special relations with both gods and demons as a means of legitimizing her rule. She apparently also maintained a retinue of assistants. Beyond the immediate circle of this corps of personal retainers, in the populace at large, the will of the paramount chief was sustained by the application of a system of formalized judgments. In short, in the range of tribal evolutionary development the society described in the *Hou-Han Shu* would seem to have inclined toward the pole of the chiefdom, technically a *system* of chieftainships exercising authority in a ranked society of regional rather than village dimensions.

The Testimony of the *Wei Chih* (chüan 30, fols. 25 verso - 31 recto)

The account of Japan incorporated in the *Wei Chih* is considerably more detailed than that of the *Hou-Han Shu*. To begin with, the *·Jwi̯e are located somewhat more precisely:

> From the commandery [of *Tâi-pi̯wang 帶方 : MSC = Tai-fang][21] the *·Jwi̯e are reached by sailing along the seacoast past the territory (*kuo*) of *γân 韓 [MSC = Han].[22] Turning abruptly to the south, [then] to the east, one arrives at the territory of the *Ḳ̯ąu-i̯a γân 狗邪韓 國 [23] on the north[-trending] coast of that country.[24] [The total distance traversed] exceeds 7,000 *li*. First crossing a sea 1,000 *li* in extent, one reaches *Tu̯ậi-ma kuo 對馬國, . . . a remote island 絶 島 more than 400 *li* square. The land is of mountain steepness and densely wooded, with trails like those of birds and deer[25] . . . Again crossing, in a southerly direction, a sea of more than 1000 *li* called the *γân [MSC = Han] Sea 瀚海, one arrives at a large country 一 大 國 . . . 300 *li* square, with numerous bamboo groves and dense woodland[26] . . . Again crossing a sea of more than 1,000 *li*, one reaches the country of *Mu̯ât-luo 末盧國,[27] . . . located on a mountainous coast where the vegetation grows so densely that one cannot keep a person in view as he walks ahead . . . Proceeding 500 *li* to the southwest

by land, one reaches the country of *·*I-tuo* 伊都國[28] . . . A hundred *li* to the southeast one reaches the country of *Nuo* 奴國 [29] . . . Proceeding eastward for 100 *li*, one reaches the country of *Pi̯ə̯u-mji̯ẹ* 不彌 (Jap. Fumi) . . . Traveling southward by water for twenty days, one reaches the country of *D'ə̯u-ma* 投馬[30] . . . Proceeding to the south, one arrives at the country of *I̯a-ma-·i̯ĕt* 邪馬壹國, which is where a female ruler has her seat of government 女王之所都.[31] By water [this journey] takes ten days, by land a month.

At this point a note is inserted to the effect that, from the country of the female ruler northward, populations (in terms of households) and distances can be stated in summary fashion but that the countries beyond are too remote to be described in detail. Then follows a schedule of twenty-one *kuo* lying beyond the female ruler's territory but still subject to her dominion.[32] Finally,

To the south [even of this zone of subject peoples] is the country of *Kə̯u-nuo* 狗奴國, with a male ruler 男子為王 . . . not subject to the female ruler.[33]

The times and distances incorporated in the preceding passages[34] have given rise to a voluminous literature of explication concerned primarily to elucidate the location of *I̯a-ma-·i̯ĕt/*I̯a-ma-d'ə̯i*.[35] A great many of the arguments advanced have been settled to their authors' satisfaction in the light of much later evidence from the Japanese chronicles, but in this section, restricting our discussion to the implications of the relevant passage in the *Wei Chih*, we shall attempt to reconstruct conditions in the Japanese islands purely as they were perceived by Chinese officials of the time.

As far as the island of Iki (cf. note 26) the stages of the itinerary would seem to be secure on directional and phonetic grounds, though even here the recorded distances are seriously discrepant. For instance, the distances of approximately 70 and 40 nautical miles between the mainland and Tsushima and between Tsushima and Iki are both stated as 1,000 *li*, a round figure which must be not only disproportionate in one case but also exaggerated in both.[36] Nor does it inspire confidence in the distances cited in the text when we find that the voyage from Iki to one of the main islands, almost certainly Kyūshū, is also quoted as 1,000 *li*. The plain truth is that the distances and directions composing the itinerary are such that one or both — and most likely both — must be adjusted before they can be made to yield meaningful inferences.

If the distances and directions recorded in the *Wei Chih* are plotted as an itinerary on a featureless and uniform surface, a route something like that depicted in figure 2A is implied. As the direction taken from the island of Iki is not specified, reconstruction of the itinerary must begin at *Muât-luo*, the landfall on Japan proper. The actual distance from Gōnoura on Iki to Nagoya in Higashi Matsura District is only 15 nautical miles; but even a voyage of a full 1,000 *li* (measured either as a proportion of the 7,000 *li* allotted to the journey from the commandery seat of *Tâi-pi̯wang* to the region of the *Ki̯əu-i̯a ɣân*, or in terms of Ishida's estimation of the *li* in Wei times)[37] would have resulted in a landfall somewhere in Kyūshū or, just possibly, at the extreme western tip of either Honshū or Shikoku. Under these circumstances there seems to be no compelling reason to reject the received identification of *Muât-luo* with Matsura in north Kyūshū.[38] Thence the direction of advance is predominantly southward, with only two stages of 500 *li* and 100 *li*, respectively, diverging to the southeast. It is evident, however, that if both the distances and the directions in the passage cited above are retained in unamended form, then *I̯a-ma-·i̯ĕt*, located explicitly some 12,000 *li* from the commandery seat of *Tâi-pi̯wang* and, by inference, 5,000 *li* from the southeastern angle of the Korean peninsula, must be sought somewhere in the Pacific Ocean to the south of the Japanese archipelago, or, by stretching a point or two, in the Ryūkyū chain. This was, in fact, the conclusion of the compiler of the *Wei Chih*, who remarked that, "Calculation of distances would seem to imply that [the territory of the *·Jwi̯e* ruler] is situated to the east of Tung-chih 東 治 (for Tung-yeh 東 冶) in K'uai-chi 會 稽," in what is now Che-chiang. By retaining the distances while rotating the directions through approximately 90 degrees, *I̯a-ma-·i̯ĕt* could be made to lie in Honshū, but such egregious inaccuracies in directional information, though not unknown, are not all that common in contemporary Chinese topographical reporting. And extremely seldom do directional errors of such magnitude occur in a mutually reinforcing sequence as it would be necessary to postulate in the present instance. The third alternative is to retain directions but adjust distances, an expedient which positively encourages the location of *I̯a-ma-·i̯ĕt* in Kyūshū.[39]

This attempt to assess the implications of an itinerary illustrates the manner in which the problem of locating the *·*Jwiḙ* has customarily been approached (see figs. 2B and 2C). There is, however, the possibility that the schedule of names represents not an itinerary but a simple enumeration. There is nothing in the text to prevent its being read in this way, and one particular turn of phrase may in fact give some support to this interpretation: the stages of the voyage from the Korean peninsula, which are obviously conceived as a sequence, are introduced as "First (女台) crossing . . . again (又) crossing . . . again crossing," but after the landfall at *Muât-luo the notion of repetition is dropped from the phrasing. This construction may have been a merely fortuitous accident of compilation, but that the distances and directions should be read as originating at a common point, presumably either *Muât-luo or *·*I-tuo*, is by no means an impossibility, in which case the argument for locations in Kyūshū, and possibly on the western fringes of Honshū and Shikoku, is considerably strengthened.[40] The journey by water to **I̭a-ma-·i̭ĕt*, which could also be accomplished by overland travel, was presumably a matter of cabotage along the coast of Kyūshū, but the stage from **Pi̭ǝu-mji̭ḙ* to **D'ǝu-ma*, which was by water only, could conceivably — though only by positing a gross directional error — have brought the traveler to one of the other main islands. In this connection, though, a distinction must be drawn between the territories of Great *·*Jwiḙ* under the hegemony of the ruler of **I̭a-ma-·i̭ĕt/d'ậi* and those of the *·*Jwiḙ* at large, which were "located on islands, both isolated and in chains, scattered through the distant sea" 倭地絕在海中洲 島之上或絕連 . A tour through all of them would, according to the *Wei Chih*, have necessitated a round trip of some 5,000 *li*.

We incline at this time to favor an interpretation along the lines suggested by Okubo Izumi (fig. 2D), in which **I̭a-ma-·i̭ĕt/d'ậi* is located in eastern Kyūshū, all or most of its dependencies are in other parts of the same island, and the vaguely mentioned *·*Jwiḙ* groups not subject to Pimiko are strung along the shores of the Inland Sea, that is, along the axis of third-century development attested by archeology and discussed in some detail in the next section. In this way the distances recorded in the *Wei Chih* (which in any case cannot have been more than relatively casual estimates) are not grossly distorted, directions are fairly

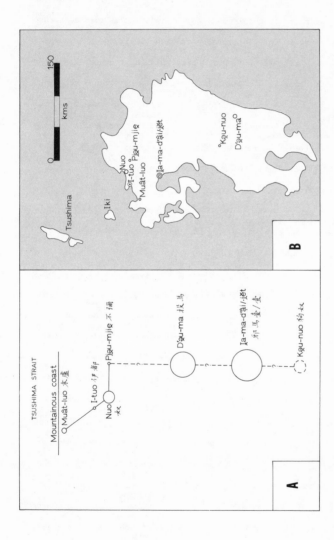

Fig. 2. Some representative identifications of the locations of the main *ʔwiɐ (Wa) settlements known to the Chinese prior to the fifth century A.D.

A. Schematic representation of the schedule of place names interpreted as an itinerary. This reconstruction is based on information in the *San-Kuo Chih*; in the *Hou-Han Shu*, *Nuo is located to the south of *I-tuo. Circles are proportional to recorded populations.

B. A fairly representative type of reconstruction by a modern Japanese scholar of the *ʔwiɐ (Wa) settlements mentioned in the *San-Kuo Chih*. Redrawn from Maki Kenji 牧健二, *Nihon no genshi kokka* 日本の原始国家 (Tōkyō, 1968), p. 289.

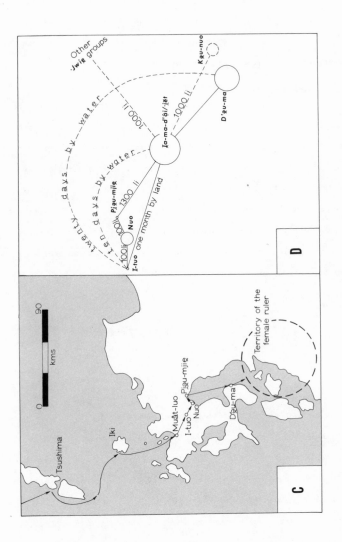

C. A somewhat unusual reconstruction based on information in the *San-Kuo Chih*. Redrawn from a restoration in Kishimoto Fumiaki 岸元史明, *Heian-kyō chishi* 平安京地誌 (Tōkyō, 1974), p. 17.

D. Schematic representation of the schedule of place names interpreted partly as an enumeration. Adapted from a reconstruction in Okubo Izumi 久保泉, *Yamataikoku no shozai to yukue* 邪馬台国の所在とゆくえ (Tōkyō, 1970), p. 231. Circles are proportional to recorded populations.

consistently rotated counterclockwise through some 20 to 30 degrees, the territories well known to the Chinese are assigned locations to the north of *Ia-ma-
·iĕt/d'âi (as the *Wei Chih* requires), and the whole reconstruction is in reasonable accord with available archeological evidence.[41] However, while adopting
this style of interpretation as a provisional operational expedient, we realize
that philological considerations will probably play as large a part as Chinese
topographical descriptions in finally determining the location of Pimiko's chiefdom.

Whatever may have been the precise locations of the *·Jwie territories, the
account in the *Wei Chih* firmly reinforces the general implications of the *Hou-Han
Shu*. A good deal of the ethnographic material in the latter work is repeated in
the *Wei Chih*, together with some significant additions. Where descriptions are
elaborated, though, it is not always possible to be certain whether the incremental material derives from a century or so of institutional change or is simply
the result of a more detailed record. One class of information that is undoubtedly the result of the greater detail provided by the *Wei Chih* is the record of
population for certain named territories lying between the coast at *Muât-luo and
*Ia-ma-·iĕt/d'âi, namely:

*Muât-luo	more than (餘) 4,000 households (戶)
*I-tuo	more than 1,000 households (戶)
*Nuo	more than 20,000 households (戶)
*Piəu-mjie	more than 1,000 households (家)[42]
*D'əu-ma	possibly (可) 50,000 households (戶)
*Ia-ma-·iĕt/d'âi	possibly 70,000 households (戶)

It goes without saying that these figures could not have been other than approxi-
mations, but the likelihood that they may have been firsthand observations is
implicit in the fact that the governor of the commandery of *Tâi-piwang used to
send his legate 使 on tours through at least some sectors of the *·Jwie territories, on which occasions he would put up (駐) at *I-tuo. Furthermore, two
embassies from the Wei court traveled through these territories to *Ia-ma-·iĕt/
d'âi just before the middle of the third century and doubtless contributed to the
Chinese store of knowledge of the *·Jwie.

The simple existence of status distinctions among the *·Jwie (尊 卑 各 有

差序)[43] that was recorded in a rather similar phrase in the *Hou-Han Shu* is given additional emphasis in the *Wei Chih*, both by the remark that some men become clients of others 足相臣服 and by a subsequent description of the quasi-ritualized behavior of a common man (戶) when encountering an important personage (大人) on the road ("he is abashed and withdraws into the bushes") or when addressing a superior ("he either squats or kneels with both hands on the ground").[44] At the summit of the sociopolitical hierarchy implied by these comments was the ruler-priestess *Pi̯ĕt-mji̯e-χuo, who also figured in the Han annals discussed above. The substance of the information is essentially the same in both accounts, but the *Wei Chih* elaborates on a few points. It does state explicitly, for instance, that prior to *Pi̯ĕt-mji̯e-χuo's assumption of power the *·Jwi̯e had been ruled by a male chief 其國本亦以男子為王. It also lengthens the period of disruption that preceded *Pi̯ĕt-mji̯e-χuo's reign from just over forty years to seventy or eighty, and it adds a significant snippet of information completely lacking in the *Hou-Han Shu*, namely, that the shamaness was assisted in the government of the country by a junior kinsman, classificatorily a "younger brother" 有男弟佐治國 .[45] She herself was again reported as being almost totally secluded from the populace while yet being served by a thousand female attendants together with one male, who provided her food and transmitted her pronouncements (this time the phrase used is 傳辭出入).[46]

The organization of the territorial units comprising Great *·Jwi̯e is also treated a little more fully in the *Wei Chih*, albeit by implication rather than explicit statement. From a fortified and securely guarded retreat,[47] the paramount chieftainess held sway over *I̯a-ma-·i̯ĕt (or *I̯a-ma-dʻậi) and a fairly extensive zone of surrounding territories, of which more than a score are named. The *Wei Chih* notes baldly enough that taxes and imposts (probably implying land taxes and poll taxes) were levied 收租賦 , and that there were, presumably in the chief settlement of *I̯a-ma-·i̯ĕt/dʻậi, both assembly halls, for gatherings of subordinate rulers, and council chambers 有邸閣 .[48] The only relevant information of a purely economic character in the whole of this account is a brief notice stating that each territorial grouping supported a market 市 where transactions were supervised by a Great *·Jwi̯e[49] official. The wording of the passage

31

is insufficiently precise to warrant any conclusion as to the precise nature of the exchanges that took place in the "market,"[50] much less as to the possibility of a market system, but it does attest the pervasiveness of *Ia-ma-·$i\breve{e}t/d'\hat{a}i$ control over surrounding communities. It is also likely that the representatives of Great *·$Jwi\ę$ who supervised the transactions not only maintained order, and possibly regulated exchange rates, but also exacted a commission on behalf of the paramount ruler.

The *Wei Chih* repeats the remarks of the Han text on designated punishments which we have already interpreted as implying a system of formalized judgments designed to maintain a degree of order at the societal level. In the political sphere it is probable that *$Pi\breve{e}t$-mjie-χuo's praetorian guard was by no means powerless to enforce her commands, but there are fragmentary indications that she could also call upon personal representatives for the same purpose. In *·I-tuo, for example, she had stationed an official, whose title the Chinese rendered as *$d'\hat{a}i$-$siu\breve{e}t$ 大率 , with the special charge of exercising surveillance over the communities (*kuo*) from *Ia-ma-·$i\breve{e}t/d'\hat{a}i$ northward to the coast. "All these groups," adds the *Wei Chih*, "went in fear and dread of him" 諸國畏憚之 . There was also an official whom the Chinese compared to their own governor of a department, namely, the Inciting Notary 刺史,[51] whose business it was to supervise the diplomatic traffic between the *·$Jwi\ę$ groups on the one hand and the Chinese and various Korean governments on the other. Envoys were constrained to submit to examination at the landing point 津 so that "despatches and gifts might reach the ruler without going astray."

In one direction the authority of *$Pi\breve{e}t$-mjie-χuo abutted on the territory of *$K\partial u$-nuo,[52] but in which direction is disputed, the *Hou-Han Shu* prescribing an easterly location "across the sea" and the *Wei Chih* a position to the south of *Ia-ma-·$i\breve{e}t/d\hat{a}i$. War between this *kuo*, the domain of a male ruler, and the chiefdom of Great *·$Jwi\ę$ appears to have been frequent if not endemic. However, structural oppositions of this sort between male and female principles are not rare in East Asia,[53] and one may be permitted at least to speculate on the possibility that the Chinese chroniclers were here rendering as political fact what was in effect a ritual situation.

The implication of some of the preceding remarks that traditional authority in at least one part of the Japanese archipelago was, by the third century A.D., evolving toward patrimonialism is reinforced by hints of a development of a personal administrative staff under the control of the paramount chief. Two such officials have already been mentioned, and an unspecified number of others were implied in our comments on local market exchange. In addition to these more or less incidental references, the following hierarchy of officials (官) is recorded for *Ḭa-ma-·ḭĕt/dʻḁi: at the top the *·i-kʻjḭę-ma 伊支馬; below him in order the *mjḭę-ma-ŝiəng 彌馬升, the *mjḭę-ma-ɣwɛк-kʻjḭę彌馬獲支, and the *nuo-kai-tiei (or -dʻiei)奴佳鞮.[54] Nor was this personal staff restricted to the level of the chiefdom itself, for abbreviated official hierarchies were also ascribed to the constituent chieftainships. In *Dʻəu-ma, for instance, the chief officer was styled (官) *mjḭę-mjḭę 彌彌 , and his assistant (副) was styled *mjḭę-mjḭę-nâ-lji彌彌那利.[55] In *Pḭəu-mjḭę the chief official was the *tâ-muo 多模; his assistant was the *pjḭę-nuo-məu-ljḭę卑奴母離.[56] In *Nuo the principal official was the *zi-ma-kuo 兕馬觚,[57] and his assistant was also known as *pjḭę-nuo-məu-ljḭę卑奴母離(assuming that this term is not here a dittography). In *·I-tuo a *ńĝḭę-kʻjḭę爾支was assisted by a *sḭät-muo-kuo 泄謨觚 and a *piwɒng-gʻiwo-kuo柄渠觚.[58] Even in the relatively small communities on the islands in the Korea Strait such officials apparently existed. On both *Tuậi-ma (Tsushima: more than 1000 families) and *·Ḭĕt-kjḭę (Iki: more than 3,000 families) the chief official (大官) was styled *pjḭę-kəu卑狗,[59] and his assistant *pjḭę-nuo-məu-ljḭę, precisely as in *Pḭəu-mjḭę and *Nuo. That the existence of such officials was a feature common to *·Jwḭę culture and not a politically inspired imposition restricted to territories subject to *Pḭĕt-mjḭę-χuo is attested by the record of a *Kəu-kuo-t̑ḭę-pḭĕt-kəu狗古智卑狗in the independent country of *Kəu-nuo.

The combined testimony of the *Hou-Han Shu* and the *Wei Chih* would seem to project the image of a number of *·Jwḭę chieftainships of varying size integrated into a chiefdom under the religiously validated authority of a paramount ruler. Allowing for a mean of three persons per household, the figures previously cited would imply a range of population aggregates for the several territories that

appeared to the Chinese to range from 3,000 up to 200,000 or so persons. Judged
both from the numbers of households registered in the various provinces of the
developed bureaucratic empire of Han China and from such archeological evidence
as is available, the *·Jwię̆ figures must be regarded as inflated, at the upper
end of the scale grossly so. Yet the evidence, imperfect though it be, attests
to a by no means negligible institutional development. A paramount chief claiming special, and presumably exclusive, relations with both gods and demons controlled a centralized administrative staff, furnished with specific offices in
*I̯a-ma-·i̯ět/d'ẫi, that collected revenues, organized markets, and inflicted pun-
ishments. It is unfortunate that the precise relationship of the administrative
staff to the ruler is unspecified, but superficially it seems to have conformed
fairly closely to the extension of the paternal authority obtaining within the
household of a ruler that lies at the heart of patrimonial domain.[60] Certainly
*Pi̯ět-mjię̆-χuo and her, possibly classificatory, kinsman, if not the male prede-
cessors mentioned in the Chinese accounts, had broadened the range of arbitrary
power beyond the capacity of a purely patriarchal ruler.

The incipiently bureaucratic character of the rule of *Pi̯ět-mjię̆-χuo is
reflected in the regularized diplomatic exchanges that took place between the
*·Jwię̆ and the Chinese government. In the sixth month of the second year of the
Ching-Chʻu 景初 period (A.D. 238), *Pi̯ět-mjię̆-χuo dispatched an embassy under
the chief (大夫) *Nân-śiəng-miei 難升米 [61] to the Chinese court to present
(獻) four male slaves (男生口) and six female slaves (女生口), together
with two lengths of multicolored cloth (班布二匹). As tribute offerings went,
these were modest gifts, presumably reflecting the relatively low level of *·Jwię̆
craft specialization (importations were another matter) that is implied by the
perfunctory treatment accorded this aspect of Japanese ethnography in the Chinese
histories. However, the Chinese court recognized only too well the dual function
of "tribute" as a mode of international trade and political integration and
accordingly bestowed on the *·Jwię̆ ruler gifts many times more valuable than her
tribute offerings.[62] Perhaps more significantly, the emperor admitted the *·Jwię̆
to the comity of nations by conferring on *Pi̯ět-mjię̆-χuo the title "Ruler of
*·Jwię̆ friendly to Wei" 親魏倭王, together with the gold seal with the purple

ribbon. Nashonmi, the chief envoy, and his second-in-command were given honorary appointments in the imperial guard appropriate to their status (率善中郎將 and 率善校尉, respectively) and received the silver seal with the blue ribbon.

Subsequently, embassies passed back and forth between the two countries with some degree of regularity. In the first year of the Cheng-shih 正始 period (A.D. 240) the governor of the *Tâi-p̯iwang Commandery sent a commandant of the imperial guard to present gifts to the *·Jwi̯e ruler, a gesture to which *P̯iĕt-mji̯e-χuo responded by dispatching an envoy to express her appreciation of the imperial beneficence. In the fourth year of the same period (243) she sent another embassy to China under the leadership of a chief (大夫) whose name (or perhaps title) the Chinese transcribed as *·I-śi̯äng-g'ji̯-i̯äk-i̯a-kəu 伊聲耆掖邪狗 .[63] Two years later, by imperial decree, Nashonmi, the chief who had led the successful mission of 238 and who had perhaps played some part in the organization of subsequent embassies, was granted a yellow pennant 黃幢, the award being conferred through the office of the governor of *Tâi-p̯iwang Commandery. In the eighth year of the Cheng-shih period (247) *P̯iĕt-mji̯e-χuo solicited the good offices of a new governor in settling her continuing dispute with the ruler of *Kəu-nuo. When the acting secretary of the border guard visited *I̯a-ma-·i̯ĕt/d'ậi, he, in a manner not uncharacteristic of a Chinese frontier official, advised reconciliation between the two groups.

According to the passage in the *Wei Chih* in which all this is related, *P̯iĕt-mji̯e-χuo was ruling vigorously in 247. According to the *Hou-Han Shu*, she had assumed power after terminating some forty years of turmoil toward the end of the second century A.D. The *Wei Chih* almost doubles the length of the period of disruption. Two interpretations of these accounts are possible. Either the compiler of the *Hou-Han Shu* was drawing anachronistically on materials relating to a period after the fall of the Han, or *P̯iĕt-mji̯e-χuo enjoyed an unusually long rule, possibly from the last decade of the second century until the middle of the third or, in any event, if Fan Yeh's account is indeed restricted to Han times, from a date prior to 220. On the evidence at present available, this matter cannot be resolved with certainty, though there is no compelling reason to assume that Fan Yeh extended his account beyond the Han period. What can be accepted with complete confidence is the existence in the middle of the third century of a chiefdom, probably at the threshold of statehood, which constituted a developing, if not yet powerful, component in the political hierarchy of East Asia.

In a concluding passage the *Wei Chih* implies that the rules of succession to the paramount chieftainship had not yet been securely institutionalized, lineage considerations still being in conflict with bureaucratic or appointive succession.[64] The death of *Piĕt-mjiᶒ-χuo, presumably not long after 247, was attended by obsequies that were not untypical of such events during the formative phases of state and urban genesis in other cultural realms. More than a hundred male and female attendants (奴婢) accompanied her into the grave, over which was raised a mound more than 100 paces in diameter 大作冢徑百餘步. But it appears that the authority and power of the ruler-priestess were temporarily buried with her. The rejection of a male successor initiated, in the words of the Chinese chronicler, a period of assassination and murder, which was brought to a close only when *·Iĕt-iwo 壹與,[65] a thirteen-year-old girl of *Piĕt-mjiᶒ-χuo's lineage (宗), was confirmed as paramount chief (王), possibly with the help of the Chinese acting secretary of the border guard from *Tâi-piwang. In any event, it was this official who issued a proclamation to the effect that *·Iĕt-iwo was the new ruler of *·Jwiᶒ, upon which *·Iĕt-iwo regularized her accession to power by sending a delegation of twenty persons to the Chinese court with a tribute of gems, textiles, and thirty male and female slaves 男女生口. Henceforth, an organized and continuing polity located in the Japanese archipelago was to figure more or less continuously in official Chinese historiography.

THE ARCHEOLOGICAL EVIDENCE

Although discoveries of stone and bronze artifacts had attracted more than local attention almost from the beginning of Japanese written history, and although the study of ancient epigraphy (*kinsekigaku* 金石學) had flourished during the latter part of the Tokugawa period, archeology as a modern science owed its inception to the initiative of Western scholars during the second half of the nineteenth century. Publication of the pioneer investigations of such men as William Gowland, Baron Henry von Siebold, Edward Morse, Ernest Mason Satow, and Romyn

Hitchcock[66] inspired similar researches by Japanese associated with both the
Tōkyō Imperial University and the Tōkyō Imperial Museum. Archeologists from both
institutions, it should be noted, were government servants and consequently obli-
gated to support Meiji policy, a fact that assumed considerable importance whenever the study of ancient Japan threatened to subvert what was conceived to be
the dignity of the imperial lineage.[67] From 1874, when excavation of tumuli was
first made contingent on official permission, through a series of decrees in
1882, 1899, 1929, and 1933, the central government came to exercise increasingly
rigid control over both excavation and the disposal of finds. Throughout the
first half of the present century Japanese archeologists continually protested
what they regarded as excessively restrictive regulations hampering the systematic study of prehistoric times,[68] and not a few transferred their attention to
the early cultures of Korea, Manchuria, and North China. Not until the end of
World War II were Japanese archeologists accorded greater freedom of investigation and interpretation, though even today there are restrictions on the study of
the early imperial tombs, potentially the principal source of information about
the beginnings of the Japanese court. Nevertheless, something of the order of
100,000 archeological sites have been explored to date. Probably three-quarters
of them are Neolithic, but the overwhelming majority of the remainder have
yielded materials relevant in one way or another to the transitional phase that
witnessed the rise of the earliest Japanese urban centers. What follows is a
distillation of the information that they have provided.

The Middle and Late Yayoi Periods
Our concern here will be with the archeological basis for the reconstruction of
the relatively advanced paleotechnic ecotype, sometimes generalized as the level
of Developed Village Farming Efficiency, that provided the cultural matrix within
which urban forms crystallized. To that extent we can ignore both the exiguous
remains of the preceramic cultures associated with the earliest inhabitants of
Japan and the vastly more abundant evidence of the hunting-and-gathering cultures
that, from a distinctive marking commonly imprinted on the outer surface of their
pottery, are known collectively as Jōmon (繩 紋 = "cord-patterned"). The period

of primary significance for present purposes is termed Yayoi 彌生, after its
type site excavated in the Hongō section of Tōkyō in 1884. It lasted for some
five or six hundred years, from some time in the third century B.C. to about A.D.
300, and is customarily divided — on good trinitarian, but possibly less compelling archeological, grounds — into an early period (third century - second century B.C.), a middle period (first century B.C. - first century A.D.), and a late
period (second century - third century A.D.).

The main way in which the Yayoi ecotype differed from the preceding Jōmon
was that it was primarily agricultural. It is true that the collecting, fishing,
and hunting characteristic of Jōmon times had been supplemented toward the close
of that period by limited modes of crop production, but to the end they had never
become more than minor adjuncts to a terminal food-gathering manner of life.
Millet (*Setaria italica*, Beauv.) had been grown in at least a few places, and
buckwheat (*Fagopyrum esculentum*, Moench.), sesame (*Sesamum orientale*, Linn.), and
the hairy-podded kidney bean (*Phaseolus angularis*, W. F. Wright) had probably
been raised as garden crops; at least this is what seems to be implied by their
occurrence in the peat layer of the Shimpukuji shell mound in Saitama. However,
the transition from the Jōmon to the Yayoi ecosystem was not everywhere abrupt,
and it is not unlikely that the limited crop-raising undertaken at the end of the
former era was itself the result of initial contacts with the Yayoi. Complemen-
tarily, the dawn of the Yayoi period did not inevitably entail the abandonment of
all the old Jōmon ways, as the not infrequent discoveries of Yayoi shell mounds
testify. At Nishishiga in Aichi, for instance, *padi* (rice in the ear) was being
grown by a community that still consumed an enormous quantity of shellfish.

In its full development, however, the Yayoi ecotype was structured about a
system of permanent-field agriculture based on wet-padi cultivation. Virtually
all the major Yayoi archeological sites, including Uriwari, Nishishiga, Urigo,
Toro, Karako, and numerous others, have yielded either rice imprints on pottery
or traces of carbonized rice chaff or, frequently, both. The grains are of at
least two *Japonica*-type varieties, one found on sites in North Fukuoka and the
other in the south of the same prefecture. Both are close to races traditionally
grown in east-central China. At Toro, to the south of Shizuoka city, the most

elaborate excavation ever undertaken in Japan revealed thirty-three padi fields,
each enclosed by bunds reinforced with cryptomeria battens. Nine of the fields
conformed closely to the average size, namely, 1,580 square yeards (or about 500
tsubo 坪), but one was as large as 2,765, and another as small as 790, square
yards. Irrigation appears to have taken the form of a simple but effective allocation of rain- and river-water to selected fields. It is usually believed that
direct seeding of padi, rather than transplanting, was customary. At Toro,[69] at
Karako in Shiki county of Nara prefecture, and elsewhere the wooden implements
traditionally associated with padi farming have, by great good fortune, been preserved in the mud of the padi fields. They include spades, rakes, hoes, mortars
and pestles for milling the grain, baskets, and huge clogs for use in the flooded
fields. Clearly, between the Jōmon and the Yayoi periods there had supervened a
major transmutation of the ecotype. Expediential adaptation to the constraints
of the natural environment had been superseded by a thoroughgoing remodeling of
the landscape, a transformation summarized succinctly enough as the conversion of
a generalized to a more specialized ecosystem.[70] Where exigencies of terrain
inhibited such a total reorientation, dry-field crops assumed greater importance
in the farming cycle,[71] though it is remarkable to what extent wet padi was
adopted in regions of only marginal suitability — such, for instance, as Tennōzan in the upland country of Fukushima (a site within the confines of present-day
Shirakawa city).

The population of Yayoi times was apparently disposed in nucleated villages,
of which the Middle- and Late-period settlement at Toro was probably fairly representative. The dwellings,[72] eleven of which have been excavated, in this
instance were located on rising ground to the northeast of the padi fields, where
they would have been not only relatively secure from flooding but also conveniently situated to exploit the resources of a varied terrain. In any case, the
invention (or adoption) of the simple shaft well now allowed a wider choice in
the selection of settlement sites. The fairly typical grouping of three or four
houses ranged about a somewhat larger building has been interpreted as representing a hierarchically structured kinship unit.[73] Close to the dwellings at Toro,
and easily accessible from the fields, were granaries, each raised on eight piles

about five feet high. A storehouse of this type was also depicted in relief on a bronze bell reputedly from Kagawa in Shikoku, while a scene incised on a pottery sherd from Karako shows two men ascending a notched log at the entrance to such a structure.

There has been considerable debate among Japanese prehistorians as to the manner in which this new padi-based ecotype arose. Some have maintained that it evolved sequentially when padi and other grains were integrated with the Jōmon cultivation of root crops. They can then point to the Shimpukuji site mentioned above as representing an incipient stage in the adaptive process and to the fact that the earliest Yayoi artifactual assemblages are not easily distinguished from their Jōmon analogues. There is, of course, no question of padi having been domesticated in Japan, since wild strains were not endemic to the islands. This has led a second group of scholars to argue that wet padi was not simply adopted by indigenous husbandmen, who thereby initiated a series of changes that ultimately transformed their whole culture,[74] but was actually brought to Japan by immigrant farmers who settled there.[75] They assert that the degree to which not only the technique of padi cultivation but also a whole complex of associated customs, traditions, and rites was assimilated to the structure of Yayoi culture is incompatible with the simple adoption of a farming technology. Among those who advance this thesis there are further disagreements as to the character and provenance of the immigrants. It is not at all clear, for instance, to what extent the social differentiation implied by Yayoi archeological assemblages inhered in the structure of immigrant agricultural groups themselves, to what extent it arose through the superimposition of a farming elite on a hunting and gathering society, or if — as seems most likely — it was a function of both circumstances. Egami Namio, a noted proponent of the migration theory, expresses a point of view that has attracted considerable support when he characterizes Yayoi culture as a highly integrated amalgam of

> on the one hand, the wet-rice culture from central eastern and south-eastern China and, on the other, Jōmon culture, with added elements of the polished-stone culture of southern Korea and the metal cultures of northeastern Asia; the whole being given still greater complexity by variations peculiar to Japan and, in some fields, by the adoption of culture-elements from Han-dynasty China.[76]

However that may be, the Yayoi period witnessed the diffusion throughout southern Japan (Kyūshū, Shikoku, and southwestern Honshū) and southern Korea of a continental-style agrarian technology.

So far as Japan was concerned, the Yayoi culture is generally considered to have manifested itself first in northern Kyūshū, whence it diffused eastward along the shores of the Inland Sea, presumably in search of more extensive padi lands than were available in Kyūshū. By the second century B.C. it had reached into the Chūgoku and the Kansai, in less than another century into southern Tōkai, by the beginning of the Christian era into the Kantō, and ultimately, by the opening of the second century A.D., into the southern tracts of the Tōhoku.[77] By the third century A.D. the focus of the culture itself had shifted from its original hearth in northern Kyūshū to the Setouchi and Kinai districts. Wherever Yayoi peoples established themselves, rice became the dietary staple. Conversely, in terrain unsuitable for padi farming, Yayoi culture seldom achieved its full development, and, consequently, it managed to penetrate little more than the southern half of the Tōhoku. Although the culture exhibited a considerable degree of structural uniformity wherever it set its imprint on communities from Kyūshū to the Kantō, certain very significant regional traditions can nevertheless be discerned within its spatial extent. To these we shall now turn our attention.

Generally speaking, the several Yayoi industrial technologies seem to have advanced eastward at roughly similar rates as constituent elements in a coherent cultural system. Stone continued to be used for axes, adzes, and arrowheads and for copies of imported metal weapons. These last (eneoliths) are believed to have been manufactured in accordance with a practice common in Korea, so that it is not altogether surprising that, within the Japanese islands, they should occur most commonly in Kyūshū. One stone innovation that was clearly a response to developments in the ordering of the padi ecosystem was the lunar or roughly trapezoidal harvesting knife, usually about six inches in length (though much larger ones were not uncommon) and perforated to allow for the attachment of strings to fit round the hand. The fact that a convex or straight blade with two perforations was customary in both Kyūshū and Korea, whereas concave-bladed knives, sometimes with three holes, were common in the Kansai is only one among many indications of the close relations that obtained between the former two regions. Another new ceramic form was the pot with perforated base, suitable for the steaming of rice.

Early Yayoi ceramics are almost indistinguishable from those produced in northern Kyūshū during the terminal stage of the Jōmon, but the adoption of the wheel, probably from Korea, eventually imparted a distinctively continental utilitarian quality to virtually all pottery forms. By the Middle Yayoi it was used uniformly throughout southern Japan. The resulting pottery was prevailingly reddish in color, of comparatively pure though somewhat variable paste, relatively thin, and fired under more closely controlled conditions than in Jōmon times. Strong regional traditions developed in Kyūshū, in Kansai and neighboring districts, and in Kantō and the southern Tōhoku, with minor variations in other localities, such as Shikoku, the Tōsan, and central Tōhoku.

Another technological advance that is believed to have derived from the Asian continent by either primary or secondary diffusion during Middle Yayoi times was in the field of textile manufacture. Not only have clay spindle-whorls and components of looms been discovered in the Toro excavations, but fragments of the cloth they produced have been found in burial jars, notably at Miai village in Saga, and at Sugu, where a length of cloth had been wrapped round a mirror. Imprints of what appears to have been hemp cloth have been recorded on the base of a pottery jar from the Nishishiga shell mound and imprints of what were probably cloths of wild ramie fiber from Nozawa in Tochigi. Both warp and weft in these ancient fabrics were S-twisted and ranged in ratio from 7 x 11 per centimeter at Nozawa to 10 x 24, 8 x 16, 7 x 13, and 7 x 14 in the Nishishiga imprints.[78]

From the point of view of our present inquiry, the most significant regional distinction is that manifested in the tradition of metal technology. Bronze weapons were first imported into northern Kyūshū in the Middle Yayoi, and the flow continued until about the middle of the first century A.D. By the end of the pre-Christian period, foundrymen, either native or immigrant according to one's interpretation of the evidence, were casting three of the four classes of weapons that were being imported, namely, halberd blades that were made to be hafted at right angles to their handles, tanged spearheads, and socketed spearheads. In each class the weapon of Japanese manufacture was invariably larger and dispro-portionately broader-bladed than the original continental import. The foreign halberd blades seem to have been of Chinese provenance, while the spearheads had affiliations with both China and Korea. The fourth class of weapons, those which were never, so far as is known, manufactured in Japan, comprised double-edged swords with slender blades and narrow handles. They were among the earliest bronze objects to be introduced into the islands, probably dating to the second or first centuries B.C., when similar weapons from Late Chou times were still current in Han China. A sword of this type that came to light at Kōtsugu is identical with one from southern Manchuria, while another from Kashiwazaki is of a type that was used in both China and Korea.[79]

Distributionally, what is of interest here is that all these classes of weaponry were restricted to southern Japan (figs. 3A and 3B). As might have been expected of early imports, the double-edged swords, a relatively small number of which have been found in any case, were confined to the prefectures of Fukuoka, Saga, and Nagasaki in Kyūshū and to Yamaguchi in lower Honshū. The halberd blades were almost equally severely restricted in their distribution. Although imported examples are occasionally found along the western shores of the Inland Sea, indigenously cast models do not extend beyond Kyūshū. Locally manufactured tanged spearheads are distributed around the shores of the Inland Sea, with a particularly dense concentration in northeast Shikoku. Imported ones are rather rare. The socketed spearheads, which are thought to have been among the later products of Yayoi bronze foundry (one was found in a cist grave on Tsushima Island in association with Late Yayoi, Haji, and grey Korean pottery), have the widest distribution, occurring from Kyūshū to the Kinai. Longer versions are found from Nagasaki to the central sector of the Inland Sea, wide-bladed ones on Tsushima, in northern Kyūshū, and, somewhat unexpectedly, in southwestern Shikoku. Molds for casting the latter type have come to light on the Chikushi plain of northern Kyūshū. It is thought that there were probably only one or two centers of manufacture of this particular weapon and that they were in Fukuoka and/or Saga.

43

The circumstances of weapon finds are also of considerable relevance to the present inquiry. The tanged spearheads tend to occur in groups of up to ten, unassociated with other objects, and buried on slopes affording views over stretches of lowland. The socketed versions also occur in hoards, usually of four or five, though bundles of up to sixteen are not uncommon, that have been deliberately interred on isolated hill slopes. The implication that these bronze pieces were employed for symbolic and ceremonial purposes is supported by the fact that those manufactured in Japan became progressively more impracticable as weapons by reason alike of the lightness of their metal and the increasing breadth of their blades. The idea that sacred power inhered in a spear was not alien to Japan in ancient times. Amaterasu, the Sun Goddess herself, progenetrix of the Japanese royal line, was often symbolized by the Sun Spear (*hiboku* 日矛). In ancient mythology the very islands of Japan were created when the god Izanagi and the goddess Izanami, standing on the Floating Bridge of Heaven (*Ama no uki-hashi* 天浮橋), thrust a jeweled spear (沼矛) into the primal ocean.[80] Of an at least quasi-historical character is the statement in the ancient Japanese chronicle *Nihon Shoki* that under Emperor Seimu provincial governors (*miyatsuko-wosa* 造長) and village headmen (*inaki* 稲置) were assigned shields and spears as insignia [of authority]賜盾矛以爲表.[81] In the adjusted chronology commonly applied to the earlier chapters of the *Nihon Shoki*, Seimu Tennō was ruling during the first half of the fourth century A.D. Another passage, ascribed by Kidder to the *Tsushima kiji* (a work we have not been able to consult), notes that shields and spears bestowed on officials were placed in stone chests and interred in the sacred hills of Tsutsu and Sago in order to ensure the integrity of the boundaries.[82] Even if this is not a record of an actual event, it is presumably what later chroniclers conceived to have been a proper use of spears, and there is no reason to doubt that the caches of Yayoi bronzes that have been excavated in southern Japan played their part in this or a similar complex of ritual actions.

In marked contrast to the distribution of weapons is that of bronze bells (*dōtaku* 銅鐸), a wholly indigenous development in Japanese bronze technology. In fact the total evolution of these artifacts is displayed in the archeological record, from the craftsmen's early and not altogether successful attempts to cast

a complicated shape through to complete mastery of the technical process. The

bells are found through much of western Honshū and eastern Shikoku but are com-

pletely absent in Kyūshū, the region where most Yayoi imports from the continent

initially established themselves and underwent the first in a series of modifica-

tions that would ultimately lead to the emergence of indigenous traditions. The

most archaic type of bell, which most closely approximates a musical instrument,

is especially common in the San'in district, so that it is not unreasonable to

suppose that models of Chinese *to* (denoted by the 鐸 of *dōtaku*) first reached

that part of Japan by way of Korea. A small specimen has in fact been unearthed

near Kyŏngju in the southern part of the peninsula.

The vast majority of the bells are usually attributed to the Middle Yayoi

period, that is, they overlapped with the main period of spear manufacture but

continued somewhat later. Their eastward diffusion appears to have been closely

coordinated with the extension of Yayoi pottery. The bells, some 300 of which

have been found so far, exhibit a chronological progression from small size

(beginning with a length of less than five inches), a relatively crude casting

technique, and perhaps a minor degree of functionalism to large size (nearly four

feet), a mastery of sophisticated metallurgical skills, and almost total unsuit-

ability for use as sounding instruments. At the same time, they extended their

range from a focus in San'in outward into the Chūgoku and eastern Shikoku. The

latest ones are from the Kansai (fig. 3C).

There is every reason to suppose that the bells, like the spears, served a

ritual purpose. This inference from their lack of functional utility is rein-

forced by their deliberate burial, singly or in caches, usually on rising ground

commanding a view over the countryside. Later specimens often bear panels

depicting predominantly activities such as the getting or preparation of food,

so that they have usually been interpreted as offerings by communities of hunters,

fishermen, or farmers designed to secure the cooperation of nature spirits in the

provision of abundance.[83] However, more than thirty years ago Jean Buhot pro-

posed an alternative interpretation that has something to recommend it in some

instances. He suggested that the bells may have been placed as protective symbols along trails and in certain propitious locations (most have been recovered singly), and further — though this is highly speculative — that they may originally have covered stone phalli such as are known to have bordered some roads in Japan as late as the nineteenth century. The perforations in the shoulders of the bells occasioned by the need to tie sections of the mold together might then have served the symbolic purpose of facilitating communication with the spirit of the phallus, while the notches in the base could have been used to secure the bell to a wood stand.[84] Whatever may be the truth of the matter, there is no doubt that *dōtaku* served some ritual purpose. The fact that there are today no surface indications of the spots where they lie buried, so that they are chanced upon only by accident, affords some measure of the huge numbers that must have been cast in Middle and Late Yayoi times.

A third type of bronze import that was ultimately reproduced by Japanese bronzesmiths — though mostly after the close of the Yayoi period — was the mirror, one surface of which was highly polished, while the back was decorated in relief. All together, more than a thousand of these have come to light on Japanese soil, from Kyūshū to the Kantō region. Almost all have been recovered from burial sites, where they had been placed close to the corpse, as if highly prized by the deceased. The elaborate typologies developed by Japanese archeologists need not concern us here; suffice it to emphasize the ceremonial significance of mirrors as repositories of magical power.[85] The earliest imports from the continent, of Han-dynasty times, were restricted almost exclusively to Saga, Fukuoka, and Nagasaki prefectures in northern Kyūshū (fig. 3D). A large proportion of these Han-type mirrors were recovered from burial urns. During the first half of the second century A.D. the importation of Chinese mirrors practically ceased, only to be revived during the period of the Three Kingdoms (A.D. 220–265). Whereas few of the earlier examples are dated, certain of those from the states of Wei and Wu are attributed to specific year-periods. It is interesting to note that not all foreign models had a Chinese provenance; one particular genre of presumed Middle Yayoi date, and bearing a profusion of fine lines fitted into a framework of triangles (sometimes called a saw-tooth pattern), had a Korean or Manchurian origin.[86] The four specimens of this type of mirror recovered to date are from Fukuoka, Yamaguchi, Ōsaka, and Nara prefectures.

For some three centuries the needs of Japanese symbolism were satisfied by imports from the continent, primarily China. Long after Japanese craftsmen had mastered the techniques of halberd and spear casting, however, they were inhibited from reproducing mirrors, presumably by the alien symbolism and perhaps by an inherent reverence for this particular brand of exoticism. Not until about the middle of the third century A.D., when Chinese production of these articles started to shrink as a result of Buddhist imprecations, did indigenous bronzesmiths begin to cast their own mirrors, the *bōsei kyō* 仿製鏡 of Japanese archeologists. The decorative reliefs that they employed were mostly adaptations of the Taoist divinities and fabulous creatures that had figured on Han and, in accentuated form, on Wei mirrors.

Another category of archeological find that has been reported over a wide area in Japan is the Huo-ch'üan 貨泉, a type of coin minted in China in A.D. 14 but circulated both there and in Manchuria in succeeding centuries. Specimens of this coin have been found at four sites in Japan, namely, Haranotsuji on Iki island, Matsubara in Fukuoka prefecture in Kyūshū, Hakoishihama in Kyōtō prefecture, and Uriwari in Ōsaka prefecture. At Matsubara the find was associated with both a stone arrowhead and iron slag and at Hakoishihama with stone, bronze, and iron arrowheads — circumstances which themselves provide a pertinent commentary on the interdigitation of technologies in Yayoi times.

One artifact allegedly discovered in 1784 on Shiga Island, off the coast of Kyūshū, has prompted more discussion than any other archeological find of the Yayoi period. It was a gold signet of pure Han-dynasty style, in perfect condition, and bearing the characters 漢委奴國王, which have usually been construed as reading "the ruler of the *·Jwiə* territory of *Nuo* subject to the Han (*χân) [dynasty]."[87] Earlier commentators virtually to a man identified this object with a seal bestowed by the Chinese emperor on the ruler of *Nuo* in A.D. 57 (see p. 23 , above), but the extreme improbability of a particular recorded artifact's being recovered under the circumstances related at the time, together with the curiously unliterary phrasing of the inscription, makes it more than likely that we are here dealing with a forgery. In short, we are inclined to agree with Saku

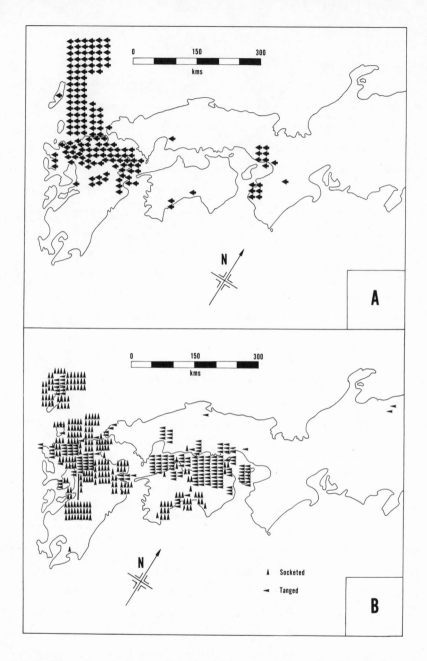

Fig. 3. Distribution of pre-fifth-century bronze artifacts found in southern Japan:

    A.   Bronze halberds (*dōka* 銅戈).

    B.   Bronze spearheads: tanged (*dōken* 銅劍) and socketed
       (*dōboko* 銅鉾).

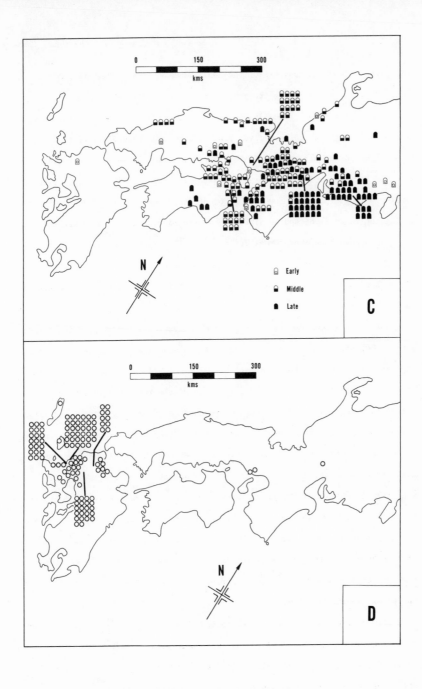

C. Bronze bells (*dōtaku* 銅鐸): early, middle, and late.
D. Han-dynasty mirrors (*kagami* 鏡).

Tatsuo that the whole business of the Han seal from Kyūshū, despite the contrary
opinions presented in a fine study by Murayama Yoshio, is so much nonsense.[88]

A high proportion of the inventory of Yayoi artifacts has been recovered
from burial sites, which themselves exhibit a marked regionality of type.
Although the dead were interred in a number of different ways, the prevailing
modes of burial involved cist graves and pottery jars. The former, comprising
boxlike arrangements of a few thin slabs of stone, were introduced from Korea
during the Early Yayoi and persisted until the Middle Yayoi. Although they are
thought to have been the prerogative of a chiefly class, the majority are devoid
of funerary furnishings. They occur only in northern Kyūshū, the extreme western
tip of Honshū, and the islands of the Korea Strait. The densest concentration is
on Tsushima Island.

Jar burials took two main forms: the enclosure of the corpse either in two
jars placed neck to neck or in a single jar furnished with a wooden lid. They
began to take place in Japan in Early Yayoi times and continued into the sixth
century A.D., but the great majority were of Middle Yayoi date. This was the
period when imports from the continent reached their maximum volume, and large
numbers of such items have been found in association with jar burials, among them
glass beads, *pi* 璧 disks, iron and bronze axe-heads, halberds, daggers, spears,
bracelets, and bronze mirrors. The burials themselves, though, bear only slight
typological resemblances to those known from Manchuria or Korea. In fact, it has
been suggested that the idea of urn burial was adopted directly from China and
was only subsequently diffused back to the northeast Asian mainland.[89] A feature
of some burial sites that was certainly adopted from Korea was the erection over
the jars of a dolmen in the form of a single massive stone slab supported by a
number of smaller ones arranged more or less in a circle. In Korea, however,
such dolmens usually enclosed a cist rather than an urn, and there are in fact
two sites in Japan, Ishigasaki in Fukuoka and Suwaike in Saga, where this is also
true. Presumably this particular practice was adopted while cist graves were
still popular in Kyūshū and was subsequently adapted to urn burials when cist
tombs went out of favor.

Jar burials usually occur in groups averaging about ten to a site, though

fields of thirty or more are not uncommon. They were customarily placed on
slopes above the village, presumably so as not to preempt high-quality padi land
and in order to avoid flooding. In a community cemetery excavated in Iizuka city
a group of urns that had been buried at the highest available point on the site
had been segregated from other interments by a wall of large stones. Presumably
this was another indication of Yayoi status differentiation -- at least so far as
Kyūshū was concerned. Variations in ceramic types in a single field sometimes
indicate continuous and prolonged use of a particular site.

The distinctive feature in the distribution of these Yayoi urn fields is
their restriction to the island of Kyūshū. This is usually explained by postulating that, being generally of a later date than the cist graves,[90] jar burials
were confronted in their eastward expansion by the more impressive tumulus mode
of interment that was contemporaneously spreading westward from a locus of origin
in the Kansai. This will be the subject of discussion in the next section.

The Early Tumulus Culture

The Yayoi was followed by the Tumulus culture, out of which were to crystallize
both the Japanese state and its earliest urban forms. A majority of Japanese
scholars divide this period into the three eras of Early, Middle, and Late, but
here we shall follow Professor Egami Namio in recognizing a simple dichotomy into
Early and Late.[91] In this section we shall be concerned mainly with the Early
period, which extended from late in the third century A.D. until near the end of
the fifth century, and shall have relatively little to say about the Late Tumulus,
which ran on until the second half of the seventh century. Moreover, whereas the
culture of the Early period can reasonably be viewed as essentially a prolonga-
tion of the Yayoi, between the Early and Late periods there was a cultural dis-
continuity of such magnitude that it is difficult to conceive of it as representing a completely internally generated transformation.[92]

Like that of the Yayoi period, mortuary furniture during the Early Tumulus
consisted not of articles of everyday practical use but of those symbolizing
authority, those possessing magical properties, and others probably expressive
simply of wealth. These now included, in addition to mirrors of Chinese manufac-

ture and *magatama* (勾玉)-[93] and pipe-shaped beads, jasper bracelet-type objects in wheel, ring, and so-called hoe shapes.[94] The bells, swords, and spears so characteristic of Yayoi times were completely abandoned as burial accoutrements, their place being taken by bronze mirrors, beads, and various highly wrought stone artifacts. Invariably these objects reflected advances in technology beyond those attained in Yayoi times, the quality of the materials being improved, designs becoming increasingly sophisticated, and the execution more assured. The manufacture of bronze mirrors made particularly rapid advances in the Late period. Whereas during the Yayoi almost all those found on burial sites had been imported from China, now they were commonly cast by indigenous craftsmen. At first they were simply copies of Chinese models, which would seem to indicate that the Chinese imports were conceived to be themselves invested with authority, but subsequently they came to incorporate distinctively Japanese designs. They were buried, as was the case a century earlier in the Yayoi tombs of Kyūshū, as the personal property of chiefs in the great mound tombs of the period. One class of mirrors that were imported from China during the Wei dynasty are today known to Japanese archeologists as *shōhōsaku shinjin gazō kyō* 尚方作神人畫象鏡. It has been established with a reasonable degree of confidence that some of these were cast from common molds, from which it is inferred that they were hoarded by a privileged group (or perhaps groups) and then distributed in some manner to local representatives.

Iron, which had been a relatively minor industrial medium during the Yayoi — it is uncertain whether it was imported or locally wrought — now assumed enhanced importance. Early in the Yayoi period it had been cast into scraper-like tools for the fashioning of agricultural implements. By the Middle Yayoi it had already diffused eastward to the Kantō, where axes have been recovered in association with pottery of that period at Akasaka in Miura city, Kanagawa — a region, incidentally, which bronze had failed to penetrate in significant quantities. Although the vast majority of the iron artifacts that have come to light in tombs are chiefly accoutrements of symbolic value, very occasionally a farm implement is recovered. Such a find is usually considered to denote the working of padi land.

Finally, in the roster of industrial technologies, mention must be made of a tradition of miniature stone replicas of iron, bronze, and wooden utensils that is specifically Early Tumulus in its occurrence. Usually modeled in green steatite and sometimes painted red, these little reproductions occur in such numbers as often to constitute the dominant artifact in a tomb assemblage. They are especially prevalent in the Kansai and in both the Kantō plain and the uplands bordering it on the west. It is evident that in the majority of instances, and particularly so far as wooden implements were concerned, the fashioning of the replicas must have required a far greater investment of time and skill than did manufacture of the originals. At the present time opinion is divided as to whether this commitment of energy to the production of miniature stone replicas in such quantities should be attributed to the desire to provide the dead with indestructible articles for their long journey or to a not unnatural wish to avoid interring metals in limited supply and thereby denying the living in order to provide for the dead.

Despite the prodigious number and prevailingly high quality of the workmanship of many of the funerary relics that have been recovered, it is the eponymous earth-covered mound tombs (Jap. *kofun* 古墳) themselves that are visually the most impressive remains of the Tumulus period. At about the turn of the fourth century, this mode of burial was introduced into the Kansai region, probably from Korea. Within a century it had spread westward along the shores of the Inland Sea to Kyūshū and eastward beyond the Kantō. By the end of the fifth century five regional concentrations of such tombs had developed, namely, the Kansai, the territories bordering the constriction of the Inland Sea, northern Kyūshū, the Sadowara Plain in southeast Kyūshū, and eastern Gumma-Saitama. The first three regions had been foci of cultural evolution in Yayoi times, but the latter two were assuming a new prominence. Tottori and Shimane, too, if anything enhanced their standing. The Kōchi district of Shikoku, by contrast, which had been in the forefront of cultural developments during the Yayoi, now sank to a backwater status. All together, more than 10,000 large and small *kofun* were raised during the Tumulus period, over 4,000 in Okayama prefecture alone and an even larger concentration in present-day Nara prefecture.

Tombs of the Early Tumulus period were sited on hill slopes, where they dominated, without preempting, the prime agricultural land of the plains and valleys.
At the beginning of the Late period, massive mounds, typified by those attributed,
mainly by Meiji bureaucrats, to the emperors Ōjin (who probably ruled at the end
of the fourth century) and Nintoku (beginning of the fifth century),[95] were constructed in the midst of lowland padi fields. The latter tomb, situated on the
Sakai plain near Ōsaka, occupied, including its moats, some eighty acres and rose
to a height of ninety feet. Toward the end of the Late period, increasing pressure of population caused tumuli to be raised on hill and plain alike, wherever
land was available.

These mounds were constructed in a variety of forms. Circular ones of all
sizes and proportions were raised throughout the Tumulus period, sometimes ter-
raced, sometimes moated, occasionally in pairs or with a square projection on one
side. Square examples can also be found throughout the period, but they became
more fashionable in the later phase, when they were occasionally built in threes,
a large central mound being flanked by smaller ones on opposing sides. It is
also not unknown for a square base to support a circular superstructure. But the
specifically Japanese form, upon which the received developmental scheme has been
based, is the circular mound with a more or less rectangular projection. This is
the *zempō-kōen fun* ("square-front, round-rear tomb前方後圓墳) of Japanese
archeologists, the "keyhole tomb" of Western writers.[96] The reasons that prompted
the development of this shape remain obscure. Some have thought that the projection originated as a flat surface for the holding of ceremonies in front of the
tomb, while others have regarded it simply as yet another manifestation of the
tendency, already noted in connection with bronze weapons, of Yayoi and Tumulus
craftsmen to lengthen and widen their creations.[97] In more prosaic fashion,
Suenaga Masao has demonstrated that in some cases the square end was created when
a hill spur was sliced through to isolate a mound.[98]

There is reason to believe that, when the Japanese islanders adopted the
tumulus tomb, what really appealed to them was its form and that they had only an
imperfect awareness of its function. On the Asian continent, mound tombs were
invariably piled above a coffin placed either at, or in some instances below,

ground level, but in Japan the tumulus was raised first and the coffin was subsequently inserted in a pit excavated in the top of the mound in a typical Yayoi manner. It may not be without significance that the groups who initially espoused the mound burial were located in central Japan, remote from northern Kyūshū, the region where continental influence was experienced most immediately. It is not unreasonable, therefore, to assume that the earliest mound-builders had little direct knowledge of continental mortuary practices. Wooden coffins made from the hollowed halves of a split log or of plank construction were customary in the Early period, with more substantial stone types predominating during the fifth century. In the Late period, sarcophagus burials in stone chambers became common, often with a passageway leading to the vault proper. They might be erected in dolmen form in the lowlands or tunneled into the hill slopes above. In northern Kyūshū more than fifty tombs of the Late corridor type, mostly datable to the sixth century, have carved or painted (often both) walls.

The alleged presence or absence of orientational uniformity in the spatial positioning of the tombs is a puzzling problem, probably exacerbated by changes in practice with time. The predominantly north-south alignment of the large fourth-century moated tombs that occupy the foothills northwest of Nara city, for example, would seem to have been imposed by the trend of the hill spurs from which several of them were cut. The tumuli, protecting the remains of mostly fifth-century rulers, that protrude from the plains in the angle between the Yamato and Ishi rivers in Ōsaka prefecture by contrast show little directional uniformity, apart from a tendency for certain of the smaller moated ones to face southwest. The thirty-three circular and keyhole tombs on the Tamate upland constitute a group for which it is impossible to discern any dominant orientational pattern whatsoever.

Whatever may have been the precise form of a tumulus, it is evident that it represented a considerable concentration of political and social power. In the case of one of the larger tombs, floating and dragging into position the slabs that were to form the burial crypts, raising the mound itself (or in some instances cutting through a hill spur in order to isolate it), and excavating the moat must have required a very considerable investment of labor. It has been calculated that the mound alone of one tomb, fairly representative of this type — that of Tsukuriyama in Takamatsu township, just west of Okayama — would have required the work-equivalent of a thousand laborers each piling a cubic meter of earth a day for four years.[99] The precise manner of solving the logistical problems inherent in an undertaking of this magnitude is probably forever lost to us, but presumably the peasantry was assembled under corvée during one or more slack farming seasons. It may also be significant that most rulers were interred several months, and occasionally years, after their deaths. Extrapolations from the magnitude, number, and artistic elaboration of monumental structures to the sociocultural and political features of the societies constructing them are notoriously hazardous, but it is nevertheless true that in paleotechnic ecotypes human labor is the only available substitute for advanced technology. And the organization of human labor on a large scale necessitates a sociopolitical structure that is efficient in one way or another, whether it be through the agency of coercive political institutions, strong reciprocative bonds, a kinship system that incorporates a ranking principle concentrative of power, or some other means. Nor must we overestimate the complexity of the architectural principles involved in the construction of these tombs, which required only the repetition of essentially simple procedures. It is not so much the quantitative aspects of a construction project which bear witness to a focus of power but rather the complexity of the task.[100] Clues to the mechanisms devised to cope with such undertakings in the Tumulus period of Japanese history will be examined in the next section of this work.

By way of summary, it can be said that during the more than half-millennium known as the Yayoi period an ecotype developed in Japan south of the Tōhoku that was structured primarily (though, needless to say, not exclusively) about the twin organizational foci of wet-padi cultivation and the use of metals. This does not mean that these two nexuses of activity were in close functional association. In fact, until late in the period the metal artifacts that figure so prominantly in the archeological inventory played little or no part in the field operations through which Yayoi communities adapted to their natural environment. Padi farming, as well as the cultivation of dry-land crops, were undertaken for

most of the period with wooden and, to a lesser extent, stone tools. Metals, by
contrast, were important not so much in the adaptive subsystem of Yayoi society
as in those sectors concerned with integration, pattern maintenance, and, possibly to a lesser degree, goal attainment. They were employed almost exclusively
as symbols of social authority or as objects for ritual use. As such they functioned as system-maintaining mechanisms in Yayoi communities rather than as
environment-shaping tools.

Although the basic Yayoi ecotype appears to have maintained a reasonably
uniform pattern from northern Kyūshū in the west to the Hokuriku and Chūbu in the
east, several regional modes of social integration are reflected in the archeological record. The primary distinction was perhaps between an eastern zone in
which *dōtaku* seem to have served as objects of community ritual, and a western
zone in which bronze weapons apparently symbolized the prestige of tribal chiefs.
It must be emphasized, though, that in numerous interstitial and peripheral areas
older Jōmon cultures persisted virtually intact or were only slightly modified by
contacts with Yayoi communities. This was particularly true of the remoter parts
of Kyūshū, San'in, Hokuriku, and the Tōhoku. Indeed, the northern tracts of this
last district remained to the end of the period under consideration alien Ezo
蝦夷 territories, totally uninfluenced by Yayoi or even Tumulus cultures.

The most impressive relics of the Yayoi period are bronze objects used
either in community rites and festivals or as symbols of authority. From the
middle of the period these bronze artifacts were imported from the mainland in
two streams: weapons of predominantly Korean manufacture, though modeled on generalized northeast Asian prototypes, and mirrors from China of the Han and Three
Kingdoms periods. Sooner or later all were reproduced in Japan, but the insular
bronzesmiths, especially those of northern Kyūshū, exhibited an unfailing tendency to transmute a foreign object of practical use into something numinous, or
at least of symbolic significance. And in so doing they invested it with a distinctively Japanese form, as if they might never have been cognizant of its practical purpose. It is evident that for the Japanese craftsmen the value of the
foreign artifact initially resided in some inherent magical quality that it was
deemed to have acquired by virtue of its provenance rather than in an utilitarian

function it might have had. This was especially true of the bronze mirrors that were imported from China and which served as emblems of personal authority. It is certainly not without significance that the mirrors were first used in this way in northern Kyūshū, the region that had previously inaugurated the Japanese Bronze Age by adopting the double-edged sword and that had also enjoyed a virtual monopoly of halberd blades, both of which artifacts were employed as symbols of individual power. It is to be inferred that it was in this extreme southwestern corner of the Japanese archipelago that a true authority, in the sense of an office independent of the person occupying it, first emerged. The customary interpretation of the northern Kyūshū cist graves as the prerogatives of a chiefly class in no way conflicts with this inference.

For much of the Yayoi period Kyūshū served as a vestibule through which innovations entered the Japanese culture realm and where they began to undergo a process of adaptation to the Japanese idiom. The main exception to this general-ization was provided by the predominantly Middle Yayoi *dōtaku*, the idea of which seems to have passed from Korea into the San'in district, thereby illustrating the gradual eastward shift in the focus of development that was evident all through the period. In the Late Yayoi the centroid of growth reached beyond the Setouchi into the Kinai district. In the Early Tumulus period the process by which power and authority came to inhere in certain individuals and institutions continued apace and was manifested preeminently in the tumulus burials described above, but the locus of innovation was now the Kansai region. The mortuary fur-niture accompanying these mound tombs bespeaks a strongly religious, or at least magical, dimension to the authority of the personages buried within them, and it was this, in a broad sense sacrally derived, authority that legitimized their right to have these artificial hills piled above their mortal remains. If in death they could command such an investment of labor, there is no reason to doubt that in life their power over their communities was no less absolute.

THE TESTIMONY OF INDIGENOUS LITERATURE

The Ancient Chronicles of Japan

Only two ancient Japanese records have much bearing on the matters discussed in the present section, and neither was anything like contemporary with the events

that we are here seeking to understand. Both were compiled to validate the

interests of a particular power group, for which purpose highly heterogeneous

classes of material — myths, historical narratives, anecdotes, songs, genealo-

gies, and etymologies — were subsumed within loosely organized ideational frame-

works. The earlier parts of both works are so purely mythological that their

structural analysis inevitably contributes more to our understanding of Japanese

thought patterns than to our knowledge of social change in the archipelago in

early times. Then follow sections that preserve a core of actual events in the

form of archetyped actions, idealized values, and heroized characters, all fur-

thur selected and edited to substantiate the preeminence of the Yamato lineage.

Finally, there are accounts, still not entirely free of miraculous interpolations

and equally heavily edited, which may be legitimately categorized as chronicles.

Cultural influences from China and the Korean kingdoms are especially apparent in

the myths, legends, and annalistic materials of the later of these works.

These two main sources are supplemented in a minor way by a number of other

ancient works, among them the *Kogoshūi* 古語拾遺 (*Gleanings from Ancient Tales*),

a collection of traditions preserved by the Imbe lineage and brought together in

their present form in 807. Some of the traditions there recorded had been omit-

ted from both Yamato corpora.[101] In addition, certain official liturgies (*norito*

祝詞) included in the *Engi Shiki* 延喜式 (*Procedures of the Engi Period* [901-

922]) may incorporate formulae of great antiquity. Certainly they antedate by

several centuries their commitment to writing.[102] Then there are the *fudoki* 風

土記, compendia of local lore compiled by an imperial order of 713. Although

only four now survive, fragments of others are quoted in later works. Together

they provide a rich source for provincial mythology. The only complete example,

that for Izumo, is discussed below. Finally, there are some mythological ele-

ments dating from ancient times in the great eighth-century anthology of poems

entitled *Man'yōshū* 萬葉集 (*Collection of Myriad Leaves*).[103] But all four of

these types of sources are, *for our immediate purposes*, secondary to the two

great chronicles.

The earlier of the two main sources is the *Kojiki* 古事記 (*Record of*

Ancient Matters), which was completed in 712.[104] The circumstances of its compilation are recounted in the preface composed by the chief redactor, Ō no Yasumaro 太安萬呂:

> Hereupon the Heavenly Sovereign [Temmu Tennō] commanded, saying: "I hear that the chronicles of the emperors (*teiki* 帝紀) and likewise the original words (*honji* 本辭) in the possession of the various families deviate from exact truth, and are mostly amplified by empty falsehoods. If at the present time these imperfections be not amended, ere many years shall have elapsed, the purport of this, the very warp and woof of the country, the grand foundation of the monarchy, will be destroyed. So, now I desire to have the chronicles of the emperors selected and recorded, and the old words (舊辭) examined and ascertained, falsehoods being eliminated and the truth determined, in order to transmit [the latter] to subsequent ages." [Transl. Chamberlain, mod.].[105]

After the lapse of a quarter of a century, an interruption occasioned almost certainly by the death of Emperor Temmu, the text of the *Kojiki* was copied down by Yasumaro[106] in the reign of the Empress Gemmyō. The language and script were both Chinese, with the vocabulary supplemented by a considerable admixture of Japanese words, written phonetically. The main sources that were used in the compilation were the *sendai no kuji* (先代の舊辭: old annals; lit., old dicta of former ages)[107] and, particularly, *teiki* 帝紀: (imperial chronicles),[108] also called *teiō no hitsugi* (帝皇日繼: imperial genealogies). The narrative began with the creation of heaven and earth and was carried down to the death of the thirty-third ruler, Empress Suiko, in the middle of the seventh century, though only genealogies are recorded for the period subsequent to the death of Kenzō Tennō in about 487.

It has often been pointed out that the character of the *Kojiki* changes rather radically between the section dealing with the fourteenth ruler, Emperor Chūai, and the fifteenth, Emperor Ōjin. After that time the imperial style changed, the honorifics such as *Kami*, *Mi*, and *Ō* that had previously been attached to royal names were omitted, at the same time as political and official matters tended to be accorded less prominence than the private affairs of the imperial household.[109] It is as if information of a more immediately experienced sort, possibly extracted from then extant records, had replaced the old archetyped accounts of a world no man could remember. Moreover, five Japanese rulers whose styles have been recognized in garbled form in the official history of the Chinese Liu Sung dynasty[110] fall between numbers sixteen or seventeen and twenty-one in the canonical genealogy, depending on the identifications adopted.[111] In other words, independent confirmation of historicity occurs at the very point in the genealogical table when the nature of the record descends to the human plane. The Sung history deals with the period from 420 to 478, so it would seem reasonable to regard the *Kojiki* as purveying quasi-historical, as opposed to mythologized, information, at least from the middle of the fifth century. It is also implicit in this argument that the *Kojiki* can be used only with extreme caution as a source for the period presently under discussion.[112]

The second of the indigenous records of relevance to the present section of this work is that known alternatively as the *Nihon Shoki* 日本書紀 (*Chronicles of Japan*) or *Nihongi* 日本紀. According to the *Shoku Nihongi* 續日本紀 (*Continued Chronicles of Japan*), which was compiled in 797, the preparation of the *Nihon Shoki* was ordered by Empress Gemmyō in 714, as soon as it had become apparent that the *Kojiki* was not entirely adequate to the purpose for which it had been commissioned. Its coverage of recent events was certainly deficient, it had been compiled hastily in a mere four months, and it failed to reflect the Chinese influence on court life that had become increasingly apparent during the two centuries prior to its completion. The new synthesis was under the direction of Prince Toneri 舍人親王 (traditionally ascribed the dates 676–735) and the same Yasumaro who had produced the *Kojiki*. After six years of work they were able to present the completed *Nihon Shoki* to the empress.

Like the *Kojiki*, the *Nihon Shoki* professed to chronicle events from the beginning of time, but it also carried its narrative down to the close of the seventh century A.D. It drew on Chinese and Korean sources[113] as well as on the surviving fragments of the *Kujiki* and other Japanese materials. Rather surprisingly, the *Kojiki*, despite Yasumaro's involvement in both enterprises, seems to have contributed little to the making of the *Nihon Shoki*. Although the editors clearly sought to shape the thirty books into a unitary whole, the work has the

stamp of a compilation rather than a composition. It consists essentially of a
series of discrete passages whose coherence derives solely from their chronological arrangement. A book of imperial genealogies which originally formed part of
the *Nihon Shoki* is now lost. However, a corpus of what appear to be addenda to
the original text by subsequent, though still early, commentators has for long
been accepted as an integral part of the work. The language and script are Chinese, except when verse is being quoted, in which case the original Japanese
sounds are conveyed by means of Chinese characters used phonetically.

The compilers of the *Kojiki* had eschewed any attempt to furnish their work
with an absolute chronology. Not so the editors of the *Nihon Shoki*, who, following the pattern of Chinese historiography, established — to their satisfaction
— exact years, months, and even days as far back as the equivalent of 660 B.C.
Not unexpectedly, anachronisms and inconsistencies abound. A Japan without rice,
bronze swords, and mirrors was unthinkable even in the Age of the Gods (*Kamiyo*
神代). Boats were used before they were invented during the reign of the
tenth emperor, Sujin, who also had dealings with Korean kingdoms, even though it
is subsequently affirmed that such places were totally unknown to the Japanese as
late as the time of the fourteenth emperor. More surprising are the discrepancies between the ages of the emperors as they are recorded in the *Kojiki* and the
Nihon Shoki, with the latter work manifesting a tendency to shorten very long
lives (Sujin, for instance, is reduced from a grand old age of 168 at the time of
his death to a mere 120 years) while yet lengthening a fairly high proportion of
shorter life-spans (as in the case of, say, Suizei Tennō, who was given a new
lease on life that raised him from 45 to 80). Clearly, discrepancies of this
character and magnitude were intentional rather than accidental, introduced into
the record for the express purpose of rearranging the genealogy of the imperial
lineage. Since the publication of Naka Michiyo's analyses of the chronological
structure of the *Nihon Shoki* at the end of the nineteenth century it has been
customary to revise the dates attributed to the earlier rulers by subtracting 600
years or so and, we may add, at the present time to reject them altogether as
fabrications of Yamato genealogists.

As repositories of myths and legends, the *Kojiki* and the *Nihon Shoki* are not vastly different. The *Kojiki* does incorporate certain materials, usually of an excessively fanciful kind even by eighth-century standards, that are entirely omitted from the *Nihon Shoki*, but the latter more than compensates by providing variant versions of many of the myths. When the two records are evaluated as archives of historical materials, the balance swings clearly toward the *Nihon Shoki*. It is more detailed, draws on a wider range of sources, and also covers the sixth and seventh centuries, which have no place in the *Kojiki*. Yet it must not be forgotten that both works, but particularly the *Nihon Shoki*, were prepared to substantiate the authority of the royal lineage by documenting, in a manner consonant with the temper of the time, its antiquity, its continuity, its claims to divine protection, and its incontestable martial superiority. An impressive feature of the chronicles is the skill with which virtually all important local deities, including many who had once opposed the gods of Yamato, were ultimately integrated into the imperial genealogy. There is no shortage of evidence to show that, to attain their goal, the compilers engaged in a good deal of selection, adjustment, emendation, elimination, and, without doubt, addition as well,[115] so that the onus is on him who would use the *Nihon Shoki* as a historical source to evaluate its evidence both skeptically and contextually.[116]

The Evidence of the Chronicles

In pursuance of the aims defined above, the compilers of the *Kojiki* and the *Nihon Shoki* crammed the earlier sections of their works with etiological myths explaining how the gods of Japanese Shintō, the Japanese islands, the Japanese people, and the Japanese state came into existence. Having fitted these fundamental matters into a reasonably coherent cosmogonic framework, they then turned their attention to the sociopolitical basis of Japanese life and explained how the Great Sun Goddess (*Amaterasu Ōmikami* 天照大御神) had become the supreme deity of heaven, how she entrusted the overlordship of the Japanese archipelago, symbolized by the Three Imperial Regalia (*Sanjū no shinki* 三種神器), to her descendents, how this lineage established itself on the Yamato 大和 plain, how other subordinate, but still noble, lineages came to be entrusted with high government offices, and why they were assigned specific traditional duties. Within this corpus of myths it is possible to discriminate five separate, though often interlinked, cycles associated with three different regions of Japan.[117]

1. The most primitive, in the sense of least differentiated, of the myths treat of the most fundamental of matters, namely, the primal cosmogonic act which brought heaven and earth, including the Japanese islands, into being — what the preface to the *Kojiki* calls "the dimness of the great beginning" (太素杳冥: Iwanami text pp. 42 and 43). This cycle, which bears the cultural imprimatur of a maritime people, is said to resemble in substance, if not necessarily in structure, others formerly current among certain Southeast Asian and Pacific folk. When it narrows down its focus to Japan, it does so through the agency of the deities Izanagi no Mikoto伊弉諾尊(traditionally explicated as the August Male-Who-Invites), and Izanami no Mikoto伊弉冉尊(the August Female-Who-Invites), the *-nagi* and *-nami* elements in whose names are said to signify, respectively, "tranquil waters" and "waves." As this group of myths is the most highly archetyped, so also is its geography the most generalized. Onogoro石殼馭盧, traditionally identified as an islet off the coast of the larger island of Awaji, was selected as the *axis mundi* (國中之柱), and the rest of the eight "islands" of traditional Japan were created round about. The only regional focus that can be deduced from this cycle of legends is the broad one of central Japan. As the royal court was established on the Yamato plain at the time the chronicles were compiled, it is not altogether unexpected that the center of creation should have been located nearby. Evidently this was less a decision of the gods than of Yamato literati.

2. A second cycle of myths, also with a strong maritime flavor, recounts the descents of superior beings (*kami*神) from the Plain of High Heaven (*Takama-gahara*高天原) to various parts of Japan, often referred to as the Central Land of Reed-covered Plains (*Ashiwara no naka tsu kuni*葦原中國).[118] Most of these tales are located in Kyūshū, mainly in Himuka (Archaic Jap. = *Pimuka*) no kuni 日向國, meaning Sun-facing Country, and subsequently known as Hyūga no Kuni. However, the implications of this ascription have been disputed. Some see the text as preserving a folk memory of a culture hearth of the Japanese people (or perhaps of one element among them) in southeast Kyūshū. Others maintain that it is at least as likely that the Japanese of historical times, regarding their

rulers as descended from the Sun Goddess, should simply have assumed that their divine ancestors had first set foot in a land long known as the Sun-facing Country.[119] Such support as there is for the first of these interpretations is presented in paragraph 5, below.

3. A third corpus of myths appears to have been formulated by an agricultural people in order to explain the cycle of the seasons. In a tale that is usually regarded as pivotal to the structure of Japanese mythology, it is related how the unseemly and impious antics[120] of Susa no wo no Mikoto (須佐乃烏尊: The August Impetuous Male, that is, the Storm God), so alarmed his sister, the Sun Goddess (Amaterasu), that she retreated into the Heavenly Rock-Cavern (*Ama no iwaya* 天岩窟), from which she was persuaded to emerge only after the other deities had performed various dances and sacrifices. Several aspects of this cycle would seem to imply that it was originally evolved by a padi-cultivating people within reach of mountain terrain (not a difficult juxtaposition to find in southern Japan), and the toponyms mentioned point to a community in the vicinity of Yamato. Generally speaking, the component elements in this group of myths appear to be of more recent origin than those comprising cycles 1 and 2.

4. The fourth group of myths tells of the exploits of the lineage of Susa no wo no Mikoto in Izumo no Kuni. The descendants of this Storm God, who were apparently deities (*kami*) of water, rain, thunder, and various occult practices, originally ruled over southern Japan (the Central Land of Reed-covered Plains) from a base in Izumo. So powerful was one particular ruler of this line, Ōkuninushi no Kami (大國主神: the Divine Lord-of-the-Great-Land), that even the Sun Goddess was obliged to negotiate with him when she wished to send her grandson to rule over Yamato. By a combination of force and persuasion, Amaterasu Ōmikami finally prevailed on Ōkuninushi to relinquish secular power in return for a status in the Shintō pantheon second only to that of the Sun Goddess herself.

Only fragments of the Izumo cycle have been preserved, and those in two main versions that are not wholly accordant. One of them is incorporated in the *Izumo Fudoki* 出雲風土記, a topographical report compiled under the general supervision of the high priest and *kuni no miyatsuko* 國造 of Izumo in 733.[121] Not unnaturally, it tends to depict an independent Izumo. The other group of extant

Izumo myths, which on the whole are in fair agreement among themselves, are those which were selectively accepted into the *Kojiki* and the *Nihon Shoki* in justification of the Yamato hegemony.[122] These were almost invariably modified in the interests of the royal lineage. In particular, the Izumo gods were relegated to the Realm of Darkness (variously *Yomi no Kuni* 黃泉國, *Ne no Kuni* 根の國, *Ne no Kata su Kuni* 根堅州國);[123] this reflected their powerlessness, as contrasted with the Yamato deities, who disported themselves in the bright light of Heaven. Most modern scholars have seen in this latter sequence of tales a validation of the right of the Yamato court to exercise secular power over the Central Land of Reed-covered Plains while yet reserving a high degree of ceremonial prestige to a powerful priestly lineage in Izumo, whose ritual authority the court was never able entirely to destroy.[124] An anomalous aspect of both the mythic cycle and its interpretation is the relative lack of independently (which means, here, archeologically) attested cultural development in Izumo, particularly in the western tracts known as Kizuki 杵築, prior to the rise of the Yamato court and even afterward. None of the archeological distributions discussed in the preceding pages exhibits particularly dense or otherwise distinctive concentrations in that region. Perhaps its importance in ancient times derived from the exploitation of its iron-ore deposits, as is possibly reflected in a myth that has the Izumo culture hero Susa no wo no Mikoto discovering an iron sword in the tail of a serpent he has slain.[125]

5. The fifth cycle relates how a descendant of Amaterasu's August Grandchild, who had been deputed to rule over Japan, the Emperor Kamu Yamato Iware Biko, better known under his posthumous style of Jimmu Tennō,[126] set out from Hyūga in southeast Kyūshū on the voyage that would bring "the blessings of imperial rule" (霑於王澤) to a "fair land to the eastward that is encircled on all sides by blue mountains" (東有美地青山四周).[127] Traveling first to northern Kyūshū, Jimmu Tennō then sailed through the Inland Sea, coasted round the Kii peninsula, and finally, with divine assistance, imposed his authority on the peoples of the Yamato plain. On the first day of the first month of spring in the year Kanoto Tori, Jimmu Tennō was enthroned in the Palace of Kashiwara (*Kashiwara no Miya* 橿原宮) at the center of the land. In a speech that is anachronistic by a

millennium, Jimmu claimed, in an authentically Chinese idiom, that by "reverently assuming the Precious Dignity" he was bringing peace to his subjects. "Above," so he is reported as saying, "I should then respond to the kindness of the Heavenly Powers in granting me the Kingdom, and below, I should extend the line of the Imperial descendants and foster right-mindedness."[128]

With the exploits of Jimmu Tennō, both the *Kojiki* and *Nihon Shoki* narratives assume a quasi-historical, as opposed to purely mythological, character. Toponym by toponym the topography of the Yamato kingdom is established; item by item the cultural inventory of Archaic Japan is accounted for in etiological myth. But all that this comprehensive schedule amounts to is a projection into the past of conditions in central Japan early in the eighth century. It is a register of cultural traits familiar to the compilers of the chronicles rather than an actual evolutionary sequence.

Both wet-padi and dry-field crops had already been produced from the lifeless body of the Food Goddess (Ukemochi no Kami保食神) and their seeds prepared for sowing by the Sun Goddess.[129] Now it remained only for the government to encourage good farming practices. To that end Suinin Tennō, in the thirty-fifth year of his reign, commanded his provincial officials "to excavate reservoirs and irrigation channels to the number of 800 or more." A great deal of attention, the *Nihon Shoki* adds, was paid to husbandry, so that "the people enjoyed abundance, and the empire was at peace."[130] Under the preceding Emperor Sujin the same officials had been ordered to construct boats to facilitate coastwise transportation between districts.[131] At about the same time, a count of the populace was undertaken, and a male "bow-end tax" (弓弭調) and a female "finger-end tax" (手末調) were instituted.[132] In an effort to arrive at a more comprehensive understanding of the resources of his realm, Keikō Tennō sent Takeuchi no Sukune武内宿禰to inquire into the topography of the northern and eastern regions[133] and ordered that granaries (*miyake*屯倉) be erected in the provinces for the storage of grain from the imperial padi fields.[134] All these activities were doubtless familiar enough events at the beginning of the eighth century.

Nor were the ritual underpinnings of polity neglected. In his seventh year Sujin Tennō founded shrines to the deities of heaven (*ama tsu yashiro*天社) and earth (*kuni tsu yashiro* 國社), dedicated public lands for their worship (*kamu-dokoro* 神地), and assigned their upkeep to hereditary corporations (*kamube* 神戸).[135] On the very day on which Emperor Jimmu inaugurated the Heavenly Institution (Yamato rule), he bestowed on Michi no Omi no Mikoto 道臣命 the divine secret of employing incantations and magic to dissipate evil influences. "The use of magic formulae (倒語)," notes the *Nihon Shoki*, "had its origin in this."[136] Under Suinin Tennō weapons were first presented as offerings to deities (*kami*).[137]

The Yamato state itself was conceived as having been established by Jimmu Tennō in all its imperial maturity without any previous developmental phase. Provincial chiefs (*kuni no miyatsuko* 國造) and district overseers (*agata nushi* 縣主) had been first appointed, allegedly, by Seimu Tennō.[138] It is true that the frontier lands were "still unpurified, so that remnants of their spirit populations continued to be refractory"[139] for some time after the arrival of Jimmu Tennō at Yamato, and there were to be revolts (or, possibly more likely, raids) by the Kumaso 熊襲 of southern Kyūshū and the Earth Spiders (Tsuchi gumo 土蜘蛛),[140] probably Ezo pit-dwellers, for a long time to come; but the prevailing tenor of even the legendary reigns reflects fairly faithfully the territorial domain of the high Yamato polity. It also implies close relationships between Yamato and a group of chiefdoms in south Korea that were known collectively as Mimana (任那).[141] Whether this relationship was one of political conquest by the Japanese as their chronicles claim, or simply one of voluntary submission by Korean chieftains, perhaps with the aim of securing protection against Mimana's northern neighbors and facilitated by shared cultural values deriving from common ethnic origins, is still a matter for debate, but all available evidence points to the presence of *·Jwiẹ (Wa) in the general region of the Naktong River in the middle of the fourth century. Whatever the reason for their foothold on the Korean peninsula, an inscription on a stone stele, the Hot'ae-wang-pi 好太王碑 erected in the Koguryŏ capital of Kungnaesŏng,[142] attests that Wa (*·Jwiẹ) were present, and ostensibly (though see p.84 below) raiding northward, at the end of that century.

At home, in Yamato territory proper, the royal residence supposedly was relocated on the accession of each new emperor. The usual formula announcing the change in the *Nihon Shoki* reads: "The seat of government was removed to ————. It was called the Palace of ————"遷都於——.是謂——宫.[143] The names and locations of the royal residences recorded in this way, from the time when Jimmu Tennō "reared aloft the crossed roof timbers [of Kashiwara in Unebi] to the Plain of High Heaven" until the erection of the several palaces of Emperor Ōjin, were as follows (though it would be a matter of no little interest to discover why these particular names and sites were chosen by the compilers of the *Nihon Shoki*):

Name of palace (miya)	Location	Emperor
Different formula		Jimmu
Takaoka 高岡	Kazuraki 葛城	Suizei
Ukiana 浮穴	Katashiro 片鹽	Annei
Magiriwo 曲峰	Karu 輕	Itoku
Ikegokoro 池心	Wakigami 掖上	Kōshō
Akitsushima 秋津嶋	Muro 室	Kōan
Ihoto 廬戸	Kuroda 黑田	Kōrei
Sakahihara 堺原	Karu 輕	Kōgen
Izakaha 率川	Kasuga 春日	Kaika
Mitsukaki 瑞籬	Shiki 磯城	Sujin
Tamaki 珠城	Makimuku 纏向	Suinin
Hishiro 日代	Makimuku 纏向	Keikō
Toyura 豐浦	Anato 穴門	Chūai
Different formula		Ōjin[144]

There were, moreover, what were termed specifically "traveling palaces" 行宫 where the emperors and their courts would reside from time to time,[145] as well as provincial residences scattered throughout the realm. Empress Jingu and Emperor Ōjin allegedly made more use of them than previous rulers had.

One aspect of the process of societal differentiation that we have seen to be implied by both Chinese and archeological sources is also hinted at in the *Nihon Shoki* (Aston trans., vol. 1, pp. 151-52). Until the reign of Sujin Tennō, so the story goes, the Great Sun Goddess (Amaterasu Ōmikami) had been worshiped within the palace of the emperor. Fearing that a pestilence that had afflicted the land had been occasioned by his presumption of undue proximity to his most powerful ancestor, Sujin commanded his daughter, Toyo Suke Iri-hime no Mikoto, to transfer the mirror that embodied the spirit of the Sun Goddess, together with the sacred sword discovered by Susa no wo no Mikoto, to the village of Kasanu-hi.[146] While explaining in mythological terms what became the traditional practice of committing the ritual worship of the Sun Goddess to a daughter or grand-daughter of the emperor, this tale also reflects what the Yamato court late in the seventh century perceived as a degree of separation of secular from sacral power. This has, in fact, been a common enough occurrence in numerous other cultural realms at comparable phases in their societal development.[147] Although the chronicles attribute these events to the reign of Sujin Tennō, whose adjusted dates fall in the first half of the third century, this is no guarantee of the period when the separation of powers actually occurred. In fact, on the evidence that has been presented in the two preceding sections, it would seem likely that a rather later date is to be preferred, perhaps the first half of the fifth century.

Earlier scholars invariably accepted the view propounded by the *Kojiki* and the *Nihon Shoki*, which was the dogma current at the eighth-century Yamato court, that the sequence of rulers listed in those records constituted a single unbroken dynastic line. A representative version of this approach to the dynastic history of early Japan as it culminated in the earlier decades of the present century is that presented by Kuroita Katsumi.[148] Since World War II, however, the Yamato version of events has been exposed for what it is, neither more nor less than a comprehensive, though not infrequently fictitious, set of formulations underpinning the political legitimacy of the court that created it. The scholar who has based his reevaluations most directly on the literary records is probably Mizuno Yū.[149] By comparative analysis of the *teiki* (cf. p. 60, above) incorporated in the *Kojiki* and the *Nihon Shoki*, Mizuno has been able to demonstrate that the very idea of dynastic continuity was itself hardly more ancient than the chronicles to which it was so central. Briefly, and shorn of its wealth of documentation, Mizuno's thesis is that the compilers of the *Kojiki* and *Nihon Shoki* drew on at least four discrete lists of rulers. He has noted discrepancies in dates and styles between the king lists and the chronicles and, significantly, has observed that certain rulers who figure in the chronicles are absent from the king lists.

Further, he has proposed that, prior to the seventh century, three successive
dynasties ruled over Yamato, of which only the first is of concern to us at the
moment. According to Mizuno, the putative founder of this, the first dynasty to
hold power in Japan, was Sujin, the tenth ruler in the traditional list. On this
interpretation, he probably ruled during the earlier part of the fourth century,
as contrasted with Naka's scheme, which assigned him to the first half of the
third century.

At some points Mizuno's analysis of the literary records accords fairly
closely with Egami Namio's interpretation of the archeological evidence. Egami
postulates a complete break in the dynastic line late in the fourth century, when
first Kyūshū and then Yamato were conquered by a horse-riding folk who spilled
out of Manchuria into the Korean peninsula and finally into the Japanese archipelago. Egami further identifies this invasion from the Asian continent with the
so-called second conquest of Yamato by armies from Kyūshū, which the chronicles
attribute to the beginning of Ōjin's reign.[150] Egami sees Sujin playing much the
same part as that assigned to him by Mizuno, but he restricts his realm to Kyūshū.

These two interpretations are still highly controversial.[151] They are,
moreover, only samples, though admittedly among the intellectually more stimulat-
ing, from a rather large number of explications of the chronicles proposed during
the past quarter-century, all of which are so far no more than paradigms for
thought about the origins and early development of the Japanese state — so many
frameworks for research, in other words. Clearly, not all of them will ultimately prove to be equally illuminating; in fact, in their present forms several
appear to be mutually exclusive. Almost the only thing they share in common is
the conviction that the early chronicles of Japan must be read, not as records of
events or indeed for the most part wholly as myth, but as one eighth-century view
of the world propagated by a politically powerful lineage. They constitute a
cocoon of mythological and historical significances that the Yamato court spun
around itself to protect its legitimacy.

THE PROTO-URBAN PHASE: THE RISE OF THE CEREMONIAL CENTER
What sort of picture emerges if we attempt to combine the material provided by

71

the bodies of evidence summarized in the preceding pages, namely, the simple
descriptions of the Chinese chroniclers, whose ostensible objectivity was inevitably subverted to a greater or lesser degree by culturally biased preconceptions;
the inherently mute archeological evidence that speaks only through the mouths of
trained, but by no means accordant, interpreters; and the Japanese records themselves, episodic rather than epic in character, in which the course of development during the four centuries under discussion has been irreparably skewed by
the purposeful idealizations of the Yamato court?

In the first place, it is evident that during the first four centuries of
the Christian era Japan south of the Tōhoku was occupied by a mosaic of tribal
groups. These were distinguished by widely differing levels of technological
achievement, but, as far as can be ascertained, the main thrusts of social and
political advance were invariably associated with an ecosystem founded on wet-
padi cultivation, with all that that implies as to permanence and concentration
of settlement. By the third century A.D., if not earlier,[152] a score or so of
segmentary tribes in one part of the archipelago had been integrated into a chiefdom, the *system* of chieftainships that is a precursor, either potential or actual,
of statehood. Summarizing the salient characteristics of the chiefdom, Flannery
has written:

> Chiefs in rank society are not merely of noble birth, but usually
> divine; they have special relationships with the gods which are denied
> commoners and which legitimize their right to demand community support
> and tribute. Frequently, they build up elaborate retinues of followers
> and assistants (often relatives) — the chiefly precursors of later
> state bureaucracies. Often, chiefdoms have not only elaborate ritual
> but even full-time religious specialists; indeed, the chief himself may
> be a priest as well. Further, the office of "chief" exists apart from
> the man who occupies it, and on his death the office must be filled by
> one of equally noble descent; some chiefdoms maintained elaborate gene-
> alogies to establish this . . . Finally, high-ranking members of
> chiefdoms reinforce their status with sumptuary goods, some of which
> archeologists later recover in the form of "art works" in jade, tur-
> quoise, alabaster, gold, lapis lazuli, and so on.[153]

Perusal of the preceding discussions reveals a more than casual congruence
between this conceptualization of the chiefdom and the sociopolitical entity presided over by *Pi̯ĕt-mji̯e-χuo. From a Weberian point of view, the evidence, inadequate and ambivalent though it be, points firmly toward patrimonialism, a type
of domain in which governmental and court administrations coincide.

By the Middle Yayoi the incipient status differentiation that had been dimly discernible in Late Jōmon archeological assemblages had crystallized into a pyramidal society with a paramount chieftainess at the apex claiming supernatural powers and exercising control over something in the nature of a praetorian guard, possibly a limited number of specialized craftsmen, and a broad understratum of peasantry. The significance of the fact that the paramountcy was in the hands of a woman who, while dwelling in a seclusion worthy of a Yoruba *ọba* in his *afin*, was "assisted" (the Chinese text uses the graph *tso* 佐, which conveys strong overtones of assistantship and subordination) by a younger "brother" has not been adequately evaluated. Possibly the personage that the Chinese knew as *Pimiko* was invested with sacral authority, while her junior kinsman, whether classificatory or otherwise, held secular power. The former might well have subsumed the delicate and quasi-ritual matter of tribute offerings to the Chinese court, in which case Chinese officials, ceremonially received at Pimiko's court, might have had little opportunity to discover her precise role in the conduct of affairs. Moreover, one of the myths incorporated in the Japanese chronicles does associate such a separation of secular and sacral powers with the reign of Sujin Tennō (p. 69, above). Against this it can be argued that envoys from the Chinese commandery capital of *Tâi-piwang traveled fairly regularly among the *·*Jwiẹ*, apparently operating from a temporary base at *·*I-tuo* in Kyūshū, and that a Chinese acting secretary of the border guard was actually present in *Ia-ma-·iĕt/d'ậi* at the time of a disputed succession in about the middle of the third century. Indeed, it is not unlikely that he had a hand in the settlement. Presumably he could not but have acquired a reasonably accurate idea of the manner in which power and authority were deployed at that time, if not at an earlier period.[154] Whatever may have been the truth of this relationship between sacred and secular jurisdiction, by the third century A.D. at the latest the paramount ruler was controlling an administrative staff capable of collecting revenues, supervising what appears to have been a form of market exchange, organizing the corvée,[155] assigning punishments according to a corpus of judgments,[156] and negotiating with the Chinese central and border governments. In fact, certain of these officials were honored by the Chinese government, a circumstance which is itself powerful testimony to the organizational status of Pimiko's chiefdom.

The references in the Chinese histories to the manner in which Pimiko secured her authority, namely, by making offerings to the lower and higher spirits (or to earthly and heavenly spirits 事鬼神道), [157] are the earliest extant mentions of the nexus of ideas which, several centuries later, and under the influence of foreign ideologies, became formalized as the Shintō 神道 faith. It was within this cultural context that the function and form of bronze artifacts acquired from the Asian continent were redefined so that what had originally been objects of practical use acquired ceremonial significances. Sometimes these objects assumed the functions of propitiatory offerings, at others of sanctification, and at others of legitimation of personal status. In terms of Robert Bellah's scheme of religious evolution, the period extending from terminal Jōmon to Early Tumulus witnessed a transition from Primitive to Archaic religion. [158] From the standpoint of religious symbolism this was a period when the paradigmatic figures of tribal religion with whom men had formerly identified in ritual were accorded specific, and often characteristic, attributes. Such figures became objectified and were conceived as actively involved in the ordering of both the natural and human worlds; that is, they assumed the role of gods and, incidentally, disposed themselves in a hierarchy closely parallelling that obtaining in the Yamato court. Although the prevailing world view in both the Primitive and Archaic phases was monistic, by the Early Tumulus it had been cast in terms of a more highly differentiated monism in the sense that a single all-embracing cosmology was being invoked to justify the existence of all things, both divine and terrestrial. In this schema it was the gods of High Heaven, and particularly Amaterasu Ōmikami, who held supreme power.

Religious action at the beginning of the period under discussion was characterized by identification and participation. In Bellah's words, it was ritual par excellence. [159] By the end of the period it had come to take the primary form of cult, a response to an ever deepening distinction between gods and men, which in turn predicated the establishment of channels of communication — in the form of worship and sacrifice [160] — between the planes of existence. So far as *religious organization* was concerned, political authority and religious authority were poorly discriminated (despite whatever implications may be deduced from the legend of Sujin Tennō's daughter, cited above); for even at the end of the period it was the higher-status groups who monopolized the superior religious ranks. It will be recalled that, in both Yamato and Izumo,[161] priestly roles were the prerogatives of noble lineages which asserted their divine descent. It is doubtful, moreover, if there was any significant development of adherents, as opposed to priests, within the religious collectivities of the time.[162] The *social implications* of the Archaic phase were not greatly different from those of Primitive religion. The important feature of both periods was that social structures and social practices were both subsumed within a divinely ordained cosmic scheme, so that there was little tension between religious prescription and social conformity.

The organizational focus of Pimiko's chiefdom was her court at the place whose *·Jwi̯e name the Chinese transcribed as *Ia-ma-dʿậi or *Ia-ma-·i̯ět. This site has not been identified archeologically, so that we are entirely dependent on the Chinese records for an appreciation of its morphology.[163] Unfortunately, they are not particularly informative. The royal residence 宮 室 itself was protected by towers and other defenses and furnished with appropriate ceremonial chambers which may have taken the form of *muro* (see note 48 to this chapter). Yet, although this description is meager, even by the standards of the dynastic histories for describing foreign courts, the function of *Ia-ma-dʿậi/·i̯ět is clear enough. It was the locus of a set of functionally interrelated institutions that, from our present vantage point, are recognizable as having attained an at least proto-urban level of differentiation and integration and that combined together to promote regional integration and to organize surrounding territories. In short, the court of Pimiko exhibited the functional characteristics of a developmental phase of urban evolution that has elsewhere been categorized as that of the ceremonial center:

> Operationally [such centers] were instruments for the generation of political, social, economic, sacred, [and other] spaces, at the same time as they were symbols of cosmic, social, political, and moral order. Under the religious authority of organized priesthoods and divine monarchs, they elaborated the redistributive sectors of the economy to a position of institutionalized regional dominance, functioned as nodes in a web of administered trade,[164] and served as foci

> of craft specialization . . . Above all they embodied the aspirations
> of brittle, pyramidal societies in which, typically, a sacerdotal élite,
> controlling a corps of officials and a palace guard, ruled over a peas-
> antry whose business it was to produce a fund of rent which could be
> absorbed into the reservoir of resources controlled by the masters of
> the ceremonial center.[165] [Wheatley, *The Pivot*, pp. 225-26, modified.]

So far we have discussed the rise of the ceremonial center in Japan as if it
took place within a single region. However, this is almost certainly not the way
it actually happened, which brings us face to face with a problem that has probably occasioned more discussion than any other single topic in early Japanese
history, namely, the relationship of the *Ꞩa-ma-d'ậi* mentioned in the *Hou-Han Shu*
to the Yamato (strictly, Yamatö) which was the seat of the imperial court when
the early chronicles were compiled. Without pursuing the tortuous and often cas-
uistical arguments of Japanese historians from medieval to recent times, suffice
it to say that three main alternatives, each subsuming a range of emphases and
nuances appropriate to a particular author's circumstances and predilections,
have been proposed at different times: *Ꞩa-ma-d'ậi* was the Yamatö of the chronicles and had always been located in the Kinki; *Ꞩa-ma-d'ậi* was the Yamatö of the
chronicles but had been transferred from Kyūshū to the Kinki; and *Ꞩa-ma-d'ậi* and
Yamatö were separate and unrelated places.[166] *For our present purposes*, which
constitute an attempt to elucidate structural changes in early Japanese society,
the question whether the transformations took place in one region or several is
not critical; but, for what it is worth, our view is as follows.

In the first place, only by doing gross violence to the directional information in the Chinese histories could *Ꞩa-ma-d'ậi* be equated with the Yamato of the
Kinai. In our opinion an unbiased reading of these sources must point to some
locality in Kyūshū as the site of Pimiko's court. Second, *Ꞩa-ma-d'ậi* (or
——d'ə [g]: see note 14) would probably have constituted an accurate transcription of Yamatö in the third century A.D. More important, however, is the
fact that the form *Ꞩa-ma-d'ậi* is found only in the *Hou-Han Shu*; in the expanded
account in the *Wei Chih* the form *Ꞩa-ma-·i̯ĕt* is used. Nor is there any reliable
means of determining which was the correct transcription, though it might be
argued that *Yama[w]i* (山 妦 = mountain spring: the form presumably rendered as
Ꞩa-ma-·i̯ĕt) is less common as a place name than Yamatö.[167]

By placing Pimiko's court in Kyūshū we are locating it in that part of Japan which archeology attests to have been technologically the most advanced in the early centuries of the Christian era. The island functioned as an antechamber within which technological borrowings from the Asian continent were adapted to the Japanese cultural style before diffusing eastward along the axis of the Inland Sea toward the Kansai. In this connection it is pertinent to recall the myth of Jimmu Tennō's migration from Kyūshū to Yamato, elaborated in considerable detail in the chronicles and often assumed to have been inspired by some folk remembrance of just such a movement or, more likely, series of movements, as is implied by the archeological record. The repetition of the myth as an exploit of Ōjin's reign reinforces the probability of such a migration and, in this latter guise, may even be a resonated echo of the truth. On the other hand, it is not wholly impossible that the name Yamato could have been adopted by a rising chiefdom in the Kinai seeking to appropriate the prestige and authority of an earlier polity located in Kyūshū without any migration having taken place — in which case the Jimmu and Ōjin migrations would have to be construed simply as etiological myths developed as a means of linking the two regions.

We are not here pretending to resolve these ambivalences in the available evidence. We are simply assuming that the proto-urban ceremonial center first manifested itself in Kyūshū as the result of a process of urban generation stimulated by the adoption of certain cultural traits from already urbanized regions on the Asian mainland and that, in a manner yet to be elucidated, the style of life thus created diffused eastward to the Kansai. Subsequently, a powerful group based in the Kinai extended its control, and, with it, an urban-based sociopolitical organization, over the whole of Japan south of the Tōhoku.

Throughout this transformation there is evident the dialectical interplay of the antithetical processes of segregation and centralization described in chapter 1. Nor is it difficult to discern at least some of the mechanisms by which these processes operated, though it is seldom easy to specify precisely which were the socioenvironmental stresses selecting for them. The rise to prominence of a paramount chieftainess during the Late Yayoi period, for instance, is presumably to be interpreted as the upward translation from one level in the control hierarchy

77

to a position at a higher level of the role of informal headman characteristic of earlier times. The fortified palace-like residence of Pimiko and the moot halls that constituted an incipient bureaucratic complex in *Yamatai* similarly represented institutionalized promotions of functions that had formerly been combined within the chief's dwelling, while the great tumuli that were raised throughout southern Japan signified the elevation, to a higher control level, of the old chiefly plot within a village cemetery. It is noteworthy, though, that the military, in the form of Pimiko's palace guard, was still a system-serving, special-purpose institution and that selection for the office of paramount chief was apparently effected by means of some special-purpose ritual procedure, at least at the accession of this particular ruler. There are indications that, at her death, an external agent in the person of a Chinese acting secretary of the border guard may have prevented a special-purpose leader from promoting himself to a general-purpose office (or a self-serving one: see p. 12), but the matter is very obscure.[168] In any case, there is no reason to suppose that the trend toward segregation was dominant over the process of centralization. Both processes were in a state of generative tension, with the latter, already manifested in the imposition of Pimiko's political control over a score or so of dependent territories, being reinforced by such linearization mechanisms as the payment of taxes directly to a central authority (though whether by individuals or corporate groups is not clear) and the supervision by Great Wa officials of local market transactions. The increased tensions inherent in the interplay of segregative and centralizing processes, and the manner in which these contributed to the evolution of the Yamato state, will be discussed in the next chapter.

3 The Early Capitals (From the Beginning of the Fifth Century to the Middle of the Eighth)

THE EVOLUTION OF THE YAMATO COURT

We saw in chapter 2 that, during the later Yayoi and Early Tumulus periods, there came into being in southern Japan an unspecified number of ceremonial-administrative centers that functioned as organizing foci for chiefdoms of varying size. One of these, which was probably located in Kyūshū, figured specifically in certain Chinese histories, while the general level of sociocultural development that it represented was attested by a reasonably full archeological record and was reflected, though much less faithfully, in later literary accounts. Up to this point the process appears to have been largely autochthonous and self-generating, but at the beginning of the Late Tumulus period there is reason to suspect the intrusion of external forces. The documentation for this is almost wholly archeological, although, with this evidence to hand, it is sometimes possible to elicit support for such an interpretation from the written sources.[1]

The scholar whose name is customarily associated with this reading of events is Egami Namio.[2] His argument is roughly as follows. Large tumuli continued to be raised over the graves of chiefs, but toward the end of the fourth century the character of the funerary furniture that accompanied these chiefly burials changed abruptly. During the fourth century it consisted mainly of ritual paraphernalia, but in the fifth century it was dominated by military accoutrements exhibiting stylistic affinities with those of certain equestrian cultures prominent in Northeast Asia at the time.[3] Included in these mortuary assemblages were swords with pommels of gryphon or phoenix design, whistling arrows (*nari kabura* 鳴鏑矢),[4] decorated saddles, bridle bits, and a variety of horse ornaments. The same impression of a horse-riding military elite is conveyed by the garments, personal ornaments, weapons, and armor depicted on the clay figures known as *haniwa* 埴輪 that were placed in rows on the slopes of tumuli, particularly in the Kantō and neighboring parts of Gumma and Tōhoku.[5] According to Egami, the most plausible explanation of this transformation is a hypothesized extension of the conquests of militant horse-raising peoples, already securely documented on the northeast Asian mainland, into the Japanese archipelago. In north China, toward the end of the fourth century, the primarily Turkic tribal federation of the

T'o-pa (*T'âk-buât 拓跋) established a dynastic fief that ultimately developed
into a bureaucratic empire lasting well into the sixth century.[6] In eastern Manchuria and north Korea as early as the first century A.D. the Koguryŏ (高句麗),
a branch of the Tungusic Puyŏ (扶餘) people, founded a polity that remained a
power in eastern Manchuria and neighboring areas until the second half of the
seventh century.[7] In southwestern Korea during the first half of the fourth century the kingdom of Paekche (百濟: Jap. Kudara) was founded by a prince also
claiming descent from a former royal house of the Puyŏ.[8] It is a similar process
of tribal migration that is invoked by Egami in his attempt to account for the
continental, martial, and equestrian character of tomb furniture during the Late
Tumulus period.

The significance of this cultural transformation is that it corresponds
chronologically to an event of signal importance in the evolution of the Japanese
state, namely, the rise of the imperial court in Yamato, the establishment of
which Egami does in fact attribute to mounted warriors who, from a base in Korea,
invaded Kyūshū and thence extended their control to the Kinki. In some of his
writings Egami appears to envisage these invaders as a tribe, occasionally
almost as a horde, establishing itself on the Yamato plain. Basing our views
both on the social organization of the stock-raising peoples of northeast Asia
and on what can be inferred about the familial relations of the Yamato court in
the fifth and sixth centuries,[9] we think that the marauding force should more
realistically be conceived as a fairly tightly knit group of lineage heads —
dissident nobility from one of the Korean kingdoms, perhaps — possibly approxi-
mating to a conical clan[10] and accompanied by their families, clients, bondsmen,
and probably slaves. It is not unlikely, moreover, that in their several roles
the invaders had already acquired a certain familiarity with the bureaucratic
procedures currently employed in the states on the Korean peninsula. It is our
opinion that, in this modified form, the theory of foreign influence during the
Late Tumulus period has much to recommend it. In particular, it is not wholly
irreconcilable with the dynastic structure revealed by Mizuno Yū's analysis of
Kojiki and *Nihon Shoki* genealogies.[11]

Egami has been able to adduce some support for his thesis from both mythological traditions and historical circumstance. For instance, the dualistic

quality in the former, a quality that often opposes the power of heavenly gods

(*ama tsu kami* 天神) to that of earthly gods (*kuni tsu kami* 國神), is readily

intelligible as an ideational sanction for the imposition of quasi-military rule

on a population of peasant agriculturalists. More specifically, there is the

persistent tradition, which was incorporated in the early chronicles in two sep-

arate contexts, of the seizure of power in Yamato by invaders from Kyūshū (cf.

note 128 to chapter 2). The first of the dynasts credited with this achievement

was the patently legendary Jimmu Tennō;[12] but the second was Ōjin, who, though

the object of much subsequent mythologizing, may have had some basis in fact.[13]

His adjusted dates fall within the second half of the fourth century, and Naoki

Kōjirō has given reasons for believing that he may at one time have been regarded

as the founder of the Yamato kingdom.[14] Third, there are pronounced similari-

ties, both substantive and structural, between some of the etiological myths of

Yamato, as preserved in the *Kojiki* and *Nihon Shoki*, and those current in Korea

during the first half of the first millennium A.D. The similarities are espe-

cially striking between elements in, respectively, the Yamato mythic corpus and

that of the Tungusic rulers of Koguryŏ and Paekche.

Even before this postulated invasion, close relations had obtained between

the **·Jwię* and several ethnic groups on the Korean Peninsula. We have already

examined the archeological evidence for these links which predate the beginning

of the Christian era, to which may be added the testimony of the *Wei Chih* (chüan

30, fols. 23a-b) that during the third century A.D. **·Jwię* were among those who

came to acquire iron in Pyŏn-chin (弁辰出鐵韓濊倭皆從取之).[15] We have

also had occasion to comment on both the epigraphic evidence for the presence of

Japanese armies on the peninsula early in the fifth century and the vaguer sup-

porting references in the ancient chronicles. There is no doubt that **·Jwię* con-

tacts with the people of the lower Naktong Valley were especially close from

early times as master strands in a more extensive web of maritime trade rela-

tions. In the third and fourth centuries these relationships took the form (de-

pending on whether one relies on Korean or Japanese sources) of the **·Jwię* exact-

ing, from the group of chieftainships known collectively in somewhat later times

as the Kaya (伽耶),[16] tribute in return for military aid against the depreda-
tions of the latter's neighbors, or of the outright conquest of the Kaya by the
*·Jwię, who established garrisons of occupation at strategic points such as
T'aksun (卓淳: Jap. Tokushu).[17] In view of the stylistic similarities that
have been posited between items of material culture in fifth-century Japan and
Koguryŏ, it is interesting to note that the Pyŏn-han people, from among whom the
Kaya emerged, are thought to have once been closely related to, if not part of,
the Koguryŏ confederacy.

Egami has carried this line of reasoning somewhat farther. He attaches considerable importance to the fact that the five fifth-century rulers of Yamato who
petitioned the Chinese emperor for validation of their claims to sovereignty each
requested that recognition be extended retroactively to the third century, that
is, prior to the establishment of the Yamato court itself. In their claims to
territorial jurisdiction they listed all the Korean polities of that century,
with the exception of Pyŏn-han, which Egami thinks was omitted because, in the
fifth century, it was still considered as Yamato territory, but under the name
Mimana.[18] He then points out that Sujin Tennō who, like Jimmu Tennō, was styled
the First Ruler of the Land (*Hatsukuni Shirashishi Mimaki no Sumera Mikoto* 知初
國之御真木天皇: *Hatsukuni Shirasu Sumera Mikoto* 始馭天下之天皇, and
similar expressions)[19] and whom some scholars have regarded as the founder of the
so-called Old Dynasty[20] (one of our *·Jwię chiefdoms), bore the personal style
Mimakï Iri-Biko Iniwe nö Sumera Mikötö (御間城入彦五十瓊殖天皇),[21] the
first element of which has sometimes been associated with the Mimana territories
in south Korea.[22] If this chain of reasoning were to prove sound, then it would
presumably imply that Sujin, hypothesized founder of the third-century dynasty,
was either a Korean prince or at least a fief-holder on the peninsula. Egami
himself has given reasons for tentatively suggesting that Sujin may have been the
last paramount chief of the Chin-Han who, after establishing the principality of
Mimana, extended his conquests to Kyūshū.[23] Whether or not these particular
highly speculative interpretations are ultimately substantiated, there is a good
deal of trustworthy evidence that groups of *·Jwię (Wa) in south Korea were from
relatively early times closely allied with others in southern Japan, perhaps as a

result of having once formed part of a common southward migration,[24] perhaps as
interdependent components in a skein of maritime commerce. To that extent,
Egami's Tungusic invasion at the end of the fourth century may have been very
largely an intra- (rather than inter-) ethnic transfer of power, an interpretation which is wholly consonant not only with the consensus of cultural historians
that the fundamental pattern of Japanese life was laid in Yayoi times but with
the implications of the Chinese sources that the $*\cdot Jw\underset{n}{i}e$ of the third century A.D.
were already speaking a language recognizably Japanese.

Very recently Gari Ledyard has published a reconstruction of events on the
Korean peninsula and in the Wa archipelago during the fourth century A.D. which,
while retaining in modified form Egami's notion of a military invasion from the
mainland, is cast in even more radical terms.[25] Beginning with the situation on
the Korean peninsula during the fourth century, Ledyard accepts Egami's view that
Mimaki (he who was subsequently designated as Sujin Tennō) was in some way connected with Mimana. But Mimaki was no martial equestrian invader; rather, he is
to be envisaged as a Wa chieftain constrained by disturbances consequent on the
great *Völkerwanderung* that affected all northeast Asia in the third and fourth
centuries to transfer his base of operations from the mainland to the islands,
where he seems to have founded a dynasty that endured until the second half of
the fourth century.[26] This was the so-called Old Dynasty, designated as ritual-
religious by Mizuno.[27] Although its founding appears to have constituted little
more than an internal redisposition of power and authority within the Wa culture
realm (which, incidentally, Ledyard characterizes as a thalassocracy),[28] its
demise was the result of an invasion from the continent much on the pattern postulated by Egami.

One of Ledyard's major achievements in his campaign to expose the fabrications and equivocations of the Yamato scribes has been to demonstrate, largely
from analysis of the internal structure of the *Nihon Shoki* and the *Samguk Sagi*
三國史記,[29] that the alleged Wa invasion of the Korean peninsula in the second half of the fourth century was probably a Yamato transmutation of the genea-
logically inconvenient circumstance that both the Ma-Han and the ethnically Wa
territory of Mimana had been overrun by the Puyŏ during the latter's founding of

83

the Paekche state.[30]   Subsequently the Puyŏ extended their conquests to the

southern half of the archipelago, where they established their base of power at

Yamato in the Kinai.[31]   During the last quarter of the fourth century, Puyŏ rule

in one form or another stretched in an arc from the Han River in the center of

the Korean peninsula, through Mimana and Kyūshū, to the Kinai. However, pressure

from Koguryŏ began to undermine the stability of the northern flank of the con-

federacy even before the end of the fourth century,[32] with the result that during

the fifth century Mimana had little choice but to merge its interests with those

of the insular focus of Puyŏ power at Yamato. Ledyard follows Mizuno Yū in

attributing leadership in the conquest of Yamato to Ōjin (Homuda), though he

associates the analytically separable myth of heavenly descent with Jimmu, "an

impersonation of our Puyŏ warriors," as he calls him.[33]

In this interpretation of events, it was the Puyŏ conquest dynasty estab-

lished in Yamato — but exercising power over all southern Japan, from Kyūshū to

at least the Tohōku — that inaugurated the Late Tumulus culture. For our pres-

ent purpose, one of the more significant of Ledyard's numerous interesting sug-

gestions is that the labor required for the construction of such mausoleums,

which are thought to have attained their largest mean size in the early decades

of Tomb Culture II, was assembled less by means of an internal bureaucratic reor-

ganization than by the massive importation of labor from the mainland, in the

form, in the author's words, of "prisoners, captives, dragged behind Puyŏ horses

from conquests in Manchuria and Korea."[34]   This perspective on the origins of the

Late Tumulus culture naturally casts the whole question of Paekche immigration

into the islands in a new light, transposing it from a transcultural to a primar-

ily intracultural transfer of population.[35]

Radical though it may be in its implications for our understanding of early

Japanese history, Ledyard's reconstruction is not incompatible with the interpre-

tation of urban genesis advanced in the present work. Both presentations envis-

age essentially the emergence of a series of chiefdoms focused on ceremonial and

administrative complexes which were subsequently subsumed within a larger polity

forged through external conquest. What Ledyard has done is to devise a much more

precise, though in many respects still tentative, reconstruction of events than

84

has hitherto existed, relate it more closely to available literary records, furnish adequate documentation, and indicate both where we might seek for more certain information and how to interpret it when we find it. The main incongruity
between the two interpretations, as at present conceived, lies in the differing
locations assigned to Pimiko's seat at *Yamatai*, Ledyard firmly identifying it
with the Yamato of the fifth century in the Kinai, while we incline, though without great conviction, to a site in Kyūshū.

We are not able, on the evidence at present available, thoroughly and defin-
itively to evaluate the theories and interpretations outlined in the preceding
paragraphs. In any case, there is virtually no contemporary documentation of the
manner in which the invaders, whether from Korea or more immediately from Kyūshū,
established their hegemony over the network of ceremonial centers that had
attained its maximum development during the Early Tumulus period.[36] Such evidence as is available would seem to imply that the transfer of power involved a
measure of secularization. The new rulers were no longer ritual experts controlling both gods and demons and monopolizing the channels of communication between
earthly and heavenly polities; rather, they appear to have been essentially lineage chiefs whose tribal mores had been considerably modified by some generations
of state-building but whose powers of coercion and exploitation were still
severely limited.[37] Essentially the ruler was *primus inter pares* among a group
of chiefs, and the distinction between royal and nonroyal seems to have been but
weakly developed.[38] In the event — according to Cornelius Kiley, who has
devoted a paper to the structure of the Yamato court in its earlier years —
despite the low degree of functional differentiation manifested by the nobility,
two lineages managed to appropriate supreme power during the first half of the
fifth century. Even so, succession to the throne was indeterminate, almost every
reign being followed by a period of unrest during which the eventual successor
eliminated rival claimants. Not infrequently, members of nonroyal lineages
(meaning, probably, old *•Jwię ritual leaders in the style of Pimiko) played significant roles in the succession process.

The reasons for the fall of this dualistic, perhaps even tanistic, regime[39]
near the turn of the sixth century are impenetrably obscure but were almost cer-

tainly connected with the emergence of a service nobility. In Weberian terms,
the rise of this group signified the beginning of a transition from "traditional"
to "rational-legal" authority, a transition effected in the following way: an
administrative staff that had predominantly owned its own means of administration
was gradually transformed into one that was decisively separated from those means
(though personal service to the ruler remained fairly common virtually to the end
of the sixth century).[40] Just such a noble, Ōtomo no Kanamura 大伴金村 was in
fact instrumental, after the usual interregnum, in securing the throne of Yamato
for Keitai Tennō, whose accession, in the opinion of Mizuno Yū, inaugurated a new
dynasty.[41] In the view of scholars such as Mizuno and Kiley, it is this dynasty
which has retained sovereignty until the present day. Soon after the founding of
the dynasty, the authors of Chinese official histories began to use the term *Jih-
pen* (日本: Jap. = Nippon or Nihon) instead of Wa (*·*Jwie̯*), from which it may
be inferred that they too probably recognized a change in the ruling line.[42]

The fact that Keitai was himself a chief, though undoubtedly a "royal" one,
from beyond the borders of Yamato territory is only one of several indications,
inadequately disguised by the eighth-century chroniclers, that, at the beginning
of the sixth century, regional nobles had not yet been effectively assimilated to
the Yamato court structure.[43] Half a century later, however, these regional
chiefs had been incorporated into the developing Yamato bureaucracy as *kuni no
miyatsuko* 國造, that is, minor members of the nobility who, as representatives
of the court in local areas, performed the generalized functions that the Western
world often associates with the office of magistrate. In addition to their
administrative duties, the *kuni no miyatsuko* in earlier times also functioned as
Shintō high priests for their districts. The titles (*kabane* 姓) that they
received when they acknowledged the authority of the Yamato court reflected in a
very general sense the degrees of loyalty that might be expected of them; and,
not unexpectedly, the closer to the central government the *kuni no miyatsuko*'s
district was situated, the more loyal he was presumed to be.[44]

These changes in territorial administration were but one manifestation of a
total reconstitution of the Yamato court that took place during the sixth century.
During the four decades of interlineage conflict that intervened between the

death of Yūryaku in about 479 and the accession of Kimmei in 539, which set the
seal of legitimacy on the dynasty established by Keitai, the rough parity of
status that Kiley and others have recognized as existing between the early
descendants of the invaders seems to have been to a very great extent replaced by
a highly segmented court organization capable of accommodating, potentially if
not at that time in actuality, a spectrum of degrees of nobility.[45] At the same
time, the various branches of the Yamato lineage began to expand their roles in
the centripetal redistributive process that had underpinned even the old ritual
courts of Yayoi and Early Tumulus times. To control of this appropriational
apparatus they now added, particularly in the second half of the sixth century,
an interest in production in the form of special crown lands known as *miyake* 屯
倉 .

In these and a series of other comparable agricultural estates emphasis came
to be placed on control of land rather than labor. Estates of this type were
worked either by peasants detached from the jurisdiction of local rulers in adjacent territories or by newly created communities known as *tomo-be* 伴部, and
they were managed either by special agents of the Yamato court or by delegation
of authority to *kuni no miyatsuko*. In the former case they exerted powerful tendencies toward "linearization," and even "meddling," as Yamato control bypassed
all intervening levels in the incipient bureaucratic hierarchy and acted directly
on the *miyake* themselves. By the middle of the sixth century the Yamato family
had acquired extensive tracts of land of this type, which were inevitably
encroaching on the territorial resources of local lineages. In a detailed study
of events in Bizen province, for example, John Hall has correlated the decline of
the Kibi family with the spread of *miyake*.[46] There is also evidence that other,
nonroyal, lineages were bringing into cultivation land that was then considered
the perquisite of the group undertaking the reclamation. And, of course, control
of adscripted cultivators in time of peace amounted to the same thing as command
of conscripted military forces in time of war. It will be recalled that the
great houses of the Mononobe no Muraji, probably, and the Ōtomo no Muraji, certainly, first achieved prominence as commanders of such forces during the period
when these houses were being "promoted" from special-purpose to general-purpose

institutions. Clearly, as property came to be regarded as private and heritable, the kin groups that had formerly exercised joint rights in labor pools were increasingly forced to face these alternatives: they could persuade the nobility to accept them as members of either secondary royal lineages or the high nobility; they could be absorbed as specialized dependent elements into a new socioeconomic structure (this was the course of action followed with examplary success by the Soga 蘇我 family, who claimed descent from an old *·*Jwię* [Wa] culture hero);[47] or they could suffer progressive disenfranchisement, sometimes to the point of extinction.

Kiley distinguishes four marriage classes within the upper stratum of the Yamato court during the sixth century, namely: the primary royal lineage, qualified to provide both kings and queens; secondary royal lineages, such as the Okinaga, qualified to provide queens only; the high nobility, qualified to provide heir-producing consorts but not queens; and the service nobility, typically *muraji* 連, who were unable to provide heir-producing consorts and who in fact supplied almost no royal consorts at all.[48] But, even through the veil of the archetyped records on which we have to depend, it is evident that numerous marked discrepancies between ceremonial status and political power were giving rise to a situation that Kiley likens to Ralph Nicholas' "segmentary factionalism."[49] Factions as envisaged here are "leader-follower groups" that come into being at the initiative of leaders competing for political power. Segmentary factional political systems, in Nicholas' words, "are frequently found in arenas where rapid social change is under way, where the rules of political conflict are fluid and ambiguous"[50] — in short, under conditions like those obtaining in sixth-century Japan.[51]

The outstanding incongruity between the status and power hierarchies defined above was probably manifested in the position of the noble Soga no Ōmi (蘇我 臣), who, by the middle of the sixth century, were serving as hereditary great councillors (*ō-omi* 大臣) at the Yamato court.[52] As such, they commanded political power far exceeding that of the secondary royal lineages, who ranked formally high above them. Or, in the terminology specified in chapter 1, a kin-based system-serving institution (the Soga lineage — or, perhaps more accurately, a particular segment of it) had promoted itself to a much higher level in the control hierarchy while concurrently arrogating to itself an almost totally self-serving (general-purpose) function. Specifically, the Soga were in charge of the three treasuries (see p. 105), in which capacity they superintended the collection, storage, and disbursement of the goods and commodities produced by a wide range of communities. In short, they managed the redistributive sector and, insofar as it had developed, the mobilizative sector of the Yamato economy. Thus, although the Soga were not formally classed with the service nobility, they in effect constituted an almost purely fiscal service corps entirely new to the developing Japanese bureaucracy. In practice these service functions were directed mainly to the management both of communities of immigrant Korean and Chinese craftsmen and of Yamato rice *miyake*. The very heterogeneity of these duties, as well as the diversity of the groups with whom they dealt, prevented the Soga from basing their relationships with producers on the familial practices common to other lineage activities. Instead they had to function as administrative chiefs whose roles were validated by the authority of the central government. Ueda Masaaki has elicited the manner in which the Soga method of fiscal administration operated in the Shirai *miyake* of Kibi, which was established in 555. In 569, when a superintendent (*tatsukai* 田 令) was appointed from one of the Soga branch lineages, his deputy was chosen from an immigrant family. As a reward for his managing ability, this deputy was permitted to use the name of the *miyake* as his own. On this particular estate, cultivators were organized into "brigades" and were assigned land, in continental style, on the basis of a cadastral register constructed in terms of *shiro* 頃 , a Korean unit of land measurement.[53]

The mention of continental practice in land management draws attention to another and even more far-reaching characteristic of the Soga no Ōmi, and that was their predisposition to adopt Chinese and Korean administrative techniques. This trait was in no way subverted by their status as a branch of the Yamato lineage, which gave them as a family a less sharply defined identity than was customary among those members of the nobility who traced their descent independently to high antiquity or who believed that from time immemorial they had ruled a choice piece of Japanese earth. Consequently, the Soga perceived few threats

to their status in their adoption of foreign institutions. As we have seen, continental influence was nothing new in Japanese history. Up to the third century
A.D. it was China, through her dependencies on the Korean peninsula, that contributed most. Subsequently, direct relations with the Middle Kingdom became
tenuous, so that Korean ties predominated. Almost at the beginning of the fifth
century, Paekche scribes, together with other Korean craftsmen, were being
employed at the Yamato court, and by the middle of that century their skills were
being applied to land management, notably under Soga direction. From the fourth
to the sixth century it was not rare for whole communities to migrate (or to be
transported) from the peninsula to the Japanese islands, so that entire villages
under direct Yamato control are known to have been composed solely of trans-
planted Koreans.[54] From the second half of the sixth century China was once
again beginning to provide the model that aspiring Japanese sought most assidu-
ously to emulate. This flow of ideas and institutions from the mainland to the
islands was especially significant in two sectors of the cultural spectrum:
institutions of government, particularly as these were developed under the Sui
(581-618) and T'ang dynasties (618-906), and the doctrines of Buddhism as these
were elaborated by the sinicized sectarian orders and institutionalized under the
power of the T'ang emperors.[55] The Soga were ardent advocates, even propagan-
dists, in both fields, but even they could hardly have perceived fully the extent
to which these two sets of institutions would prove responsive to the needs of
Japanese society. The extension of the *miyake* system, for instance, and the
expansion of the service nobility, as well as competition for reclaimed land
among local communities, raised complex issues related to the authority of the
central government vis-à-vis the interests of local communities and, in a very
imminent way, to the nature of proprietary rights themselves. The only adequate
solutions to fundamental problems such as these in the context of time and place
were Buddhist ideals of social order and Confucian precepts of statecraft. Nor
were adaptive models far to seek, for by the sixth century all the Korean kingdoms had adopted Buddhism as their state religion and were in process of adapting
a state-sponsored system of official ranks, reconstituting their governments on
the Chinese bureaucratic pattern, and applying to their own territories the land-

tax system that had been developed with considerable success by the Northern Wei
dynasty.

The adoption by the Yamato court of these alien, though by no means totally
unconformable, institutions was a process extending over nearly two centuries, of
which the recorded highlights are gross, and often archetyped, condensations,
symbols of a processual transformation rather than its substance. Buddhism was
surely known in Japan, for example, at least for some decades, and perhaps for a
century or more, before its official introduction to the Yamato court from Paekche in 552.[56] Similarly, continental administrative techniques were evident,
particularly in Soga managerial practice, for something like half a century
before Prince Shōtoku, in 604, allegedly promulgated a set of seventeen precepts
for the conduct of the ruling class, an ethical code for administrators in fact,
that replaced contextual kin-based morality by Confucian universalistic proprieties and substituted for lineage structures a centralized political organization
in which ultimate power was vested in an emperor and exercised through officially
designated functionaries.[57]

Almost exactly four decades later the Taika Reforms (*Taika no kaishin* 大化
改新) claimed, for the Yamato court, functions and prestige comparable to
those of the Chinese imperial government. Promulgated in 646 after a coup d'état
had eliminated a faction which, although conceding the virtues of a centralized
state, was willing to accord the supreme ruler only nominal powers (somewhat
ironically, led by the Soga family, the strongest proponents of sinicization),
the Reform Edict (*Kaishin no Shō* 改新詔) proclaimed the doctrines of absolute
sovereignty and eminent domain on the Chinese pattern, instituted a formula for
equitable land apportionment (*handen* 班田), reorganized the system of local
government, and instituted a new scheme of taxation. In these respects the Edict
was a bold attempt to formalize the sociopolitical changes taking place in seventh-century Yamato in terms of T'ang legal codes. There is some doubt as to the
authenticity of the Edict in the form in which the chroniclers saw fit to incorporate it in the *Nihon Shoki* but, even if radically edited, it still reflects the
dominant vectors of change as perceived by informed Japanese of the period.[58]
And it certainly provided a set of authoritative guidelines for the innovations

that slowly transformed the character of the Yamato state during the second half
of the seventh century. All the steps involved in the implementation of the
Taika program are not now recoverable, but the fact that in the deceptive perspective of time they appear to have proceeded with an inherent inevitability and
according to an intrinsic logic should not blind us to the frictions, disjunc-
tions, failures, and retrogressions that fuller knowledge would surely reveal.
Only with the promulgation of the Taihō 大寶 Codes in 702 and the Yōrō (養老)
Codes in 718[59] was the pervasive but subtle influence of Chinese political theory
temporarily and expedientially accommodated to Japanese institutional realities.
For the ensuing two centuries the Yamato court manifested a virtually total commitment in principle to the idea of imperial rule under heavenly mandate,[60]
underpinned by an ordered hierarchy of court ranks, a centralized government
bureaucracy, and a formalized legal and administrative apparatus.

Thus far we have sketched in broadest outline the evolution of the Japanese
state. Before we can relate this to the process of urbanization, we must examine
in rather more detail certain changes in social organization that were taking
place between the end of the fourth century and, say, the beginning of the ninth.
This will be the theme of our next section.

THE PROBLEM OF THE *UJI*

Central to any discussion of the changes in Japanese social organization that
occurred between the fourth and ninth centuries is the problem of the *uji* 氏 .
The Yamato court prior to the Taika Reform was itself essentially a federation of
powerful *uji* chieftains who recognized the overlordship of the chief of the
Yamato *uji*, yet the constitution and function of these social units in earlier
times is still a matter of debate — and this despite a great deal of intensive
investigation by Japanese scholars in a wide range of disciplines. The earliest
direct evidence for the existence of such units dates from about the middle of
the fifth century A.D., and there is no reference to their chiefs (*uji no kami*
氏 の 上) prior to the later decades of the seventh. Nevertheless, it has customarily been assumed that the sixth-century *uji* were survivals of a mode of
lineage organization extending back at least to the first century A.D. Although

their composition in pre-Taika times is vigorously disputed, most students of the problem would probably subscribe to the statement that the *uji* of, say, the sixth century were territorially based groups of families linked through ties of kinship, either genetic or fictive, to a powerful lineage whose authority, particularly in ritual matters, derived from consanguineal proximity to a main line of descent. Those for whom this description is too precise might still be prepared to endorse Cameron Hurst's definition of the *uji* as "heterogeneous units bound by both territorial and kinship ties."[61] But beyond formulations of this order of generality, agreement on the origin, structure, and function of the pre-Taika *uji* is unexpectedly limited in scope and somewhat sporadic in occurrence.

This is not the time to attempt to resolve the numerous and intricate problems that beset the study of *uji* origins and development, many of which are in any case probably insoluble on the basis of currently available evidence. What follows is merely a conspectus of the major issues as they bear on the evolution of the Japanese urban tradition.

In the first place, the *uji* was, or at least purported to be, an institution generating and distributing social and political power at least partly on the basis of kinship. Let us therefore begin with that aspect of *uji* functions. The implication of Late Yayoi archeological assemblages that lineages were probably assuming political importance among the *·*Jwię̑ is confirmed in the third century A.D. by the *Wei Chih* account of the transmission of authority from Pimiko to her successor,[62] but the earliest extant explicit reference to an *uji* is no earlier than the middle of the fifth century.[63] Back in the third century the *Wei Chih* also attests the existence of a by no means negligible degree of stratification in *·*Jwię̑ society.[64] Among the terms of respect (*keishō* 敬称) current in the sixth century, the ones that can be traced farthest back are **piko* and **pime* (Mod. Jap. = *hiko*, *hime*). The former actually figures in the *Wei Chih*,[65] under the Chinese transcription of **pjię̑-kạu* 卑狗 , as the title of the chief official 大官 in the communities on both Tsushima and Iki islands, while an office or title of *kokochi-hiko*[*-piko*] (**kạu-kuo-t̂ię̑-pjię̑-kạu* 狗古智卑狗) is attributed to the Kuna territory.[66] In a passage that probably relates to obscure events in about the middle of the fourth century, the *Kudara Ki* refers to a military leader under the name Satsuhiko 沙至比跪 who, significantly, in later times came to be regarded as the progenitor of the Kazuraki lineage, one of the earliest such units known to have received an *uji* name.[67] In the same connection it is probably not fortuitous that *biko* 彦 was also incorporated in the styles of two early rulers of Yamato, namely, Mimakï Iri-biko Iniwe nö Mikötö (Sujin) and Ikumë Iri-biko Isati nö Mikötö (Suinin), the former of whom is often regarded by modern scholars as the founder of a dynasty of ritual-religious chiefs, probably toward the end of the third century.[68] Finally, the frequent occurrence in the *Yamashiro Fudoki* 山城風土記 of the names Tamayorihiko 玉依日子 and Tamayorihime 玉依日賣 would seem to imply that in the eighth century the terms *hiko* and *hime* were believed to have been used in earlier times as honorary affixes to the personal names of members of the aristocracy associated with the Yamato court.[69] *Pime* 媛 was presumably the first element in the style *Pimiko (or perhaps more accurately *Pimiha) assumed by the third-century chieftainess of the territory known to the Chinese as *Ia-ma-d'ǎi.[70] Subsequently it became a frequent element in the names of Yamato ladies of high rank.

The etymology of *piko is obscure, but Motoori Norinaga, on the grounds that the *pi* 上匕 was generally rendered by 靈異 (which today would probably be explicated as *mysterium fascinans*) in the *Nihon Shoki* and that *ko* 古 did duty for *ko* 子, deduced that the honorific signified "the male child possessing supernatural power." If this argument is valid (which is by no means established), it would suggest that the highest office below that of chief in some parts of Yayoi Japan was held by a male with shamanistic powers.

That such a stratification developed within a society structured primarily on the basis of kinship should occasion no surprise. The most commonly encountered mode of organization of a chiefdom (which is the level of integration to which, on other grounds, we have assigned Pimiko's polity) is by means of distinctions in kinship grade. These distinctions are established on grounds of genealogical distance from an actual or putative ancestor. By regularly favoring descendants in the main line over those of junior of "cadet" lines in the regulation of access to social, economic, political, and even spiritual rewards, such units appear to the investigator simultaneously as descent groups and units of

political order. Such systems of hierarchically ordered familial priorities
within lineages are known alternatively as conical clans or ramages.[71] Their
significance to the present inquiry resides in the fact that, by conceptualizing
post-third-century Japanese society as a series of such units incorporating elements of both kin and class, we have been able to circumvent the debate as to
whether the early *uji* were primarily kinship groups (as Early Modern Japanese
scholarship usually maintained) or were political institutions introduced into
the *·*Jwię* territories by foreign invasion (as Egami and, before him, the Marxist
historians have implied). Our answer is that they were probably both, with the
emphasis gradually shifting between, say, the third and fifth centuries in the
direction of increased politicization.[72] In terms of the Flannery model, discussed in chapter 1, this would be a striking example of the evolutionary *mechanism of promotion* contributing to the *process of segregation* by raising an existing institution from a primarily system-serving (special-purpose) level to a more
self-serving (general-purpose) level. The difficulty in following through with
this style of interpretation lies in identifying the socioenvironmental stresses
that selected for a particular mechanism. We are not yet at the point where we
are able to do that for the development of the *uji*, but it is surely a focus for
future research.

There is no reason to suppose that the continuing operation of the twin
processes of segregation and centralization could not ultimately have induced in
*·*Jwię* society an urban/state level of integration, but, as events transpired, the
evolutionary sequence was almost certainly interrupted, probably toward the end
of the fourth century, by a still imperfectly understood alien intrusion. Possibly there were other conquests as well, at different times. The effect of this
(or these) intrusions on the development of the *uji* is still unresolved, but that
it broadened the scale of *·*Jwię* society there can be no doubt. By this we mean
that it extended the radii of societal interdependence, increased the intensity
of that interdependence, enlarged the range and content of the information flows
that integrated societal action, and expanded the sphere of compliance and control. In short, it seems (on our present understanding of events in fifth-
century Japan one can hardly ever be more definite) to have effected a major step

forward in the transition from chiefdom to state. And the main control center
for the emergent larger-scale society, the critical locality in which the organizational output of one institution became the input of another, was the proto-
urban ritual-ceremonial Yamato court. Whether or not the Puyŏ dynasty (if it was
indeed Puyŏ) survived (Ledyard thinks it did; see note 41) for only a few generations before being replaced by a native *·*Jwi̯e̯* power, it surely impressed on Japanese society the stamp of centralized leadership.[73] One manifestation of this
centralization was the style *Ōkimi* 大王 assumed by paramount rulers at least from
the time of Hanzei (whose adjusted dates fall in the first half of the fifth century) until it was replaced by Sumera Mikoto toward the end of the sixth century.

By the sixth century all social groups designated in the official records as
uji were bearers of hereditary titles of nobility (*kabane* 姓). One such *kabane*
is of particular interest in the present inquiry, for it was among the earliest
titles to be associated with an *uji*. This title was *Wake* (strictly *Wakë*: 別 and
和氣), a *kabane* held by certain families of local rulers, primarily those
belonging to collateral descent groups that claimed to have branched off from the
Yamato lineage prior to the time of Ōjin. Etymologically, the term is usually
considered to carry the implication of "youth" or "young fellow," but, more
importantly, it was the only title or rank ever to be incorporated into the personal names of supreme rulers. In fact, it appeared in the names of six of the
early so-called "emperors," specifically, Keikō, Ōjin, Richū, Hanzei, Kenzō, and
Tenchi, all of whom, with the exception of Tenchi, are assigned to the fourth and
fifth centuries, and it has been shown that *Wake* was a late addition to Tenchi's
style, made in order to render him the equal of Ōjin.[74] As far as lesser individuals were concerned, it may not be without significance that the term was
employed most frequently during the time of Keikō, a reign that allegedly witnessed a considerable expansion of the Yamato frontiers, particularly in Kyūshū
and the southern Tōhoku. Moreover, even in the sixth and seventh centuries a
preponderance of the *uji* claiming collateral descent from early members of the
imperial family were to be found in the Kinai and the eastern tracts of the
Setouchi. Consequently, it is not impossible that the adoption of *Wake* as an
honorific was in some way or other associated with the territorial expansion and

consolidation undertaken by Keikō. Perhaps it originally denoted the initiator
of a cadet line within the conical clan of Yamato, possibly a Yamato chieftain
who had distinguished himself in frontier skirmishing, as a result of which he
became the ancestor of a cadet line. In Weberian terms, such a chieftain might
have been appointed a benefice-holder under patrimonial domain, in which case the
use of a title with the etymological implications of "youthfulness" and "separation" might not have been wholly inappropriate. Moreover, *Wake* would then have
been the stem-lineage analogue of *kimi* (君, 公), a title bestowed on benefice-
holders outside the Yamato lineage.

The political effectiveness of the chiefdom in comparison with more egalitarian tribes, especially when it was structured as a conical clan, invested that
form of organization with a capacity for aggrandizement that has been documented
on numerous occasions in ethnographic reporting. Paul Kirchhoff, in proposing
the term "conical clan," emphasized the flexibility of such stratified kin groupings in the face of change, as well as their potentialities for the evolution of
socially and economically differentiated hierarchies.[75] More specifically, both
Egami and Ledyard have pointed to the propensity of Puyŏ lineages to branch and
rebranch into a sociopolitical hierarchy ranked according to genealogical distance from the parent stem. At present an interpretation along these lines can
be based only on inference and speculation, but it would seem to be a hypothesis
worthy of further investigation.

In a comprehensive and detailed study of the evolution of *Wake* titles, Saeki
Arikiyo has shown that, although the term was used only as an honorific in personal names during the fourth and fifth centuries, by about the middle of the
latter century it had come to signify a hereditary court office. In other words,
it had become a true *kabane*. Finally, during the sixth century, it was employed
not only as a title but as an *uji* name as well.[76]

Another type of native social organization that was at least partially
politicized in later times was the *tomo* (伴, strictly *tömö*). This word seemingly occurs in the *Wei Chih* account of the **·Jwię* as the title of the chief
official of **Pię̯u-mjię̯*.[77] In fact the primary meaning of the graph lies in a
range that includes "companion" and "right-hand man." By the fifth century it

had come to denote a sodality of professional functionaries, incipient bureaucrats as it were, whose fortunes were bound intimately to those of the imperial
family. The senior functionary of such a sodality was known as a *tomo no miyatsuko* (伴造). However, almost no attempts have been made systematically to
trace the institution back to its origins. When that has eventually been done,
it may be possible to elicit some connection between the *tomo* of *$P\underset{\sim}{i}\partial u$-$mji\underset{\sim}{e}$* and
the *tomo-osoi* 艫襲い who in the old Okinawan kingdom of Chūzan could be either
the steersman of a boat or an assistant to a Noro priestess (cf. note 45 to chapter 2), and this in turn raises a possible relationship with the steersman
depicted on the wall of an early rock-cut tomb at Takaida in Kashiwara[78] and the
curious, presumably allegorical, "rock boats" of early Puyŏ and *·*Jwi̯ĕ* (Wa) mythology.[79] Such connections may well not have existed at all or, if found, could
be illusory, but there is every likelihood that the earliest recorded *tomo* performed quasi-ritual functions. What is of interest in the present context is
that the *tomo* was apparently an indigenous institution which changed both its
form and function with the progressive centralization of the Yamato state and
that, through a process that is not at all clear, certain *tomo* came to bear *uji*
titles.

Some Japanese scholars have related the *tomo*, the more inclusive institution
of the *be* 部,[80] and the *uji* to the construction of *kofun*. By tracing the titles
of personages supposedly interred within the *zempō-kōen* tombs (p. 54, above),
Nishijima Sadao, for instance, was led to conclude that the deceased had always
received a *kabane* of some sort: at first *ōkimi* 大王, *kimi* 君, 公, *ōmuraji* 大
連, or *muraji* 連 but subsequently, in the provinces, *atahe* 直, *miyatsuko* 造,
or *agata-nushi* 縣生.[81] Such a title, Nishijima believed, signified the establishment of a fictive kin relationship between the paramount chief in Yamato and
the head of a corporate descent group, who was thereby permitted to construct a
tomb. On this view the early *kofun* were not simply material expressions of the
stratification of Yamato society but rather manifestations of the developing
power of the court itself. Nishijima also regarded the practice of *kofun* burial
as an attempt by the Yamato chiefs to participate, as components in the Chinese
tribute system, in the ritual of the Chinese court.

Like Nishijima, Kondō Yoshirō also regarded the *kofun* as representing a
lineage relationship which finally came to signify political legitimation,[82] but
he was prepared to derive such tombs from Late Yayoi ritual interments that often
included group burials of the type recently excavated at Hirabara in Fukuoka prefecture. When continental practice eventually reinforced indigenous custom,
Kondō discounted Chinese influence in the earlier phases in favor of Korean.

During the course of a long and detailed discussion, Harashima Reiji argued,
somewhat dubiously in our opinion, that the communal commitment involved in wet-
padi farming during the Middle and Late Yayoi prejudiced the development of the
household as a social unit in favor of a larger corporate group (*kyōdōtai* 共同
体),[83] which was under the authority of a shamanistic leader who in turn conferred rank on other members of the group. During the Tumulus period this mode
of social organization, which had evolved over several centuries of wet-padi cultivation, was also responsible for *kofun* construction. As Harashima reconstructs
the processual development of the period, the *tomo no miyatsuko* (p. 98 , above)
was an incipiently bureaucratized version of the old shamanistic leader of the
Yayoi *kyōdōtai*, who provided services related to the construction and maintenance
of the *kofun* and who supervised the associated rituals of the burial ceremonies.
While the *uji* of Ōtomo and Mononobe performed military duties, ritual matters
were the prerogative of the Imbe 齋部, the Kagami-tsukuri 王作, and the Tama-
tsukuri 鏡作, and the construction and surveying of tombs was assigned to the
Kajibe 鍛冶and the Hajibe 土師.[84] According to Harashima, the construction
of *kofun* provided (in Flannery's terms, which, needless to say, were not employed
by the Japanese author) the socioenvironmental stress selecting for the mechanisms through which the processes of segregation and centralization operated. As
we see it, the lineage chiefs, although retaining control of the more important
offices in the state, began to grant more and more minor offices for the performance of lesser services. At the same time, such primary occupations as iron-
working, on which the less powerful groups depended for agricultural implements
as well as military equipment, were kept strictly within the Yamato lineage: in
the Flannery scheme, "meddling" in no uncertain terms. In this way not only was
economic specialization promoted but the foundations of a superordinate redis-

tributive system were firmly established. It was at this stage in the process of societal change that the community deity was transformed into an ancestral deity. Thus argued Harashima. While we cannot accept his argument in its totality, we do consider it extremely probable that the *kofun* symbolized the revalorization of the old Yayoi lineage system as exemplified in Pimiko's time in the form of a conical clan, a proto-*uji*, as it were.

These are only three of the numerous studies that bear on the origin and development of the *uji*. They are no more in agreement among themselves than are numerous others which we have not discussed; yet out of a welter of conflicting exposition and explication it is perhaps permissible to elicit a developing trend of thought. If so, it can be epitomized in the affirmation that it was the development of the Yamato court that created the eighth-century *uji*, not, as has traditionally been accepted, that the court emerged as the most powerful among a congeries of competing *uji*, all fully developed on the eighth-century pattern. Our own interpretation, which has no more claim to acceptance than anybody else's, discerns an incipient centralization of authority and power among the *·*Jwie̯* in Late Yayoi times, which was probably enhanced by a Puyŏ conquest that in turn provided an impetus to territorial expansion, followed by a further intensification of the centralization process. And with increased centralization came the more pronounced stratification of society that gave rise to the *uji* in more or less the form upon which the chroniclers of the eighth century set their imprimatur and which they projected into what was, even then, a remote antiquity.

Although it would seem that the earliest *uji* recognizably congruent with those of the seventh century appeared in about the middle of the fifth century, they seem not to have been institutionalized in that form throughout the Yamato territories until the rise of a service nobility in the sixth century. In this connection it must surely be significant that all of the first *uji* to exercise a marked degree of power at the court seem to have performed distinctive service functions. It would appear that the emergence of the service nobility (cf. p. 86, above), by contributing to an increase in stratification within the ranks of the elite, tended to restrict the number of lineages whose members could aspire to the higher offices of the court. At the same time, the existence of such a service nobility enabled the court to absorb an increased number of lineages into the lower echelons of its bureaucratic apparatus, thereby inducing a greater degree of economic specialization and social differentiation over an ever-broadening expanse of territory. The implication of this type of interpretation of the transformation from *·Jwiə̯* chiefdom to Yamato state is not so much that entirely new institutions were developed but rather that the concomitant increase in societal scale (as defined above) induced a refocusing of organizational goals and a consequent reconstitution of society and polity on a more universal basis. One important manifestation of this transformation during the fourth and fifth centuries was the emergence of a new style of community in which men came to be united through a network of superior-subordinate relationships that in recent times has been aptly characterized as the Age of Loyalties 忠誠時代.[85]

As court offices became hereditary and specific groups claimed the right to perform certain functions by right of birth, the *uji* developed into a diversified and highly articulated institution. This seems to have occurred soon after the *·Jwiə̯* resurgence under Keitai (if that is what really happened; cf. note 41) during the first half of the sixth century, as the old and powerful lineages providing military and ritual services lost ground to numerous less prestigious *uji* possessing primarily economic functions. At the same time, lineage chiefs began to acquire control over various types of occupational groups bearing no blood relationship to them, namely, the *be* 部, mentioned above.[86] Concomitantly, cadet lines, which today are usually referred to as branch *uji*, began to proliferate, though it is to be suspected — but by the nature of the evidence it is invariably difficult to prove — that certain alleged collateral descent groups were in fact only fictive kin to the stem lineage. Such a practice is by no means unknown in conical clans in other parts of the world, being comparatively well documented, for example, in Arabia of the Jāhilīyah and early Islamic times, when, in extreme circumstances, a whole clan might seek the protection of, and be absorbed by, a more powerful *qawm* or *qabīlah*. It is also quite common even today among the descent groups, found primarily in rural communities in northeast Japan, to which Japanese sociologists have applied the term *dōzoku* 同族.[87] Simply by adopting chiefs of segmentary tribes into the centralized hierarchy, chiefdoms everywhere are potentially capable of transforming neighboring groups into reduced replicas of themselves and thereby extending the territories subject to the paramount chief, often at a surprisingly rapid rate. Marshall Sahlins has summarized the results of such an expansion as follows:

> To speak of the greater social scope and power of paramount chiefs does not completely document the advance. What has been wrought is not just greater chiefs but a *system* of chieftainship, a hierarchy of major and minor authorities holding forth over major and minor subdivisions of the tribe: a chain of command linking paramount to middle-range and local-level leaders, and binding the hinterland hamlet to the strategic heights.[88]

This seems to have been essentially what was happening in southern Japan during the fifth century.[89]

By the beginning of the sixth century the fabric of Japanese sociopolitical organization consisted of an immensely intricate web of lineage, occupational, and political rights and obligations, the generalized surface patterning of which manifested a replication of variable units whose shared structural lineaments designated them as *uji*.[90] The *uji* chief, supposedly a direct descendant of the lineage founder, mediated both ritually between the group and the *uji* deity and politically between the group and the Yamato court. In both roles he was simultaneously proclaiming a pervasive awareness of lineage solidarity and enhancing his own authority, both sacred and secular, within the group. At the same time, through a series of shared rituals, all members of the *uji*, each at his or her appropriate level, were afforded the opportunity to express, symbolically or otherwise, the ideational content of their mutual relationships. But these social units exhibited such signal differences in size, composition, and political power that an ideal-type *uji*, abstracted from the flux of institutional forms, would bear little relation to sixth-century reality, while a constructed type would prove inordinately unwieldy.[91] It is also to be suspected that there was no inconsiderable degree of independent variation between the phenomenological and ideational orders of society, such as Keith Brown has demonstrated for contemporary *dōzoku*.[92] Such discrepancies between the two orders, though difficult to prove across a millennium, are frequently hinted at in the genealogies of the time and would certainly repay further investigation.

This same century witnessed an intense competition for political power among

a few powerful *uji* chieftains, a multifaceted struggle which in the seventh century resolved itself into a confrontation between the imperial house and the Soga
uji. The outcome was the program of institutional innovation known as the Taika
Reform,[93] designed to replace a patrimonial-style, *uji*-based court government
with a centralized, Chinese-style bureaucracy. However, even Temmu Tennō's subsequent rationalization of the whole system of social ranking in 684 -- an
attempt to eliminate the major discrepancies between status, rank, and title that
had developed during the preceding two centuries and that would have the additional desirable effect of consolidating the status of the imperial family[94] --
failed to subvert the *uji* basis of Japanese society. What it did achieve effectively enough was a restructuring of the framework within which *uji* power could
be deployed, at the same time as it validated the new order of social precedence
with quasi-religious antecedents that rendered it virtually unassailable.[95] It
was within this rigorously ordered, yet in some respects surprisingly flexible,
social milieu that the Japanese urban tradition assumed its classical form.

EARLY YAMATO PALACE-CAPITALS

> The Land of Yamato is a land
> Where matters fall as will the gods
> Without lifted words of men.
> *Man'yōshū* 13:3250

The early capitals of the Yamato state were invariably identified with the principal residence of the ruler. In conformity with a belief widespread through
many parts of the world but accorded especial emphasis in Shintō, namely, that a
dwelling is polluted by death, each ruler at his accession constructed a new palace. Not infrequently, misfortune induced the abandonment of a palace even during a reign, followed by the ceremonial building of a new one. As construction
was always in wood, with pillars sunk directly into the earth and the frame
lashed with fiber strands, this was not, in the earlier periods at any rate, an
unduly onerous task. There seems to have been a tendency, moreover, for a newly
enthroned emperor to establish his official residence in the vicinity of his
mother's house, a reflection, perhaps, of the fact that imperial consorts almost
routinely raised their children in their private palaces, whence in fact rulers
often acceded to the throne; so that it was not unnatural for a son to incline

toward the locality in which the maternal household was situated and with which
he was most familiar. When the seat of government was located physically within
the royal household, the migration of the ruler to a new palace inevitably
entailed the transfer of his administrative apparatus as well.[93]

There is no reason to suppose that the palace-capitals of the chieftains who
imposed their rule on the Yayoi agriculturalists at the end of the fourth century
differed in their essentials from the ritual-administrative complexes of the earlier *·Jwi̯e̤ (Wa) groups as represented by the chiefdom of Pimiko. None has been
identified archeologically, much less excavated, and the purportedly specific
information contained in the chronicles is at best unreliable and at worst wholly
spurious. Nevertheless, it is reasonably certain that the core of each of these
chiefly capitals was a fortified palace that either incorporated, or was surrounded by, quarters for the patrimonial-style personal administrative staff of
the ruler. The paramount capital was simply the particular residential complex
that happened to be occupied by the chief who, by election or force of arms, had
achieved supreme rule. With the progress of the fifth and sixth centuries, rules
of succession were gradually formalized and the chiefs of Yamato established
their primacy among a congeries of competing lineages. At the same time, the
administrative staff expanded and diversified its institutional structure. To
judge from the admittedly dubious records of the *Nihon Shoki*, artisans, craftsmen,
and military retainers congregated in the vicinity of the paramount capital,
which figures in the chronicles simply as the *miyako* 都 , or seat of government.

Yagi Atsuru has attempted to elicit from the ancient records the morphologi-
cal evolution of the governmental complex that ultimately came to be such a prominent feature of the Chinese-style capitals. In early times, of course, court
functions (which were in fact those of the ruler's household) and state functions
were but weakly discriminated, but with the emergence in the fifth century of an
incipient bureaucratic apparatus, it becomes possible to distinguish between what
were styled an Inner Court (*Naitei* 内廷) and an Outer Court (*Gaitei* 外廷).
At first the Inner Court was located within the ruler's palace and was supervised
by a *tomo no miyatsuko* (see p. 98), but subsequently these two institutions
underwent a physical separation, with government offices being constructed adja-

cent to the palace. Notable among these were the three treasuries, namely, the Imikura 斎藏, which housed ritual furniture and accoutrements, the Uchikura 内藏, for the storage of tribute from foreign peoples, and the Ōkura 大藏, where the fruits of taxation and other imposts were collected. It is significant, though, that the office dealing with religious affairs was always retained within the palace precinct (cf. note 175). In Yagi's view, the functions of the Outer Court were much more widely dispersed, being distributed among the mansions of ruling *uji* chiefs, traditionally sanctioned open spaces, and, after the middle of the sixth century, lineage temples.[97]

The conventional histories relate that between about A.D. 400 and the proclamation of the Taika program in 646, twenty-three rulers held sway over Yamato from no less than thirty-one paramount capitals (fig. 4). It has traditionally been accepted that Nintoku Tennō, whose adjusted dates fall at the turn of the fifth century, ruled from the palace of Takatsu 高津 in Naniwa 難波, on a site in present-day Ōsaka on the extreme eastern shore of the Inland Sea.[98] Naniwa was for long the port of entry into Yamato for travelers arriving by sea, the "玄関口 of Ōsaka Bay," as Fujioka Kenjirō has called it.[99] It was, for instance, at this port that envoys from Sui China landed in 608, and they were lodged there in an official residence prepared for them above that of the Koryŏ (Koreans).[100] The great avenue known in later times as the Takeuchi Thoroughfare 竹内街道 is also thought, rightly or wrongly, to have been constructed during the reign of Nintoku, for the *Nihon Shoki* (vol. 1, pp. 396-97; Aston trans., vol. 1, pp. 282-83) relates that in the fourteenth year of that ruler "a highway was built within the capital" (是歳作大道於京中), extending in a straight line as far as the village of Tajihi 丹比邑. Subsequent to the reign of Nintoku, the majority of the Yamato capitals were located in the southeastern angle of the Yamato plain, a district known as Asuka 飛鳥. Not all the earlier sites can now be identified, but the capitals dating from about the middle of the sixth century can be located with some precision. Kimmei Tennō, for example, established his palace called Shikishima no Kanasashi 磯城嶋金刺 on a site at present occupied by Sakurai city; Bidatsu moved to Kudara in present-day Koryō-cho; Yōmei returned to Sakurai city (though to a site different from that chosen

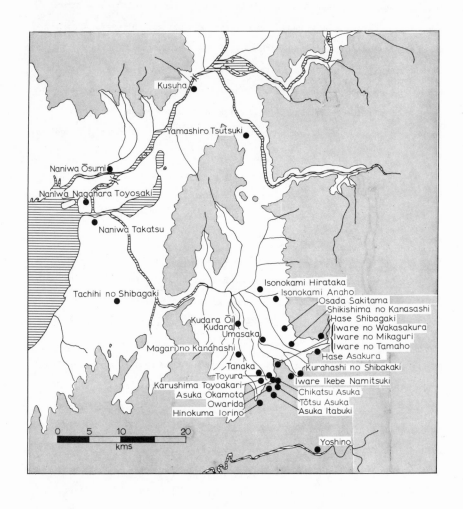

Fig. 4. Identified Yamato palace-capitals, c. A.D. 400-646. Based on
information in the *Kojiki* and *Nihon Shoki*. The river system is that of
ancient times. Stipple denotes land over 500 feet in elevation.

by Kimmei); and Sushun in turn built nearby. These sites were on the northern
edge of the Asuka region or at Kashiwara to the west, but the Empress Suiko (592-
628) transferred her residence first to Toyura Palace 豐浦 and then to Owarida
Palace 小墾田宮, both in the close vicinity of Asuka itself. Most of the succeeding pre-Taika Yamato capitals were located within a ten-mile radius of Asuka,
where they constituted a continuing, though locationally oscillating, concentration of political power and authority that attracted to itself an aggregation of
public buildings, Buddhist temples, and Shintō shrines.[101] The two former were
already being built according to continental canons of construction and taste.

The earliest palace so far identified was never the principal seat of a paramount ruler but rather a retreat constructed outside Asuka, at Ikaruga, by
Prince Shōtoku in 601 and destroyed during the factional feuds preceding the
Taika Reforms. Excavations undertaken in 1939 revealed an arrangement of buildings that bore little relation to what was soon to become the standard palace
layout. In fact, Sawamura Ji has suggested that the plan of the Ikaruga palace
was more consonant with a design of Chinese origin known as *shinden-zukuri* 寝
殿造. However, this arrangement of buildings around a garden apparently was
not well known in Japan until it was adopted by noble families late in the Heian
period.[102] By contrast, a palace complex excavated in the southern sector of
Asuka exhibited many of the features that had already been incorporated in Buddhist temple construction and which were subsequently adopted as standard practice in palace architecture. Some Japanese scholars have identified this palace
as the Asuka no Itabuki 飛鳥板蓋, built to the order of Empress Kōgyoku in 642
and occupied by her during her first reign (641-645) and again after she was
restored to the throne as Empress Saimei (655-661),[103] though the remains brought
to light thus far do not correspond at all closely with the implications of several passages in the *Nihon Shoki*. There is no sign, for instance, of the twelve
gates mentioned in the chronicle, of a Chōdō-in (朝堂院 : Palace of Administration), or of a Daigoku-den (大極殿 : literally, Palace of the Supreme
Ultimate; functionally, the Imperial Council Hall). Nevertheless, the circum-
stantial evidence supporting an identification with the Itabuki palace is sufficiently strong to suggest that the eighth-century chroniclers were not referring

to an actual historical building so much as they were projecting into the past
the practices of their own time.

The architectural canons of the earlier Buddhist temples erected in Yamato
were derived from the Korean kingdoms (fig. 5), those of the later ones, directly
from China. Even the Korean models were ultimately based on Chinese temple
architecture, which was itself an adaptation of palace architecture with the
addition of a pagoda on the major axis. During the Asuka period such temples
were of the more or less standard design represented by the Asuka-dera 飛鳥寺,
based on a Koguryŏ model,[104] which in the latter half of the seventh century
itself provided inspiration for the Kawahara-ji 川原寺[105] and, ideally, by the
Shitennō-ji 四天王寺,[106] ascribed to the year 593 and, almost a century later,
a model for the Yakushi-ji 藥師寺.[107] The exemplar for the Shitennō-ji was the
Kunsuri-sa 軍守里寺[108] in Paekche. Outside the Asuka district, near the bank
of the Yamato River, the Hōryū-ji 法隆寺 was raised shortly after 670 on the
site of an earlier temple built by Prince Shōtoku in 607. Its layout was apparently an original Japanese creation.[109] In the architectural conception exemplified by temples such as these the nucleus comprised a rectangular space surrounded by a cloister (*garan* 回廊),[110] with a Golden Hall (*kondō* 金堂, the main
hall of the temple) at its center and a pagoda (*tō* 塔)[111] on a southern extension of its longitudinal axis. Cardinal orientation was all but universal. The
main entrance to the temple precinct was by way of a Great Gate of the South
(*nandaimon* 南大門), from which one passed through a Middle Gate (*chūmon* 中門)
into the *garan*. Behind the Golden Hall was a so-called Lecture Hall (*kōdō* 講
堂) for communal study, while outside the *garan* were a bell tower (*shōrō* 鐘
楼), a *sūtra* repository (*kyōzō* 經藏), a refectory (*jikidō* 食堂), and living
quarters (*sōbō* 僧房). In the Shitennō-ji, which can serve as an ideal form for
these Asuka temples, the distances along the longitudinal axis, from the Great
Gate of the South, through the Middle Gate, the Pagoda, Golden Hall, and so to
the Lecture Hall, were in the proportions of 1.5 : 1.0 : 1.0 : 1.5 (measured from
the center of each building).[112]

There were two notable exceptions to the custom that located Yamato capitals
in Asuka. The first occurred in 645, when Kōtoku Tennō took up residence in a

new palace complex called Nagahara Toyosaki 長柄豐碕 in the old port settlement of Naniwa.[113] However, after nine years the capital was restored to Asuka,
presumably in response to clan and religious interests entrenched in that region.
Excavation at Naniwa, begun in 1952, has been severely restricted by the location
of the site in heavily built-up Hōenzaka-cho in Ōsaka city; so far it has
revealed the existence of a palace and an adjoining administrative complex, both
apparently of Chinese, or at least continental, inspiration. It seems probable
that Temmu Tennō (672-686) was the first to impose a thoroughly formal plan on
the site,[114] even though there is no reason to think that he resided there for
any length of time.[115] Certainly he constructed an "enveloping" (i.e., outer)
wall (*rajō* 羅城) enclosing either the palace complex or the whole city: the
Nihon Shoki, vol. 2, p. 438, is not explicit on this point, though it is surely
suggestive that less then a century later the Rashō Gate of Heijō marked the
outer limit of the city generally, not that of the Imperial Palace Compound. The
second occasion on which the capital was established outside the Asuka district
was in 667, when Tenchi Tennō transferred his court to Ōtsu 天津 on the west
shore of Lake Biwa,[116] in the Ōmi district; however, after a bare five years,
Emperor Temmu returned to Asuka.[117]

THE CHINESE-STYLE CAPITALS

Literary and archeological sources bearing on the capitals of the Asuka period
relate almost exclusively to the palaces and temples associated with their core
institutions, primarily those of an administrative and religious character (fig.
6). Information about the disposition of nonaristocratic residential quarters,
economic exchange systems, craft and other corporations — in fact, about all
other aspects of urban life — is virtually nonexistent. However, it is reasonably certain that in the earlier phases of the Asuka period, despite fairly rig-
orous canons governing palace and temple architecture, the surrounding settlement
was largely unplanned. There is no evidence that the capital as a whole was,
well into the seventh century, anything other than a ceremonial and administrative complex set amidst an accretion of residential and service facilities. With
the increasingly pervasive adoption of Chinese instruments of government, however,

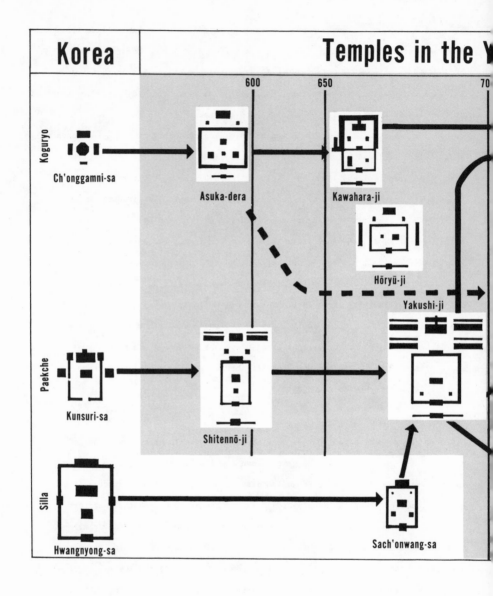

 Korea | Temples in the Y

Fig. 5. The derivation of Buddhist temple-compound layouts to about A.D. 800.
Based on Ōoka Minoru 大岡實, *Nara no tera* 奈良の寺 (Tōkyō, 1965), foldout Map I
at end of volume.

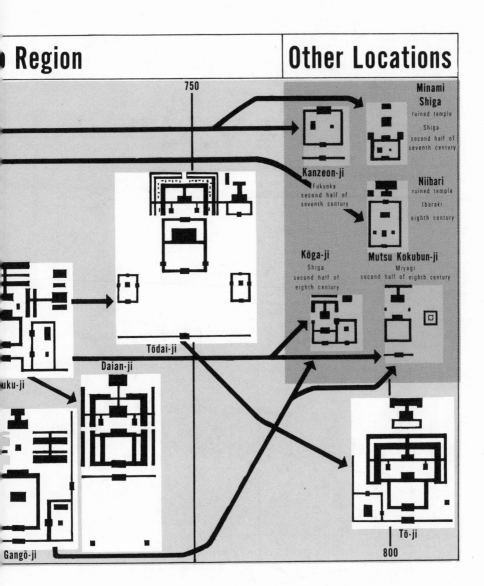

750

Minami Shiga
ruined temple

Shiga
second half of
seventh century

Kanzeon-ji
Fukuoka
second half of
seventh century

Niibari
ruined temple

Ibaraki
eighth century

Kōga-ji
Shiga
second half of
eighth century

Mutsu Kokubun-ji
Miyagi
second half of eighth century

uku-ji

Tōdai-ji

Daian-ji

Gangō-ji

Tō-ji

800

111

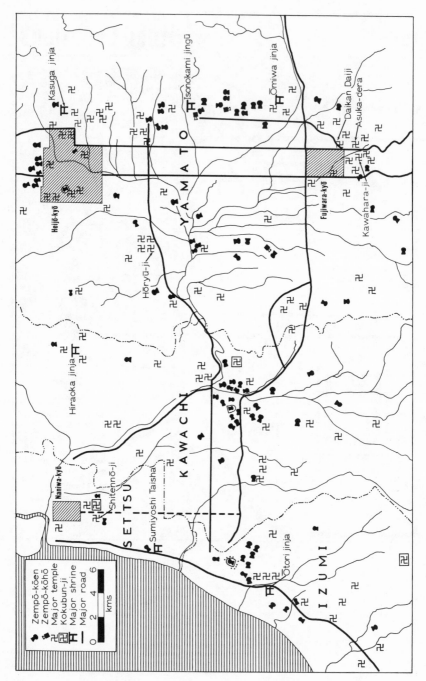

Fig. 6. The Yamato region from A.D. 646 to about 750. The river system is that of ancient times.

112

it was inevitable that the territorial locus of these institutions should ultimately have come to incorporate elements of the spatial organization of the Chinese capital that was itself both exemplar and epitome of the concept of social
order.

Precisely when the notion of a capital organized on these principles first
gained currency at the Yamato court is obscure, but it was certainly being promoted in the middle decades of the century. Article II of the Reform Edict of
646, for instance, prescribed the establishment of a metropolitan region (*uchi
tsu kuni* 内 國 [or 中 國]: lit. = the Interior [or Middle] Kingdom) focused on
an imperial city which was to be furnished with a new system of municipal government.[118] Whether this article is construed as a prescription for the future or
as a retrospective rationalization of events currently taking place will depend
on one's view of the authenticity of the Edict as presently preserved. So far,
archeology has elicited only ambivalent evidence for a regular layout in the
Naniwa contemporaneous with the Edict, which was in fact promulgated from the
palace of Nagahara Toyosaki in that city.[119] But during the second half of the
seventh century the distinctive Chinese orthogonal basis of urban design became
increasingly evident. The earliest known example may possibly have been the residential quarters surrounding the court complex of Kiyomigahara 淨御原 constructed by Temmu Tennō on his return to Asuka from Ōtsu in 672.[120] Archeology
has furnished only a minimal amount of information about this capital,[121] though
Hall, apparently quoting from an unspecified site report not available to us,
states that "Excavations of the site reveal a Ch'ang-an style plan with a division of the city into left and right halves."[122] In any case, the many mentions
of rooms and functions in the *Nihon Shoki* account of Temmu's reign would appear
to suggest an increase in the scope and complexity of palace architecture, probably in connection with the standardization of ceremonies that took place in
682.[123]

Whatever degree of overall planning may ultimately prove to have been
applied to the Naniwa and Kiyomigahara sites, the next capital of Yamato was certainly conceived as a unitary whole. This was the city of Fujiwara 藤原, which
was projected by Emperor Temmu[124] (though actually built during the reign of his

successor) when Kiyomigahara failed to provide adequate facilities for both the ramifying bureaucracy and an accompanying residential expansion. Located farther out into the Asuka plain than previous capitals, the city could also draw on a more extensive agricultural resource base. The site was inspected at different times in 690 by both Empress Jitō and imperial officials, was ceremonially purified and sacralized on at least two occasions, and was finally occupied by the court in 694.[125] Despite a decade of excavation that began in 1934 and was resumed for two years in 1966, there is still a good deal of uncertainty as to the dimensions of the city. Perhaps the most likely estimate is 2.6 km. from north to south and 1.7 from east to west, which Kojima Shunji has equated with a population of between 30,000 and 40,000 persons.[126]

Much of our knowledge of even the basic elements of the city plan is inferential, but it is usually interpreted as a reduced and simplified model either of Ch'ang-an directly or of a Sillan capital, near the site of present-day Kyŏngju, which had itself been reconstituted on the Chinese pattern subsequent to 670. The urban enceinte of Fujiwara was divided into eastern and western halves by a longitudinal avenue, the *Suzaku* 朱雀, which constituted a processional way leading up to the palace situated at the north center. All together, seven north-south avenues intersected twelve running from east to west to generate a grid of rectangular wards, sixteen of which were occupied by the palace. Twenty-four temples were eventually integrated into this design. Among these, the Daikandai-ji 大官大寺 (conceived as early as 673) and the Yakushi-ji, although begun prior to the foundation of Fujiwara, were so thoroughly conformable to the ward pattern as to leave no doubt that they were incorporated into the planning of the capital from the beginning. Finally, it should be noted that Temmu Tennō's tomb (*misasagi* 陵) was raised on an extension of the axial avenue leading southward from the palace,[127] a circumstance which has led Kishi to categorize the whole city as a Buddhist *maṇḍala*, a cosmogrammaton designed to reveal to the initiate the secret interplay of cosmic forces.[128] In this, Kishi was probably straining the evidence,[129] but what is quite certain is that the city of Fujiwara was laid out as an integrated design proximately or ultimately on the pattern of the contemporary Chinese imperial capital.

With the founding of Heijō-kyō 平城京 (or Nara 奈良) in 708 and its ceremonial occupation two years later, the court committed itself irrevocably to a mode of urban design explicitly reflective of the values of the Chinese civilization it was seeking to emulate. The location of the new capital in the center of the Yamato plain was a response to the logistical and administrative demands of the developing Japanese state, but the essentials of its form were indelibly Chinese. And that form, though not uncommon in one or another of its mutations throughout the traditional world, has until recently been fundamentally alien to the commercial-industrial urbanism of the modern world. Whereas the representative city in this latter context has most frequently been interpreted as a zonally or sectorally structured organic outgrowth from either a single center or, in one suite of interpretations, from multiple nuclei,[130] the model adopted by the Japanese in the seventh century represented the city, or at any rate the capital, as a fixed and perduring cosmion of sociopolitical order. Instead of all the potential zones of the developed city (sometimes smoothed to gradients) inhering, as it were, in an initial primitive cell that spawned its land-use patterns in a genetically programmed sequence of growth, the archetypical Chinese city of T'ang times was a rigidly articulating matrix of reduplicated units created once and for all to the preconceived design of self-confident dynasts. Growth was not, as in the representative Western city, organic and open-ended; it was allowed for, even encouraged, but only within the constraints of the cosmomagically sanctioned framework that was itself an essay in world creation. Interfaces between units were, generally speaking, stark and abrupt. The notion of gradient was morphologically (though not necessarily politically) inadmissible.

The Paradigm: T'ang Ch'ang-an

By the seventh century A.D. China had already experienced some two millennia of urban life. The earliest urban centers to emerge in the whole of eastern Asia had developed on the inner edge of the North China plain at some time around the middle of the second century B.C.[131] They took the form of ceremonial and administrative enclaves spread through an arcuate zone of the *Chung-yüan* 中原 from the neighborhood of Lo-yang in the west to An-yang in the north. Subsequently,

centers of this type diffused through most of the rest of the North China plain.
During the approximately three centuries of the Western Chou dynasty and the earlier part of the Ch'un-Ch'iu period (772-481 B.C.) the representative city seems
to have preserved the dispersed form of the Shang ceremonial center, but, from
about 550 on, a process of compaction is evident in both the literary and the
archeological records.[132]

The generalized urban form that resulted from this process was essentially a
square or rectangular walled enceinte exhibiting cardinal orientation, cardinal
axiality, and a powerful centricity generated by the authority vested in a centrally located palace (in the case of imperial or ducal capitals) or governmental
complex (in the case of lesser cities), which itself comprised an inner walled
enclave. The directional equality implicit in cardinal orientation in practice
yielded to a southerly bias, deriving from the fact that the Purple Hidden Enclosure, from which T'ai I, the Chinese cosmocrator, ruled the universe, lay to the
north of the terrestrial capital. As T'ai I, in his dealings with men, faced
south, his earthly counterpart of necessity did likewise and thereby conferred
preeminence on the longitudinal axis, the celestial meridian writ small. In conformity with this principle, all important architectural structures faced south
toward the Red Phoenix of summer. Indeed, the whole city may be said to have
assumed a southerly aspect. Within the walls, authority appears to have imposed
a fairly rigid zoning of functions. Government and administration were carried
on within the inner enceinte or ****to* 都 . So, too, were most public ritual
activities, though some important state temples appear to have been located outside the ****to*. Market exchange was confined to a designated space lying to the
north of the palace enclosure, while the sector of the city enclosed between the
inner and outer walls, and known as the ****pįəg* 鄙, housed the mass of the population and provided sites for most of the handicraft workshops serving it.

Preeminent among the sacred edifices, without which neither polity nor capital could come into or remain in being, was the state altar to the god of the
soil (****dˆįă* 社土), which was always kept unroofed in order "to receive," in the
words of the *Li Chi* 禮記, "the hoar frost, dew, wind, and rain, and to allow
free access by the influences of Heaven and Earth." The roofing-over of this

altar signified the extinction both of the ruler's line and of the state and its capital. The other essential ritual focus in the city was the temple of the ancestors (**m̯iog 廟), wherein rested the tablets of the agnatic ancestors and their wives and which provided a theater for all important state ceremonies, whether religious, political, diplomatic, or military. Between these two religious foci and the palace moved the ruler, the animating force of state and city, who, in Granet's words, "dispensed to men and things their destiny."[133] As the *Li Chi* phrased it: "When [the former emperors] presented their offerings to Shang-Ti 上帝 in the outskirts [of the capital], wind and rain were duly regulated, and cold and warmth came each in its appointed season, so that the Sage [Emperor] had only to stand with his face to the south for order to prevail throughout the world."

It was cities of this type that inspired the description that was to become the *locus classicus* for the design of Chinese capitals. This was incorporated in the *K'ao-kung Chi* 考工記, a document with some claim to antiquity which was substituted for a lost section of the *Chou Li* 周禮 during the second half of the first century A.D. The relevant passage reads as follows:

> The artificers (匠人) demarcated the [Royal Chou] capital as a square with sides of 9 *li*, each side having three gateways. Within the capital there were 9 meridional and 9 latitudinal avenues, each of the former being 9 chariot-tracks in width.[134]

On the evidence presently available, this passage can have represented only an idealized version of the manner in which Han exegetes considered a capital ought to be designed. Archeological investigation of Chou cities thus far has provided confirmation of the basic principles of the design but not of the specific internal structure implied by the *K'ao-kung Chi*. Nevertheless, the prescription has exercised a preponderant influence on the layout of subsequent Chinese imperial capitals. Certain of its design elements are apparent, for instance, in the plan of the Former Han capital of Ch'ang-an (長安: *D'i̯ang-·ân), although undulating terrain and the need to include preexisting Ch'in palaces and temples within the confines of the city precluded the laying-out of a rectangular perimeter. An effort was made imperfectly to meet the canonical desideratum of twelve gates arranged three to a side,[135] but functional zoning seems to have been enforced less rigorously than in Chou times, for some of the palaces and government offices were located in residential quarters, well away from the administrative enclave.

When the Northern Wei came to build Lo-yang 洛陽, the city that would symbolize their supremacy, they chose a locality that had already provided sites for earlier capitals, including those of the Royal Chou and the Later Han. By correlating archeological findings with literary evidence, Ho Ping-ti has been able to construct an eminently serviceable plan of the city as it existed in about A.D. 528.[136] His map shows that it occupied an area roughly 6-8 km. square and consisted of some 220 wards zoned in such a way as to segregate legally defined social groups. This principle had in fact been stated unequivocally by the official Han Hsien-tsung 韓顯宗 in a memorial discussing the proposed layout of the new capital, which read: "The separation of government offices from common dwellings and the segregation of the four classes of the populace shall forever be an immutable precept."[137] In the north-central sector of the city was a walled administrative precinct focusing on the royal palace and providing accommodation for nearly thirty government offices (fig. 7). Ten of these latter, which either served the person of the emperor and the imperial household or were functionally associated with others that did so, were located in the northern half of the enclave, close to the palace itself. In the west of the city, some thirty wards, known collectively as the Shou-ch'iu Li 壽丘里, were reserved for the imperial nobility and their relatives, while some of the most favored wards in the eastern suburbs were monopolized by officials and scholars. These same classes also shared with wealthy monasteries and educational establishments the slope leading from the southern wall of the administrative enclave down to the Lo River. The plebs were to be found mainly in the neighborhoods of the eastern and western markets[138] and in a group of wards in the northeast sector of the city. Foreigners, allegedly exceeding 10,000 households, were required to reside in the extreme south, on the far side of the Lo River, where they had set up their own market. Unlike the suburbs of most other Chinese capitals in both earlier and later times, those of Northern Wei Lo-yang were not enclosed within an outer

118

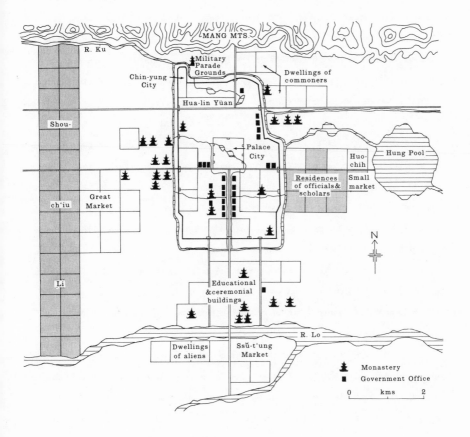

Fig. 7. The Northern Wei capital at Lo-yang in about A.D. 528. Based on a
reconstruction by Ho Ping-ti, "Lo-yang, A.D. 495–534," *Harvard Journal of
Asiatic Studies* 26 (1966): 94. Of the 220 wards (*li*) which constituted the
city, only those that have been positively identified are shown. Shaded
wards are those assigned for predominantly upper-class residences.

wall. The significance of this city in the present context resides in its having shared with the prescription in the *K'ao-kung Chi* the role of exemplar for the great capital of Sui and T'ang.[139]

When the Sui dynasts constructed a capital to project the glories of their newly united kingdom, they too, like the sovereigns of Northern Wei, chose a locality hallowed by a millennium and a half of intermittent association with royal power, namely, the Wei 渭 Valley of central Shen-hsi.[140] By reason of the potential fertility of its loessial soils wherever water could be made available, this sheltered westward extension of the North China plain had afforded a productive agricultural base for political and military power at the same time as it had provided the entrance to the main route from the Chinese heartland to Central, and ultimately to Western, Asia. In this strategic valley, near the present-day city of Hsi-an (西 安), Emperor Wen (文 帝) of Sui laid out his capital much on the lines prescribed by the ritual canon, styled it the Greatly Exalted City (大 興 城), and entered into residence there on 15 April 583. In 618 the first emperor of T'ang adopted it as his dynastic seat, renamed it Ch'ang-an (長 安) or [the City of] Enduring Peace, and initiated a series of design modifications that ultimately resulted in the layout depicted in figure 8. In its heyday the city was reputed to have had about a million inhabitants and to have occupied an area roughly six times more extensive then that enclosed within the Aurelian walls of Rome, or nearly seven times that within the extended enceinte of Constantinople constructed by Theodosius.[141]

Although the city was razed when the court moved to Lo-yang in 904,[142] traces of old walls and buildings survived to excite the curiosity of antiquarians in later centuries and to send several of them to contemporary texts in attempts to reconstruct the plan of the city.[143] The first modern investigator of the ancient city was Adachi Koroku, a Japanese schoolmaster who resided in Hsi-an from 1906 to 1910. He surveyed all the remains then accessible and correlated them with the literary evidence in a two-volume study that is still essential reading for all students of the great capital of T'ang. In 1933, Chinese archeologists undertook their first exploratory survey of the site; but not until 1956, when a program of massive redevelopment threatened to obliterate the sur-

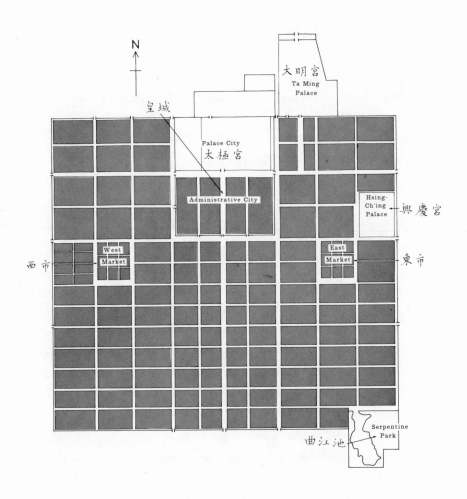

Fig. 8. Plan of Tʻang Chʻang-an during the eighth century. Based on Ma Te-
chih 馬得志, "Tʻang-tai Chʻang-an Chʻeng kʻao-ku chi-lüeh," *Kʻao-ku*
唐代長安城考古紀略 考古, no. 11 (1963), pl. 2. The overall dimen-
sions of the city were 6 x 5 1/4 miles, and the standard block was approximately two-thirds of a mile by one third. Other dimensions are specified in
the text.

viving remains of the ancient metropolis, was systematic excavation undertaken in
the form of a salvage operation. Thus far the foundations of one of the great
outer walls has been excavated and measured; most of the eleven gates have been
identified on the ground, and the northern Hsüan Wu Gate 宣武門 has been investigated in detail; the West Market 西市 has been excavated; and the architectural
complex comprising the Great Luminous Palace 大明宮 has been revealed in all
its ramifications. At the same time, incidental finds from all parts of the city
and its environs, and particularly those from tombs, have yielded a wealth of
information about the administrative geography of the metropolis and about life
in what one writer has designated as "the greatest walled city ever built by
men."[144]

The city with which the Sui and T'ang monarchs set the seal, as they thought,
on the developing tradition of Chinese urban design was of huge dimensions, a
cardinally orientated rectangular enceinte of approximately 6 miles by 5 1/4,
enclosed within walls of rammed earth, faced with ashlar and brick and reaching
to a height of nearly 18 feet.[145] Within this enclosure most of the ground was
apportioned in a grid of 110 standard spatial units (*fang* 坊), each ideally of
650 *pu* 步 x 325,[146] which was roughly equivalent to two-thirds of an English mile
by one-third of a mile. As laid out on the ground, all of these modular units
except two had at least one of the standard dimensions; but the need to incorporate the palace enclave just inside the north wall of the city[147] and the state
administrative complex (*Huang Ch'eng* 皇城) somewhat farther south, together
with the various spatial encroachments of the Palace of Exalted Felicity (興慶
宮),[148] the principal market places, the main boulevards, and the Ch'ü-chiang
(曲江) Lake,[149] ensured that exactly 60 of the units were shorter along one
dimension. The two blocks that conformed in neither direction were the Eastern
and Western markets, each of which occupied a tract 600-*pu* square[150] and was
divided into nine equal units on the pattern of the old well-field system.[151]
Each of the spatial units was surrounded by a wall possibly 9 or 10 feet high,
with gates opening into the streets on all four sides.[152] The eleven meridional
boulevards were all 100 *pu* (or 147 meters)[153] wide, and others were in proportion. The short avenue leading up to the Great Luminous Palace, the T'ang addi-

122

tion that did most to undermine the nearly perfect bilateral symmetry of the
original design,[154] was no less than 120 *pu* in width. All of the twenty-five
avenues that constituted the basic grid were flanked on each side by drainage
channels and these, in turn, by footpaths along the low walls of the *fang*, which
were often shaded by elms and pagoda trees. Between the controlled magnificence
of the framework of the urban grid and the interior of the *fang* the contrast was
abrupt and total: without was orthogonal order, within — apart from the
straight street bisecting the module from east to west, and occasionally another
from north to south — was a maze of narrow, sharply articulated lanes affording
access to the south entrances of residential and business establishments. One of
the larger mansions is known to have occupied a full half of a sector and to have
housed some 3,000 persons. Extended to the city as a whole, this residential
pattern would project a density of 56 persons per acre, but we know that population was not spread evenly through the city. Generally speaking, the upper
classes resided in low-density mansions in the eastern half of the metropolis,
the merchants and commoners in more crowded housing in the western sectors. In
any case, the more southerly *fang* were but thinly populated, being mostly under
cultivation broken only by a few scattered shrines and gardens.

The reader will have noticed that the design plan of Ch'ang-an in its heyday,
quite apart from incremental extensions beyond the boundaries of the grid,
diverged in several important respects from the canonical prescription. Perhaps
the most fundamental anomaly was the placing of the main palace complex against
the northern wall of the city, a procedure which violated the canon but was in
accord with the practice at Northern Wei Lo-yang. Nor was there canonical
authority for grouping government offices in a segregated enclave immediately to
the south of the palace precinct or for the laying-out of residential wards in a
semicircle on the east, south, and west sides of the joint palace and administrative enclaves. Finally, the markets, as at Lo-yang, were situated south of the
palace but also toward the eastern and western boundaries of the city, where they
were easily accessible to dealers and traders not only from the surrounding countryside but also from the most distant corners of Asia. Professors Ch'en Yin-k'o
and Naba Toshisada were surely correct when they attributed these divergences

from the classical design to the planners' experiences in the polyglot societies of North China under the alien dynasties that had preceded the Sui. Nevertheless, although purely Chinese traditions of urban design may have been weakened during the centuries of disunion, the innovations did not fail to dramatize the ancient hierarchy of authority. The Son of Heaven still stood, as Mencius had prescribed, in the center of the earth with, as the *Li Chi* required, his face to the south, thereby regulating the seasons and stabilizing the populace. From his ritual position in the Palace of the Supreme Ultimate he exercised authority over the bureaucrats in the Huang Ch'eng, and they in turn ruled the city in all its manifold complexities.

It is not incumbent on us here to describe the strictly architectural components of the city or to elaborate on the heterogeneity of the population that either inhabited or passed through its quarters. What the Japanese adopted, perhaps through a Korean intermediary, was not the social structure of Ch'ang-an, and certainly not its way of life, but simply its formal design, which was conceived as symbolic of a system of proprieties and governmental organization to which the Yamato court earnestly aspired. Yet it would be wrong to leave the great city without conjuring, however fleetingly, the ambience that left an indelible impression on visitors from as far away as Arabia. To that end we reproduce a paragraph from a paper by Arthur Wright:

> Tribute missions or returning provincial officials who entered the city through the monumental gate in the south wall — the "Gate of Luminous Virtue" (Ming-te Men [明德門]) — were subjected to a spatial dramatization of the powers that presided over the city and the empire. On both sides of the broad tree-lined avenue were the populous walled residential wards, then — to the right and left, the metropolitan temples of Buddhism and Taoism — centers of the state's control of these religions. Then came the great gate that led into the main north-south street of the administrative city; within, on both sides, the visitor would see ordered streets of official bureaux with officials, couriers, and mounted guards moving to and fro. Then, passing out the north gate of the administrative city, he would cross a wide glacis and pause before the imposing gates of the palace city —the "Gate of Acquiescence to Heaven" (Ch'eng-t'ien Men [承天門]). When these swung open, the splendors of the great palaces set on their ter-

raced foundations lay before him. Here was the seat of earthly power and here was the center of the cosmos.[155]

Heijō-kyō

The passage that is usually referred to as Article 2 of the Reform Edict of 646, as preserved by the Urabe family and reproduced in the Iwanami edition of the *Nihon Shoki* (pp. 280 and 281), reads as follows:

Kambun	*Transcription into Classical Japanese*
初修京師置畿内國司	初めて京師を修め畿内國司…置け

Initially [or for the first time] the *misato*[156] is to be regulated, and provincial government (*kokushi* or *kuni no tsukasa*) established for the Kinai (or Home Provinces: i.e., the metropolitan region).

The crux in the understanding of this passage is the term *misato*, which has customarily been rendered in Western writings as "capital."[157] However, in the very next column of the text the graph 京 (*miyako*, *-kyō*: *On* reading *kei*) alone is used in the general sense of "capital":

凡京毎坊置長	凡そ京には坊

125

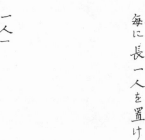

一人一

For each ward in the capital let there be appointed a headman.

Miyako 京, it would seem, was the term that had replaced *miya* 宮 as the customary designation for the seat of royal power when the palace complex of the sixth and early-seventh centuries was incorporated into a formal Chinese-style urban layout. It is to be presumed that *misato* 京師 was intended to convey something other than this, the substance of which is evidently to be sought in the 師 component of the term. One of the primary connotations of this graph in Archaic Chinese was a large number, a multitude, or an aggregation, of people — the sense in which it was used in, for example, the *Pan* 板 Ode of the *Shih Ching* 詩經 (Mao CCLIV): "The multitude [of the people] is [as] a wall" 大師維桓. This is also the meaning accorded the character by the Morohashi Dictionary (諸橋 大漢和辞典) in its explication of *misato* (京師):師は衆. In the same dictionary the complete term is defined as "The place where the mass of the people dwell" 大衆の居る所. The *Daijiten* (大字典) further defines 大衆 as "the body of followers attached to a Buddhist temple," or sometimes simply as "followers." The inference surely is that in the Reform Edict *misato* was used to denote the followers and retainers of the emperor and, by implication, the numerous retinues that accompanied them. In other words, the Edict was designed to impose order on the aggregation of population that had developed in the vicinity of the palace and its associated government offices.

The physical framework. We have already followed the earlier, and in various degrees tentative, essays in the Chinese style of urban design as they were implemented in Japan during the half-century or so following the Taika reforms. With the founding of Heijō-kyō, this tradition was realized in all its ample potential. In the third month of 707 (Keiun 4.2.19) the possibility of estab-

lishing a new seat of government was put before the empress's advisors; in the
same month of the following year (Wadō 1.2.15) officialdom was apprised that the
new capital would be located at Nara;[158] in the eleventh month (Wadō 1.9.20) the
empress officially inspected the proposed site;[159] later in the same month the
intention to build the imperial palace at Nara (*Nara no miya* 平城宮) was
announced in the Sovereign's Great Shrine (*Ise-jingū* 伊勢神宮) at Ise;[160]
the ground-breaking ceremony was held in the twelfth month;[161] and finally, in
the fourth month of 710 (Wadō 3.3.10), the grand migration of the court took
place.[162] However, the move was not viewed with favor by all sections of the
populace, as was noted in an imperial decree of 709:

> Nowadays the transfer of the Capital is causing uneasiness among the
> population. Although they have been reassured, yet they are not able
> to regain their composure. Every time We think of this We feel the
> greatest compassion. Consequently, We grant exemption from this year's
> taxes in produce and rice. [Transl. Snellen, 1937, p. 236.]

It will be recalled that there had been a similar manifestation of popular
resentment against Temmu Tennō's transference of his court from Asuka to the
neighborhood of Lake Biwa (see note 117).

Although the paradigm on which the Japanese court based its capital city was
without a doubt Chinese in origin, there is a good deal of uncertainty whether
the immediate model was Ch'ang-an itself or perhaps another city that had adopted
the design of the Chinese capital. If the latter was the case, then a likely
model would have been the capital of the Korean kingdom of Silla, which was in
close contact with the Japanese court during the seventh and eighth centuries.
Although a settlement on the site of present-day Kyŏngju in North Kyŏngsang province had served as the capital of the Sillan kingdom since its inception in the
fourth century A.D., it was only during the last quarter of the seventh century
that it had been remodeled on the Chinese pattern as one aspect of a comprehensive reconstitution of Sillan government that had made the state, as has been
said, into a little T'ang.[163] Certainly there were significant differences
between the minutiae of the designs of Ch'ang-an and Heijō, differences which the
Japanese made no attempt to eliminate when, in 794, a new capital was built at
Heian. But, on the evidence presently available, it is impossible to say whether
the Japanese *adapted* the general principles of urban design embodied in the lay-

out of Ch'ang-an to their own cultural requirements or *adopted* more or less in its entirety a Korean modification of the great Chinese imperial capital.

In any case, whatever may have been the immediate provenance of its design, it is in Heijō that the results of the injunction of 646 to "regulate the *misato*" can for the first time be evaluated in more than superficial terms. But it was no casually chosen scheme that was used to attain that end; rather, it was a plan that expressed the ambitions of Japanese society as crystallized in the values of its ruling lineages. To this extent, conceptual analogues of Heijō in the Western world should be sought among the town plans of Colonial North America, such as, for example, those for Philadelphia (1683), Savannah (1734), and Charlestown (1742), or any one of a dozen or so utopian designs reproduced in John Reps's *The Making of Urban America*.[164] In the Old World, of course, such analogues were by no means uncommon, being prescribed in canonical texts of both Hindus and Western Semites.[165] Like all these, Heijō was conceived as a bounded world, a rigorously ordered framework establishing the rules of spatial interaction within a strictly defined community. Like the American examples, it also reproduced on a varying scale an orthogonal pattern that was developed over the surrounding rural landscape; in the American West this was the grid imposed by the Land Ordinance of 1785,[166] in Japan it was the *jōrisei* 条里制 allegedly initiated by the Taika Reform of 646.[167] Like the other Old World examples, Heijō constituted a quasi-sacred enclave within the continuum of profane space, a theater of symbolic action in which man could proclaim the knowledge that he shared with the gods and dramatize the cosmic truth that had been revealed to him. What was important from this point of view was not so much the lattice that partitioned the cosmion of social order but rather the formal limits of the city as established by ritual definition. In this respect, the form of Heijō, and, as far as that goes, of numerous other Asian capitals established on similar patterns, differed fundamentally from the open-ended grids of those Hellenistic cities (Miletus will serve as an archetypal example) laid out on principles commonly (though dubiously) attributed to the Sophist Hippodamus. In these latter cities the grid was simply an expediential means of facilitating construction, and as such it was capable of indefinite extension.[168] Except in unusual circumstances, this did

not take place until already constructed sectors of the city were more or less
fully utilized. Heijō-kyō and similar cities, by contrast, were delimited once
and for all as idealized structural models for society at large. Extramural
extensions, although they did in fact occur quite frequently, were not envisaged
by the original designers, who perceived themselves as creating a unitary framework for the pursuance of a life-style and form of social organization that would
function as a mirror to the larger community, as an inculcator of appropriate
attitudes and values, and as a symbolic statement about the nature of society
which could serve as a guide to action for its constituent individuals and groups.

It was on these principles and in this spirit that Heijō-kyō was laid out
between 708 and 710. Like its paradigm of Ch'ang-an, it took the form of a cardinally orientated rectangular enceinte that was -- appropriately enough, considering the developmental levels and political scale of the two nations -- substan-
tially smaller than its model: 32 *cho* 町丁 from east to west by 36 from north to
south, or 2.5 x 3.1 miles in English measure (fig. 9). In other words, Heijō was
slightly less than a quarter the areal extent of Ch'ang-an. On the other hand,
as befitted the recently augmented prestige of the Japanese court and the accompanying increase in the size and complexity of the bureaucracy, Heijō was about
three-quarters as large again as the preceding capital at Fujiwara. Unlike
Ch'ang-an, it lacked an outer wall, a circumstance reflecting the absence in
eighth-century Japan of potential external invaders and competing internal dynasties. The enceinte thus delimited, together with the architectural features that
were raised within it, has long since been obliterated from the landscape, and
archeological excavation so far has been restricted to the palace and the bureaucratic precincts.[169] Most of our information about the city as a functioning
whole derives from written sources, principally the *Shoku Nihongi* 續日本紀
(see note 158 to this chapter), covering the period 679-791, the *Nihon Koki* 日
本後紀, the extant portions of which relate to the years 796-816 (both these
works are included in the corpus known as the *Six National Histories: Rikkokushi*
六國史), and the contemporary documents that have been assembled by Takeuchi
Rizō 竹内理三 under the title *Nara Ibun* 寧樂貴文 (Tōkyō, 1962). A certain
amount of incidental material can also be garnered from the *Nihon sandai jitsu-*

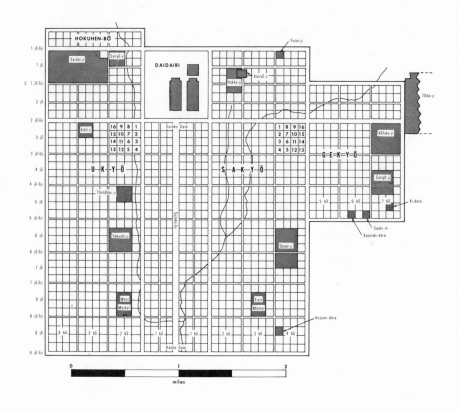

Fig. 9. Plan of Heijō-kyō. Based on Asano Kiyoshi and Kobayashi Yukio 淺野清 小林行雄, eds., *Sekai Kōkogaku Taikei* 世界考古学大系 (Tōkyō, 1964), vol. 4, fig. 24. Both *jō* 条 and their main boundary avenues (*ōji* 大路) were numbered consecutively from north to south except for the avenues bordering Ichijō to the north and south, which were called, respectively, Ichijō-kita-ōji and Ichijō-minami-ōji (North and South First Block avenues). The *bō* were numbered consecutively outward, east and west, from the Suzaku. The outermost avenue on the east was therefore referred to as Sakyō Shibō-ōji (fourth *bō* in the Left Capital), and the *bō* that formed the extreme northwest corner of the city was known as Ukyō Ichijō Shibō (fourth *bō* of the first *jō* in the Right Capital). At least some of the *ōji*, and apparently some of the minor streets (*kōji* 小路), were known by names as well as numbers; e.g., Ichijō-minami-ōji in the Left Capital was known as Saho 佐保, and Nibō-ōji in the Right Capital as Saki 佐貴. In the Left Capital, *tsubo* were numbered in boustrophedonic fashion (*chidori* 千鳥) from the northwest corner (near-est the Daidairi), with the order reversed in the Right Capital. An *ōji* was twice the width of a *kōji*, and a *tsubo* was five times wider than an *ōji*.

roku 日本三代實録, the *Kogoshūi* 古語拾遺 (p. 59, above), and the *Man'yōshū* 萬葉集, while the *fudoki* 風土記, or rather what survives of them, are use- ful mainly as implying certain relationships between the capital and the prov- inces.

Inadequate though this information is for a detailed examination of the city, it is clear that it was divided into a plat of 72 cellular units by a grid of nine longitudinal avenues and ten latitudinal ones. Whereas in Fujiwara the modular units had been rectangular in shape, with, as in Ch'ang-an, the length double the width, in Heijō the shorter (north-south) dimension of the blocks was doubled, thus converting each unit to a square and rendering the urban grid, known as the *jōbō* system of land apportionment, conformable with the *jōrisei* of the surrounding countryside.[170] Regarded from north to south, the urban blocks were referred to as *jō* 条, from east to west as *bō* 坊. The standard block was 4 *chō* 町 square (approximately 476 yards) and was subdivided into 16 square sec- tions (*tsubo* 坪). In other words, the basic unit of urban design was conceived in terms of not more than five minutes' easy walk in any direction.

The main avenue that divided the city symmetrically into eastern (Sakyō 左京:Left Capital) and western halves (Ukyō 右京:Right Capital) was known as Suzaku-ōji 朱雀大路. Running from the Suzaku Gate 朱雀門 in the north to the Rashō Gate 羅城門 in the south, it was 150 *shaku* (only a little less than 150 feet) wide, a scale of design that compares poorly with the 478-foot width of the main north-south avenues in Ch'ang-an but much more favorably with the 100- foot width of present-day Fifth Avenue in New York.[171] The other transurban ave- nues were considerably narrower; and two in particular, which ran parallel, and two *tsubo*, respectively to east and west of the Suzaku-ōji, from the southern boundary of the palace enclave to the southern edge of the grid, were narrowest of all, though they were still a good deal wider than the passageways that tran- sected the *bō*. All main avenues (*ōji* 大路, that is, those delimiting *jō* and *bō*) were lined with willow trees.

In Heijō the *bō* themselves were more consistently uniform in size than were those of Ch'ang-an. In fact, all but four within the original grid preserved the standard dimensions in both directions. The four exceptions were consolidated

into a palace and bureaucratic complex, known in Japanese as the Daidairi 大 内
裏 but usually rendered into English as the Great Palace Enclosure, which was
disposed symmetrically across the northern end of the Suzaku-ōji (fig. 9). Occupying, as it did, four mutually contiguous *bō*, this joint ceremonial and administrative complex measured 8 *chō* square, or approximately 0.5 square mile. It was
enclosed by a tamped-earth wall of unknown height, which was pierced by a total
of twelve gates, three to each side, including the north.

Within this enclosure the architectural forms transposed into spatial and
volumetric terms the structure of the central bureaucratic hierarchy, which had
been modeled in principle on the T'ang system. But this was not the first palace
enclave to take this form. In fact, archeology attests that, since the introduction of Chinese constructional technology as early as the middle of the seventh
century, at least two other palace enclosures had been laid out in this way,
namely, the Nagahara Toyosaki of Kōtoku Tennō at Naniwa and the Fujiwara no Miya
that was the seat of the court from 694 to the founding of Heijō. The references
to the several parts of Temmu Tennō's palace in the *Nihon Shoki* would also seem
to imply a series of structures on a similar pattern.[172]

In the early years of the Nara period the governmental and administrative
system adopted from T'ang China was functioning as effectively as it was ever
going to. The upper echelons of the aristocracy were benefiting materially from
the rationalization of production and distribution that resulted from the implementation of the Taihō and Yōrō codes; at the same time, they retained most of
the ancient privileges that had traditionally accrued to their lineage affiliations. That these two systems of sociopolitical integration and their associated
modes of resource distribution were fundamentally incompatible, probably even
antagonistic to each other, had not yet become as obvious as it would in the following century, and to many members of the nobility it must have seemed that a
way had been found to enjoy in perfect security the benefits of both worlds. At
the common apex of both systems was the Tennō 天皇, who, as was pointed out
above, reigned by reason of the ascriptive criterion of birth (a distinctively
Japanese emphasis) rather than, as the Chinese emperor supposedly did, by reason
of inherent virtue. According to the canons of one system, the Tennō still ruled

according to the ancient Japanese principle of corporate kinship, except that the
lineage chieftain (*uji no kami*氏の上) capable of dealing with "the upper and
lower spirits" in the manner of a Pimiko had now become the paramount chief of a
nation and premier officiant in the cult of a national deity. In the other system, the Tennō exercised supreme authority in a centralized state as an omnipo-
tent emperor served by regularly appointed officials in the Chinese manner. In
these two faces of government can be seen the lineaments of a formerly all-
powerful mode of patrimonial domain persisting side by side with a bureaucratic
system of authority relationships.[173] Despite the fact that the tradition-
sanctioned arbitrariness of patrimonial authority had been somewhat curbed by the
so-called reforms of the seventh and early-eighth centuries, and despite the fact
that the Japanese administrative hierarchy was less thoroughly bureaucratized
than its Chinese model, the two forms of government were never entirely accommodated to each other.

The central bureaucracy that had resulted from the series of reforms
reflected these two modes of "domination"[174] combined in the office of Tennō.
Immediately below the emperor were the two major departments of government, the
specifically Japanese Department of Worship (*Jingikan*神祇官),[175] which supervised all *kami* affairs both in the capital and throughout the provinces, and the
Grand Council of State (*Dajōkan*太政官), which was concerned with the secular
functions of government. Since there was no T'ang counterpart to the *Jingikan*,
there was no reason for according it the precedence over the *Dajōkan* that it did
in fact command, other than Japanese reluctance to abandon the traditional sacer-
dotal character of government. In retrospect, though, the *Jingikan* can be seen
to have acted as a powerful centralizing force in two distinct ways. At the same
time as it established the ancestral gods of the imperial lineage as the supreme
deities of the Japanese state, it also afforded a means of integrating innumer-
able minor spirits, *ujigami*, and gods of small rural communities into a single
national hierarchy. The Grand Council of State, by contrast, was in principle
almost wholly of Chinese inspiration. It was presided over by a Grand Minister
of State (*Dajō-daijin*太政大臣), who in fact delegated most of his responsibility to the Minister of the Left (*Sadaijin*左大臣) or, acting in his place,

the Minister of the Right (*Udaijin* 右大臣). The lower levels of the bureaucratic pyramid were composed of ministries (*shō* 省), important offices (*shiki*
職), bureaus (*ryō* 寮), lesser offices (*shi* 司), regional headquarters (*fu* 府),
provincial (*kuni* 國) authorities, and district (*kōri* 郡) governments. To the
ministries of Ceremonial (*Shikibushō* 式部省), Civil Affairs (*Jibushō* 治部省),
People's Affairs (*Minbushō* 民部省), Military Affairs (*Hyōbushō* 兵部省), Justice (*Gyōbushō* 刑部省), and the Treasury (*Ōkurashō* 大藏省), which were modeled
on the six T'ang boards (*Liu Pu* 六部) of Rites, Personnel, Public Works, War,
Justice, and Revenue, were added a Ministry of Central Administration (*Nakatsu-
kasashō* 中務省), which functioned essentially as an instrument of communication
between the emperor and the bureaucracy, and a Ministry of the Imperial Household
(*Kunaishō* 宮内省).[176] It is characteristic of governments of this type that
the ministries concerned with court affairs should have enjoyed a higher prestige
than those functioning on behalf of the populace at large.

In the Great Palace Enclosures incorporated in the Chinese-style capitals of
Japan this bureaucratic hierarchy was given architectural expression in the following terms. Entering the Daidairi from the south, one first passed through a
forecourt known as the *Chōshū-den* 朝集殿 or Imperial Assembly Hall, flanked to
east and west by a pair of buildings. To its north was the *Chōdō-in* 朝堂院,
usually rendered in English as the Administration Palace, though perhaps John
Hall's "Official Compound" gives a better idea of its functions. Ranged symmetrically along the east and west sides of the interior courtyard were the halls
(*chōdō* 朝堂) of the Eight Ministries, which were supplemented at the southern
end by the offices of an additional four ministries. The courtyard itself served
as a theater for a variety of installations, annual ceremonies, and other court
functions. At its northern end was a structure which, although separated from
the main courtyard by a wall or cloister, constituted an extension of the Chōdō-
in. This was the Daigoku-den 大極殿 or Palace of the Supreme Ultimate, an
audience and council hall bearing the honorific that had been bestowed on the old
Palace City (Kung Ch'eng) of Ch'ang-an in 710 (see note 147). Here, at the very
axis of the capital, the kingdom, and the universe, were conducted the great ceremonies of state. In Heijō-kyō the entire structure of the Daigoku-den was

raised on a terrace of tamped earth, so that it physically dominated the halls of
the ministries in the courtyard of the Chōdō-in.[177] Still farther north was the
Dairi 内裏 or palace proper, containing the imperial residential quarters, the
Throne Hall (*Shishinden* 紫宸殿), and shrines where the emperor, or his official delegate, performed the rituals necessary to placate the Spirits of Heaven
and Earth.[178] Much of the remaining space in the Daidairi was occupied by office
compounds of various sorts, storehouses, stables, domestic facilities such as
kitchens, and living quarters for attendants and menials; but even a measure of
congestion in the later capitals could not conceal the symbolism of the layout,
with the emperor stationed, in both his private and official capacities, at the
heart of the complex, whence, with southerly stance, he not only held sway over
the bureaucracy in the Chōdō-in and the populace of the city beyond but also projected his power along a graded surface of authority to the farthest bounds of
the realm. It was from this still point of the turning world that, as the animating force of the state, he caused nature and men to be what they were. From
the Naniwa of Kōtoku Tennō (645-654) through Fujiwara (694-710) to Heijō (710-
784) and the Naniwa of Shōmu Tennō (740s), and in the future capitals of Nagaoka
(784-794) and Heian-kyō (794-1177), in fact, as long as the Japanese court sought
to maintain itself in a city modeled on the Chinese imperial capital, the Daidairi was laid out on this pattern. Minor deviations occurred in each capital
and sometimes within the life-span of the same capital, but always the paradigm
that provided the framework for the Japanese architects was that described above.
Among the more significant modifications of the ideal-type layout was the progressive increase in size from palace to palace of the Daigoku-den (even though
the dimensions of its courtyard were being somewhat reduced in proportion to the
size of the Daidairi as a whole) in response to a continuing enhancement of
imperial prestige.

It will have become evident that the Daidairi of the representative Japanese
imperial capital was not only constructed on a smaller scale than its model in
T'ang Ch'ang-an but was also compressed within a relatively more constricted
space. Because the two contrasting modes of "domination" (cf. above) that were
exercised by the government of the time were both focused within one and the same

office, indeed, within the same person, there were few overt signs of the tension
that was generated in China between the emperor and the bureaucracy. Instead of
the separation of palace and administrative complex (the Imperial City) that was
a prominent feature of Ch'ang-an, in Heijō the two complexes were so close as to
constitute virtually a single structure.[179] There was, too, a signal difference
in the architecture of the Daidairi and its Chinese counterpart. The buildings
within the Japanese palace and administrative compounds were less grandiose than
those of Ch'ang-an. It is inferred that the Daigoku-den was constructed in the
shichū-zukuri 四注造, a style with vermilion-lacquered pillars standing in
bold contrast to white-plaster walls; but the imperial residences appear to have
still been roofed with thatch or bark rather than tile. And, since the buildings
were crowded more closely together than in the imperial administrative enclave in
the Chinese capital, there was less space for the public pageantry that so
impressed visitors to Ch'ang-an. And, of course, to the approaching visitor the
whole city must have appeared much less a fortress than did Ch'ang-an, behind its
massive outer walls. Nevertheless, in the Japan of the middle of the eighth century the Daidairi must have appeared splendid indeed.

Throughout the rest of the city architectural developments were incorporated
within the framework of standard blocks without doing violence to the main structure of the grid.[180] Figure 9 illustrates the way in which Buddhist temples, of
which there were reportedly forty-eight in 720, were accommodated to this framework. A not inconsiderable number of these had been transferred to the new capital from Fujiwara and other locations in Asuka district, including not only clan-
sponsored temples (*uji-dera* 氏寺), such as the Kōfuku-ji 興福寺 maintained
by the Fujiwara family,[181] the Kidera 紀寺 supported by the Ki and the Soga, and
the Kazuraki-dera 葛城寺 built by the *uji* of that name, but also such famous
foundations as the Daian-ji 大安寺,[182] the Gangō-ji 元興寺 or Hōkō-ji 法興
寺,[183] and the Yakushi-ji 藥師寺. Concurrently, numerous new temples were
raised, including the Tōshōdai-ji 唐招提寺, the Saidai-ji 西大寺, the
Sairyū-ji 西隆寺, the Futai-ji 不退寺, and the Kikō-ji 喜光寺. Buddhism
was a powerful political force, and the imperial government provided generous
inducements to temple construction in the form of land allotments. The Tōdai-ji

136

東大寺, under the sobriquet of Great State Temple, became the center of state
Buddhism, with its massive *Daibutsuden* 大佛殿, possibly larger than any other
wooden building ever constructed. The pagodas of these temples and others like
them were practically the only architectural features to break the evenness of
the one- or two-story rooftops of Heijō, the other main exception being the
Daigoku-den on its raised platform.

For all but the types of buildings discussed thus far, construction techniques were simple and uniform. Dwellings of polished natural timbers with roofs
of cypress shingles had long been occupied by the upper classes. Usually they
were built to a rectangular plan, the linearity of which was emphasized by the
insertion of evenly spaced rectangular windows. In 724, however, it was decreed
that all houses in Heijō-kyō should be faced with white plaster and have their
columns painted vermilion and their roofs tiled. It is not known to what extent
the order was obeyed.

Lots were assigned for life but varied in size according to the rank of the
recipients and the number of able-bodied males in the household. Nobles of the
third rank and above were allocated one *chō* (2.45 acres) each, those of the
fourth and fifth ranks half a *chō*, and those of lower rank only a quarter of a
chō. As the urban population increased during the eighth century, lot sizes were
reduced and housing densities were thereby raised. At the same time, when space
was at a premium, the storage sheds and workrooms appropriate to a rural life-
style, which had been retained in the upper-class residences, tended to be eliminated, and the city began to assume a more distinctively urban appearance.
Although the dwellings of commoners were, in any case, scarcely distinguishable
from the outhouses attached to the residences of men of rank, the reduction in
lot size affected them too, so that lots of only 1/16th or even 1/32nd of a *chō*
became by no means uncommon.

The precise manner in which holdings were allocated within *bō* is unknown,
but at least some of the lots assigned to high-ranking aristocrats may have occupied a whole block. Other less prestigious members of the nobility presumably
shared a *bō*. In any case, only nobles of the third rank and above were permitted
to hold frontage on a main avenue. But whatever the system of allocation, each

137

holding was enclosed within a wall of tamped earth or wattle and daub. It has been estimated that those surrounding the compounds of high-ranking officials might have been as much as 15 feet high and 6 feet wide at the base. Commoners, it seems, squeezed their shacks into the interstices between the building complexes of the nobility, which were often set amid gardens and lakes in a manner that prefigured the *shinden-zukuri* 寝殿造 of the Later Heian era.

Thus far we have described the layout of the city as if it were a perfectly regular grid. This it probably was in the beginning; but during the three-fourths of a century of its existence, it acquired two sizable additions that destroyed its original symmetry. The larger of these, a projection four *bō* deep extending three *bō* eastward from the northern half of the city (see fig. 9), was known as the Outer Capital (*Gekyō* 外京). It was placed under the administration of the Left Capital. It is curious that the *shaku* unit of measurement employed in the construction of this annex was slightly shorter than that used in the layout of the city proper, a circumstance that resulted in the production of rectangular rather than square *bō*. The reasons for this are obscure, though they are almost certainly associated with the establishment of the Kōfuku-ji, the clan temple of the Fujiwara, which was laid out immediately beyond the eastern edge of the grid in 710, that is, just as the Daidairi was approaching completion.[184] The most likely explanation of the slight reduction of scale in the layout of the Gekyō is that it was added at a later unspecified date in order to bring within the urban area certain settlements that had agglomerated around the Kōfuku-ji. Although the temple itself had been laid out in conformity with the *jōrisei* and with strict cardinal orientation, it was still necessary to modify the size of the unit measurement in order to accommodate the Kōfuku-ji and its appurtenances to the eastern extension of the grid.

The smaller addition to the grid was a northward projection, half a *bō* deep, of the three most northwesterly blocks of the city. Known appropriately as the Hokuhen-bō 北邊坊 (North Border Blocks), this extension was probably undertaken at some time relatively late in the eighth century in order to incorporate within the officially defined city limits the Saidai-ji, the Western Great Temple, an alleged masterpiece[185] which Empress Shōtoku had founded in 765 in an attempt to

surpass even the magnificence of Shōmu Tennō's Tōdai-ji (Eastern Great Temple) on
the opposite edge of the city. In the layout of this extension the standard
shaku was employed. It came under the administration of the Right Capital.

Social organization. The notion implicit in Jane Jacobs' work that intricate and
satisfying patterns of living cannot develop within the constraints of a preconceived and rigorously imposed physical framework, whatever its merits in the
North American context (and they are not likely to be overly numerous), had no
validity at all in eighth-century Japan.[186] All activities of living require
some sort of framework, assembled, even in the case of the unplanned city, from a
range of fairly simple formal situations. The orthogonal grid is only one such
organizing principle.[187] It is true that a strictly maintained grid acts as a
powerful force controlling the evolution of city form, but it does not of itself
prohibit social change. In Heijō, moreover, the grid, although constructed to
rigidly enforced legislative norms, signified to a high proportion, perhaps all,
of the inhabitants of the city, not personal or group restriction and deprivation
of rights but a satisfying method of defining a hierarchically ordered set of
statuses and associated privileges. In structuring urban space as an explicit
symbolic statement about the nature of society in general, and about the nature
of Japanese society in particular, the designers of Heijō created a material paradigm of approved status relationships between groups and between what Radcliffe-
Brown called "social persons."[188] For many the scale and splendor (a relativis-
tic notion but nonetheless powerful for that) of the capital, seat of a quasi-
divine ruler who symbolized a cosmically harmonized world order, were also subli-
mated projections of national and cultural ascendancy. But this orderly tradi-
tionalism, to which virtually all members of the society of the time subscribed,
was not especially inimical to change. As was to become only too evident in the
Heian period (784-1177), it did not imprison society within an architectural
past. Even during the Nara period itself, growth and change were apparent at all
levels of social organization.

Urban growth almost by definition involves an increase in population, which
can be accommodated in one of two ways: by extension of the urban area or by an
internal restructuring of that space. In Heijō, although two extensions of the

grid did impair the pristine perfection of its initial symmetry, the main means
of incorporating increments of population within the city were by one or another
process of involution: primarily by a progressive and sometimes intricate subdivision of space but also by a parallel, though less intense, elaboration of
organizational arrangements. However, most of these changes reached their maximum development only during the Heian period, with which we are not here directly
concerned.

The transfer of the court from Asuka to Heijō involved the relocation not
only of the emperor and his immediate entourage but also of a numerically impressive corps of bureaucrats. It was this aristocratic bureaucracy that dominated
the social pyramid in Heijō, controlled the exchange functions of the city, and
set the tone of its cultural life. The systems of land tenure and land taxation
that had been established under the *ritsuryō* codes ensured the retention by the
central government of administrative control over both land itself and the revenue derived from it,[189] and a good deal of the income acquired in this manner was
disseminated among members of the bureaucracy. Whereas prior to the Taika
reforms the office of lineage chief (*uji no kami* 氏 の 上) had commanded a hereditary post at the Yamato court, in the eighth century a courtier became a clan
chief (*uji no chōja* 氏 の 長 者) by virtue of being the highest-ranking member of
his *uji* in the state bureaucracy. In other words, the *uji* had been incorporated
in the structure of the state, with which it articulated through the mediacy of
the *uji* chieftain, who now assumed the dual roles of aristocrat and bureau-
crat.[190] In these circumstances an aristocratic officeholder had no choice but
to maintain a permanent residence in the capital, where he was not only close to
the source of power and authority, and perhaps to some degree able to influence
policy through personal representation, but also in a position to monitor and
evaluate the increasingly voluminous flow of information channeled into the city
as a result of the progressive centralization of government during the seventh
and early-eighth centuries. Soon after 750 no less than 130 noblemen holding the
fifth rank or higher, and including virtually all present, past, or potential
heads of departments, bureaus, or offices, were resident in Heijō, and the whole
body of officialdom is said to have numbered some 10,000 persons.[191] If we

accept what has become the standard estimate among Japanese scholars of the total population of the city *and its immediate environs* during the second half of the eighth century, namely 200,000,[192] then this tumescent bureaucracy would have accounted for one out of every twenty persons. In actual fact it is more than doubtful that what we may call "Greater Heijō" ever housed an many as 200,000 people, so that the ratio of officials to total population was almost certainly in excess of one in twenty.

Thus far we have spoken of the central administration as if it were a simple hierarchical pyramid of officials. This was far from being the case. The aristocratic governing class proper was disposed in nine ranks, which were grouped for convenience into three levels. The highest level of society consisted exclusively of those who in Heian times came to be styled *kugyō* 公卿 , that is, courtiers of the first, second, and third ranks, together with those holding the rank of imperial advisor (*sangi* 参議);[193] the second level comprised courtiers of the fourth and fifth ranks; while the lowest level was composed of those claiming ranks from six through nine. In practice these were mainly possessors of technical skills in law, medicine, and astrology. Below this ninefold structure of aristocratic administrators was a complex organization of officials, ranging from "secretaries," scribes, recorders, examiners, clerks, copyists, attendants, pages, and so on down to artisans, watchmen, and servants of various sorts. This organization varied in the details of its composition from ministry to ministry.[194] In addition there was a corps of municipal officers whose business it was to ensure the welfare of the capital, the 京, a character which, by the time of the Yōrō Codes, was being glossed as *Misato*, "the August Residence."[195] Although the organs of municipal government were structurally outside the central administration, their officials ranked relatively high in the bureaucratic hierarchy. Control of the capital was shared between the Office of the Left City (*Sakyōshiki* 左京職) and the Office of the Right City (*Ukyōshiki* 右京職), each supplied with the following personnel: a commissioner (*daibu* 大夫), charged with the maintenance of order in the broadest sense,[196] one assistant (次官), one secretary (判官), two junior secretaries (*shōjō* 少進), one senior clerk (*daizoku* 大属), two junior clerks (*shōzoku* 少属), and twelve

ward officers (*bōrei* 坊令) able to draw on the services of watchmen and aides.
For each of the two main divisions of the capital there was also a Market Office
(*Ichi no Tsukasa* [東/西]市司), under the supervision of a director (*kami* 頭),
with primary responsibility for all matters connected with economic exchange[197]
and staffed by one assistant, one secretary, five valuers (*kachō* 價長), twenty
guards, and an unspecified number of servants (*shibu* 使部).

In addition to these municipal officials, there was another large sector of
the bureaucracy that was in most respects external to the central administration;
this was composed solely of household officials. This organization had been formalized by the *Statute of Household Administrative Appointments* (*Keryō Shokuin-
ryō* 家令職員令) that was included in the Yōrō Code in response to the need of
large *kugyō* households for assistance in the management of their economic, legal,
and social affairs.[198] The *Statute* had authorized five levels of officials to
serve both imperial princes of the third rank and above and the *kugyō* nobility;
these five were steward (*keryō* 家令), in charge of the running of the household; assistant (*kafu* 家扶); inspector (*kajū* 家従; scribes (*shori* 書吏);
and, in princely households only, tutor (*bungaku* 文学). Collectively, all
these levels were known as *keryō*. Although constituted as officials by the law
codes, and indeed publicly appointed by the Ministry of Ceremonials, the *keryō*
differed in many important ways from other branches of officialdom. Their court
ranks, for instance, were awarded at lower levels than was mandatory in the central administration, their semiannual allotments were calculated at a lower rate,
they were denied the customary one day's holiday in six, and, perhaps most important, their performance was evaluated by the head of the household in which they
served rather than, as was normal in the regular bureaucracy, by the head of the
appropriate section, who in this case would have been the steward. Moreover,
they developed fictive familial ties with the house in which they served, so that
they were able to participate in family ceremonies. What this amounts to in fact,
and despite the formal public basis of their appointments, is that the *keryō* were
actually private officials in positions of clientage to noble households. Their
relationships with their superiors were based upon personal reciprocal ties of a
type wholly alien to the impersonal contract between subordinate and superior

142

that characterizes a developed bureaucratic organization. This aspect of the relationship was further evidenced by the traditional rather than legal basis of the noble's authority over his *keryō*. It was he who requested appointments from the Ministry of Ceremonials in the first instance, who was required both to recommend and to approve transfers and dismissals, and who assumed the duty of punishment, all according to custom rather than stipulated rule. The whole *keryō* system, in fact, can be construed as another manifestation of the survival of the old patrimonial values that were touched on earlier (p. 133). During the Nara period that was as far as the matter went; but in Heian times, in accordance with the expansion of familial interests into the hitherto public domain, the limited *keryō* arrangements prescribed in the codes developed into an extensive system of clientage that was beyond the power of the state to control.[199]

So far we have treated the aristocratic bureaucracy as if it were a totally urbanized group. This was far from the truth. In his role as *uji no chōja*, the high-ranking official had to maintain close ties with his ancestral estates, where, in any case, the womenfolk in his family were likely to have remained and for whose supervision he was granted fifteen-day leaves of absence in the fifth and eighth months.[200] Moreover, the wealth that accrued to the family under the *ritsuryō* system was derived primarily from the countryside, not generated within the city.

At the founding of the city, it was not only aristocrats and officials who took up residence there. They were accompanied in considerable numbers by priests and their entourages, commoner families transferred by government order, craftsmen employed in the construction of palaces and temples, peasants either forced, or profiting from the opportunity, to engage in various forms of transport, several classes of serfs and slaves attached to both government offices and private households, laborers summoned for the corvée (*kofu* 雇夫),[201] and others selling their labor on a more or less free market (*ninpu* 住夫), as well as traders of one sort or another attracted by the two great markets of the city. As might have been predicted by anyone familiar with migration theory, the vast bulk of these immigrants, both temporary and permanent, came from neighboring districts of the Kinai, though a not insignificant number hailed from the Kantō, and some even from relatively distant parts of Shikoku.[202]

That the capital city was not simply an agglomeration of independent villages grouped around a ritual and administrative center is evident from the degree of social differentiation that is apparent in the records, inadequate though they are for sophisticated analysis. One indicator of "urbanization" in its behavioral manifestations was the changing status of, and attitudes toward, labor. In response to the continuity of the demand for skilled labor for the construction of temples, palaces, and mansions that persisted throughout the Nara period, specialist workshops were set up which permitted a craftsman to work not only continuously at his trade but also independently, a development that in turn encouraged an increase in occupational specialization. Concurrently, a system of contractual arrangements took shape which permitted artisans and craftsmen to sell their skills at piece rates, all of which was made possible when the emergence of new modes of exchange liberated the court, government, and nobility from their previous almost total dependence on their own workmen, who were then often free to engage in wage labor.[203] Kishiro has illustrated this transformation dramatically enough from records of scribes preserved in the Shōsōin in Nara City.[204] The majority of the scribes mentioned in these archives were government officials of relatively low rank (though a few had achieved the higher sixth grade [*shō-rokui* 正六位]) who supplemented their modest salaries by copying Buddhist scriptures.[205] For many, the return from this copying, which, like their government work, was performed at piece rates, had actually come to constitute their primary source of income. But the supply of *sūtras* was insufficiently elastic to provide supplemental income for all the government clerks desiring it, so that we find the scribes corporately petitioning their superiors not to engage new copyists until the supply of texts should increase and, at the same time, requesting both the privilege of leave on the fifth day of each month and an improvement in the quality and quantity of food and clothing allowances. In the response of these scribes to the environmental pressures of life in Heijō can be seen the beginnings of those adjustments of personal conduct and the transformations of attitudes and values, as well as the emergence of new interest groups, new bases of solidarity, and indeed a new pecuniary nexus, that are often considered to be characteristic of urban living.

With the passage of time the *ritsuryō* system, which initially had enabled
the central government to establish a theoretically absolute control over the
land revenues of the state and had thereby made possible the construction of a
capital on the scale of Heijō, began to induce the emergence of dysfunctional
partial structures that inhibited the fulfillment of some of the social needs of
the developing city. During the second half of the eighth century, for example,
the regulative norms governing the social organization of the wards were seriously disturbed by an influx of vagabonds seeking to escape the double burden of
heavy taxation and forced labor that state and nobility alike (to the extent that
these two entities were analytically separable) imposed upon them. Population
registers from the middle of the Nara period (say about 750) make frequent reference to so-called free persons who had absconded from the settlements where they
were listed. Some simply abandoned their farms and entered into a client relationship with a powerful protector, such as a member of the nobility or the head
of a monastery, while others fled to remote areas, where they carved new farms
out of the wilderness; but some, particularly from the Kinai, where the corvée
was especially burdensome, made their way to the comparative anonymity of the
capital. In 773, alms were disbursed to a total of 9,703 destitute persons in
the east sector of Heijō and to 9,042 in the west sector.[206] Not all these were
immigrants, it is true, but the presence of nearly 20,000 indigents in a total
population surely a good deal less than 200,000 is a significant comment on the
functioning of the *ritsuryō* system. There is also evidence that crime and other
antisocial activities increased as a result of the existence of this floating and
largely destitute component of the population. Robberies and assaults in the
streets, as well as cases of arson, assumed such proportions that during the
Enryaku era (782-806) an edict expelled all gamblers and vagrants from the
city.[207]

Economic exchange. Every society employs four primary modes of exchange, each
corresponding to one of its functional subsystems, in a combination of emphases
reflective of its value system, appropriate to the degree of differentiation of
its social structure, and adapted to its external situation. The four modes of

exchange are reciprocity, which obtains primarily among those social units such
as families, neighborhood communities, and religious groups concerned with pattern maintenance and tension management; redistribution, which involves the allocation of rewards and facilities in conformity with the integrative requirements
of society; mobilization, which provides mechanisms for the acquisition, control,
and disposal of resources in the pursuit of collective goals, that is, broadly
speaking, in the political field; and market exchange, the main instrument for
the production of such generalized facilities as enable the adaptive subsystem of
society to achieve a variety of aims in a variety of situational contexts. At
any one time the subsystems exhibit not only individual morphologies but also a
particular collective configuration; but as the society evolves, the sphere of
operation of each of its subsystems changes in extent and intensity, thereby
inducing parallel mutations in its associated modes of exchange.[208]

In the present context, reciprocity, in the sense of a network of instrumental exchanges grounded in family and neighborhood morality, is not an issue.
Such exchanges were so woven into the fabric of domestic life as to be taken for
granted in much the same way as biological relationships, but there was nothing
particularly urban in their operation. On the redistributive mode of economic
integration, by contrast, the capital depended for its very existence. A system
of this type has little concern for economic calculation and price payments as
these terms are usually understood. The calculations that are undertaken, and
they are of a characteristically meticulous precision, are based seemingly on the
principle that, in the interests of societal integration, each class should be
allocated what is judged by those in control of the system to be its just share
of resources and facilities. Another mode of economic integration, which is not
always in practice easily distinguishable from redistribution, is that generally
termed mobilization. Conceptually, it differs from redistribution in that it
operates not to sustain social stratification but to channel goods and services
into the hands of those responsible for the achievement of broadly political
goals. In other words, it subordinates economic arrangements to the pursuit of
collective aims, usually the maintenance of the political integrity of the society in question. In Japan of the eighth century these two modes of economic

integration were not institutionally distinct and quite possibly were not discriminated in the minds of officials. Certainly they were administered by the
same officers of state from the same ministries and through a single chain of
command. In what follows they will therefore be treated together.

The tax system of the Nara period, which as formalized in the Taihō and Yōrō
codes was a development of that prescribed in Article IV of the Reform Edict of
646, has been the subject of thorough study by Japanese scholars and need not be
treated in detail here.[209] Suffice it to repeat that its primary purpose was to
secure for the central government administrative control over the use of land and
the peasants who cultivated it and the power to engross into the central treasury
whatever proportion of surplus production might be deemed necessary. From the
padi fields, laid out according to the *jōri* system and assessed according to land
and population registers compiled precisely for the purpose, an ever-increasing
volume of commodities flowed toward the capital in the form of three categories
of taxes modeled on those obtaining in T'ang China. The first was a land tax (*so*
租), assessed on the estimated yield of a unit area of padi-land (*kubunden* 口
分 田), levied on the household or residential group (*ko* 戸), and paid in
rice. It was in the nature of a rent charged by the state for the use of land
allocated under the codes, and it was not especially burdensome, the standard
rate being about 20 sheaves of padi to the *chō* in the inner provinces (not more
than 5 per cent of the crop in an average year), but fewer sheaves in outlying
districts — a concession to the cost of transport. The second impost took the
form of a tax in kind (*chō* 調) levied on the production of an individual according to his capacity and payable in commodities other than rice — chiefly cloth
or, in certain districts, a specialized local product. And third, there was a
work tax (*yo* 庸), which was also imposed on the able-bodied male; although it
was calculated in terms of labor duty in the capital, it was payable either in
actual labor (*rō-eki* 労役), including military service, or in some commodity,
usually cloth, at a prescribed rate of commutation. The costs of transporting
commodities to Heijō in payment of both produce and labor taxes had to be met by
members of the contributing households, and the goods had to be delivered
according to prescribed schedules. Consignments falling due in the middle of the

eighth month in fulfillment of *chō* obligations, for instance, had to be delivered
to the Treasury before the end of the tenth month in the case of the metropolitan
region, before the end of the eleventh month in the case of provinces somewhat
farther removed, and before the end of the twelfth month in the case of the most
distant provinces of the kingdom.

Ideally, the notion of redistribution involves not only centripetal movements toward a focus of authority but also a reapportionment secondarily and cen-
trifugally outward. In the case of some commodities it can require the physical
transfer of goods into the center and out again, but in other instances it can be
merely appropriational, involving only rights of disposal over goods. In eighth-
century Japan, however, redistribution was almost wholly unidirectional; its
object was to organize the whole country for the support of the capital, or at
least of the court and the bureaucracy that constituted the *raison d'être* of that
city. The land tax, it is true, was a not inequitable payment for the use of
registered padi fields, but the produce and labor taxes were severe impositions,
which brought no return to the taxpayers in the form of land or goods. Even if
the concept of redistribution be broadened, as it reasonably can be, to encompass
a transmutation of appropriated commodities and labor into centrally provided
services, it is difficult to see what benefits the taxpayer derived from the
transaction. Certainly they could not have amounted to much beyond the presence
in his neighborhood of a provincial governor, who, on the authority of the imperial government, exacted from each household sixty days of corvée labor a year
over and above that demanded by the state. For the indigent and aged who lived
in or close to the capital there were occasional disbursements of rice and
clothes; for districts afflicted with epidemics there were allocations of medicaments; for mothers of multiple births there were presents of rice and cloth; and
for those who brought auspicious occurrences to the notice of the authorities
there were likely to be rewards. Equally to be desired were the exemptions from
taxation or corvée that were sometimes granted to districts in years of exceptionally bad harvests, or to individuals performing especially meritorious services, or, very occasionally, to persons of exemplary conduct.[210] But these centrifugal movements were but a minute fraction of the massive centripetal flow of

148

goods and services that converged on the capital from all directions. Moreover, to judge from the harsh language of an imperial edict of 712, not all the benefits and remissions that were prompted by the Buddhist conscience of the court were actually communicated to the peasants; on this occasion, at least, "governors, heads of districts and village headmen, taking advantage of this favor [i.e., the remission of taxes], by cunning expedients squeezed the people."[211]

In addition to the centrally allocated *kubunden*, several other categories of land were subject to taxation under the *ritsuryō* codes, among them rank land, office land, and land granted in recognition of imperial favor, while fields that had not already been incorporated into the system in one way or another were retained under the direct management of the central government. Furthermore, although land furnished for the support of temples and shrines was exempt from government taxation, a good proportion of its revenue still found its way ultimately to the great religious institutions in the capital. J. Murdoch once calculated that in 747 two of the larger temples in Nara alone drew on the production of no less than 46 estates occupying some 5,000 acres of the most productive farmland in the Kinai.[212] In the case of some of the larger eighth-century temples the centripetal movement of commodities was of the classical type associated with the *Tempelwirtschaft* postulated for Sumeria by an earlier generation of scholars.[213] In all these instances, wherever relevant information has survived, it testifies to the fact that the centripetally induced flow of goods and services from the provinces to the capital amounted to a very sizable proportion of the total available supply of such commodities and services. But the reapportionment undertaken by the central institutions in the form of very weakly developed public services and, presumably, of communal *karma* was totally inadequate to prevent the impoverishment of the rural areas. The dysfunctional tendencies that were inherent in the *ritsuryō* system — and which were partly intrinsic to the Chinese *chün-t'ien* 均田 model, partly the result of its undiscriminating application to the Japanese situation — were exacerbated by numerous exceptions to the state control of land revenues. Almost invariably such exceptions were devised for the benefit of nobles and officials, who were, in any case, already profiting from the integrative functions of the *ritsuryō* system. The net result was that

poverty was taxed and wealth rewarded. After the middle of the eighth century
the rate of privatization of land began to increase at the same time as extragov-
ernmental offices in the hands of powerful court families began to encroach on
the domain of the formal government bureaucracy. In times subsequent to those
with which we are here concerned these two interacting processes were to destroy
the *ritsuryō* system, though not by any means did they subvert the prevalence of
the superordinate redistributive and mobilizative modes of economic integration.

A glimpse of the way in which these systems operated during the eighth century can be obtained from an archive of almost 20,000 wooden tallies recovered
from the neighborhood of the Heijō palace and from a smaller number found in the
ruins of the Fujiwara no Miya. Despite being buried in the earth for more than a
thousand years, a hundred of the tallies still bear legible characters reporting
the arrival, allocation, and inventory of commodities from the provinces. The
earliest legible record is dated to 709 A.D., the latest to 782. Two representative examples illustrated by Kidder in his book *Early Buddhist Japan* reveal
respectively that in 716-17 an individual or family in Suki county of Oki province contributed six strands of seaweed and that on 25 September 746 Emperor
Shōmu received a special gift of 2 *to* of jellyfish from Bizen province.[214] A
third tally, also pictured by Kidder, apparently recorded an internal transaction
in which a particular temple to which the empress had retired submitted a schedule of supplies for its kitchen.[215] It is apparent from the archive as a whole
that the bulk of the commodities appropriated into the Heijō palace originated in
the outlying districts of the Kinai, though, perhaps surprisingly, the Yamato
plain contributed relatively little (fig. 10). The explanation would seem to be
that the Yamato district, lying adjacent to the capital, was already being
drained of its surpluses by the exorbitant demands of its temples on land revenues and the imposition of inordinate labor taxes on its work force. However,
the districts immediately beyond were still subject to direct pressures from the
capital, were reasonably advanced technologically, and were not unduly remote
from the point of view of logistics. Most of the rice and *mugi* 麥 reaching the
palace came from precisely this area. Cotton-silk was sent exclusively from
northern Kyūshū, iron ore from Okayama prefecture, iron hoe-blades (*suki* 鋤)

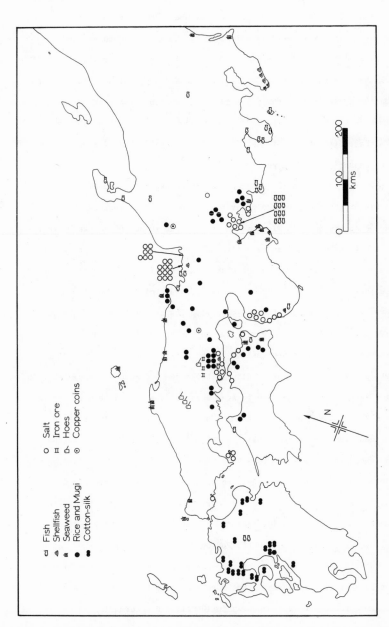

Fig. 10. Commodities appropriated for the support of the Heijō court during the eighth century. Redrawn from Tsuboi Kiyotari 坪井清足, "Heijō kyuseki to hakkutsu chōsa" 平城宮跡と発掘調査, in Kishi Toshio 岸俊男 et al., *Tenpyō Nara semināru* 天平奈良セミナール (Tōkyō, 1973), p. 117, and Yokoyama Kōichi and Narasaki Shōichi, eds., 横山浩一 楢崎彰一, *Kodaishi hakkutsu* 古代史発掘, vol. 10: *Miyako to mura no kuraishi* 都とむらの暮し (Tōkyō, 1974), pp. 50–51.

from the same region and from Hiroshima prefecture, and coins from Fukui and
Hyōgo. Fish were salted and dispatched primarily from the eastern reaches of the
Inland Sea, from Atsumi Bay in Aichi prefecture, and from the coasts of Shizuoka,
but in lesser quantities from as far afield as Kyūshū in the southwest and Iba-
ragi in the east.[216] Seaweed was shipped from widely dispersed areas, but
chiefly from the coastal tracts of Chūgoku and the Kii peninsula, while salt was
brought from the great pans on the Fukui coast, as well as from Wakayama and
northeast Shikoku. Taken as a whole, the surviving tallies provide considerable
insight into the ramifications of the redistributive system that framed the economic life of Japan in the Nara period.

The fourth mode of economic integration, market exchange, had already had a
respectable history by the time the great Eastern and Western markets (*Higashi no
Ichi* 東 市 and *Nishi no Ichi* 西 市) came to be laid out in Heijō-kyō, each occupying 6 *tsubo* divisions within its respective half of the city.[217] Or, to be precise, perhaps we should say that *market places* had been in existence for at least
four hundred years, for there is no conclusive evidence of the type of exchange
that was actually taking place at these centers. The tribal "markets" 市 supervised by *•*Jwię* officials that were recorded in the third century have already
been touched upon, and others are implied by the *Nihon Shoki*.

The ambiguities in our understanding of the mode of exchange associated with
these early markets are somewhat ameliorated when we come to evaluate the Eastern
and Western markets of Heijō-kyō. Although barter was still widely practiced in
rural areas, and even within the capital itself,[218] there can be no doubt that
transactions recognizable as market exchange *sensu stricto* also took place on a
considerable scale. In these exchanges the market mechanism was clearly demonstrated, and price was related in a general way to supply and demand; but there
are also good reasons for believing that the markets were not wholly autonomous.
They were, in the first instance, controlled by a representative of the central
government, who did not hesitate to intervene in market operations from time to
time.[219] It is sufficiently evident that when exchanges took place at a set
rate, noneconomic factors were frequently influential in determining that rate.
In any case, the markets were open for trading for only half of each month. A

proportion of the commodities offerred for sale, particularly fruits and vegetables, were brought into the markets by farmers working land adjacent to the city,
but most of the goods displayed there, including such items as rice, cloth of
various sorts, paper, iron, and different classes of ceramics, represented surpluses acquired through the several redistributive mechanisms by the central government, temples, or members of the nobility. The law codes also placed restrictions on the manner in which individuals and groups might avail themselves of the
facilities of the markets. Only those below the fifth rank were permitted to
open shops and engage personally in retailing activities. Those of higher rank
were required to conduct their business through the agency of slaves or attendants. The great monasteries and temples also employed special servants (*koeki no
tsukasa*公役使), who were often very knowledgeable in marketing matters, to man-
age their business ventures. It is significant that the sources make no reference to a class of independent professional merchants engaging in long-distance
wholesale trade, so it is to be presumed that both foreign imports and the internal centripetal movement of commodities as part of the redistributive process
were handled by agents of the central government.

   One indication of a significant degree of commercial sophistication was the
use of an indigenously minted coinage during the Nara period.[220] Rice and cloth
had long been used as media of exchange in the Japanese islands, and it is probable that Chinese coins that had filtered into the country were being used for
that purpose at the latest by the beginning of the seventh century. Shortly
after that time the T'ang-dynasty coin known as the *K'ai-yüan T'ung-pao*, first
issued in 621, circulated fairly widely in Japan. In 668, eleven plain circular
disks of silver (*mumon-ginsen*無文銀錢), probably of Korean origin, were presented at the dedication of the *Sūfuku-ji*崇福寺.[221] In 676, silver ore was
refined for the first time in Japan;[222] but, in 683, Temmu Tennō decreed that
only copper coins could be circulated. However, three days later, for unspecified reasons, the ruling was rescinded.[223] In 691, silver was sent to the court
from Iyo province,[224] and, in 694, mint officials were appointed by Empress
Jitō.[225] Copper was sent to the capital from Inaba and Suō in 698[226] and tin
from Iyo and Ise in the same year,[227] while in 708 the discovery of a rich and

easily worked copper lode in Musashi province was viewed with such enthusiasm
that Empress Gemmyō changed the era name from Keiun to Wado 和銅, meaning
"refined copper."[228] Later in that year an Office for the Promotion of the Coinage (催鋳銭司) was established, and, some six months later, coins (both copper and silver) were struck under government auspices for the first time.[229]
From the founding of Heijō two years later, commodities on sale in its markets
carried monetary prices that were fixed by the Director of the Market Office
(see p.142 , above). At the same time, many court and government employees were
paid in coin, and, in the capital itself and the surrounding Kinai (but not elsewhere), taxes could also be remitted in currency. A majority of the coins recovered from this period have come to light in the provinces surrounding the capital,
particularly in Yamato, Yamashiro, Ōmi, and Settsu, implying that barter persisted as the dominant mechanism of exchange in more distant parts of the country.
In fact, it is almost true to say that until the end of the second decade of the
eighth century, coinage was a feature of the metropolitan exchange system to the
virtual exclusion of the outer provinces. Not until 723 do we hear of provinces
paying taxes in currency instead of in commodities. But even in the metropolitan
region the management of the currency was never fully mastered during the Nara
period. During the second half of the eighth century new issues, usually of
smaller and cheaper coins, began to succeed one another at relatively short
intervals, a practice which induced a progressive devaluation of the coinage. In
Heian times this trend was to reach such proportions that the government insti-
gated a return to full dependence on Chinese currency.[230]

The Urban Hierarchy

Outside the capital the country was divided into provinces (*kuni* 國), of which
four originally, but after 716 five,[231] constituted a metropolitan region (the
Kinai 畿内). Each province was under the authority of a governor (*kokushi* 國
司), who was appointed by, and acted as the regional representative of, the central administration in all civil, military, judicial, and religious matters.
Each province was further subdivided first into districts (*gun* or *kōri* 郡),
under district governors (*gunji* 郡司), and then again into townships (*sato*

鄉),[232] each ideally comprising fifty households. Collectively, the provinces
were classified into four groups on the basis of size, namely, *taikoku* 大 國
(great province), *jōkoku* 上 國 (superior-sized province), *chūgoku* 中 國 (middle-
sized province), and *gekoku* 下 國 (inferior-sized province).[233] Until 739, in
accordance with the Taihō Code, the size of a district secretariat was proportional to the population of the district, with six officials assigned to a large
district, four to a middle-sized district, and three to a small one. After 739
the number of officials assigned to a large district was reduced to four.
Finally, the provinces were grouped topographically into seven circuits (*do* 道),
each under the jurisdiction of a particular inspecting officer; these were,
respectively, Tōkai 東 海, Tōsan 東 山, Hokuriku 北 陸, San'in 山 陰, San'yō
山 陽, Nankai 南 海, and Saikai 西 海.[234]

Within each province and district, local administrative centers were established, of which perhaps only the provincial capitals (*kokufu* 國 府) could claim
to be urban in any meaningful sense. More than sixty of these *kokufu* were established by the central government in Honshū, Shikoku, and Kyūshū, sometimes as
entirely new foundations but probably more frequently as adjuncts to existing
chiefly capitals. A typical location was a site roughly central to an intermon-
tane basin or coastal plain which took advantage of whatever local conditions
might offer in the way of productivity, defense, and accessibility. In fact,
quite a number of *kokufu* also functioned as river or ocean ports. In general,
the size of a settlement of this type, whether measured by population or areal
extent, was roughly proportional to its proximity to the capital.[235] The central
services provided by a representative example were of a primarily administrative
and ritual nature, including a provincial government headquarters (*kokuchō* 國
廳), the provincial temple (*kokubun-ji* 國 分 寺) and Shintō shrine (*sōja* 總.
社), and a provincial school (*kokugaku* 國 學). It also served as a base for a
local militia (*gundan* 軍 團). However, once established, *kokufu* tended almost
inevitably to develop supplementary facilities, the most typical of which was a
market to serve the needs of the cadre of resident officials, monks, and priests,
their retainers and servants, and eventually the surrounding population of farmers. Markets such as these were under the control of the *kokuchō*, apparently in

much the same way as, half a millennium earlier, tribal exchange marts had been under the supervision of a Great *·*Jwi̯e̯* official (see p. 31 , above).

In principle the *kokufu* were laid out as reduced models of the capital city. The one that has received most attention from archeologists is the Dazai Head-quarters 大宰府 in Kyūshū, which was hardly typical of this class of settlement. It was, in fact, the second most important, and almost certainly the second-largest, urban center in eighth-century Japan, deriving its significance from its dual roles as an administrative center for all Kyūshū and as a frontier fortress protecting the southwestern flank of the country from foreign attack. In addi-tion to the customary range of *kokufu* facilities, it was also the site of an important religious center, the Kannon-ji 觀世音寺, and of a regional college, the Gakugyōin 學業院. As in the capital, the grid plan of the city was divided into an eastern (*Sakaku* 左郭) and a western half (*Ukaku* 右郭), and an ancient text implies that each half was laid out as an orthogonal plat of at least 20 *jō* by 12 *bō*.[236] The administrative enclave, the Dazai-fu proper (though the term came to be applied to the settlement as a whole), occupied four *chō* axi-ally balanced at the north end of the city. Within this enclosure the Tofurō 都府楼 consisted of a cluster of buildings arranged in a manner that resembled a simplified version of the Daigokuden at Heijō. Five temples were incorporated into the grid of the city, and another four were erected outside the specifically urban plat, including the provincial temple itself and its associated nunnery.[237] The military function of the Dazai-fu, not only as a bastion against Korean inva-sion but also as a warning to rebellious Kyūshū nobles, was explicit in its two fortresses, one frowning over the city from a site on a mountain spur, the other protecting the maritime approaches from a point on the coast. The earthen ram-parts for the latter were constructed in 664, during the reign of Emperor Tenchi.

The only other provincial capital which is known by more than its name (other, of course, than the former capital of Naniwa, which was the seat of the specially constituted Settsu Secretariat 攝津職) is the castle fortress of Taga-jō 多賀城, built on a low hill near present-day Sendai as a means of asserting control over the Ezo. It was probably founded in about 737, when it was known as the Taga palisade, but by 780 it had become sufficiently impressive

to be called Taga fortress. Its encircling outer ramparts enclosed an area 10
chō (1,000 meters) from north to south by 8 *chō* (800 meters) from east to west.
Within it was a smaller fortified enclave, containing what is believed to have
been the government office. The temple was situated in the southeastern sector
of the citadel.

The next-lower level in the settlement hierarchy consisted of *gun* administrative centers, like the *kokufu*, either founded afresh or adapted from preexisting settlements. Little is known about them, but it is unlikely that many
achieved a true urban status. In any case, they seem to have been less closely
integrated into the administrative hierarchy than were the *kokufu*, and their
officials, often the heads of prominent local lineage segments, enjoyed considerable freedom of action. In addition, a variety of settlements were established
by the central and local administrations in the interests of external defense,
internal control, and interregional communication. These included a chain of
fortresses in the north to guard again Ezo depredations,[238] post stations along
the main roads,[239] and a series of ports that reflected a physiographically
engendered preference of the Japanese for travel by sea rather than land. Some
of these latter, such as Naniwa and Hakata, were already of respectable antiquity,
as was Ōtsu, which served as a break-of-bulk station for commodities transported
across Lake Biwa.

What all this amounted to was a rigidly controlled hierarchy of administrative centers imposed by government fiat on the mosaic of communities that had
emerged in pre-Taika times. In establishing the several levels of this national
administrative framework, the central government does not appear to have taken
particular account of the incipient marketing organization that was discernible
at least as early as the third century A.D. The result was an apparent fragmen-
tation of the potential hierarchy of market centers into small and localized
adjuncts, attached arbitrarily and adventitiously to settlements whose very
existence had been determined on other grounds. Under these restraints the evolution of a system of self-regulating markets was severely inhibited. However,
this is not to imply that economic exchange of a different type did not figure
prominently at the several levels of the urban hierarchy. Indeed, the *raison*

d'être of that hierarchy was the sustaining of a highly developed system of redistributive and mobilizative exchanges that had been given formal expression in the legislative norms of the *ritsuryō* codes. In other words, the main centers of redistribution were also the main centers of decision-making, so that locational isomorphism between administrative and economic hierarchies was almost perfect. Moreover, by decreeing that the range of the highest-order functions in both these hierarchies was coincident with the maximum extent of society as a whole (in this case the state), the codes of the seventh and eighth centuries ensured a strongly developed primate distribution in the settlement hierarchy; that is, the largest city (in this instance the capital) was several times more populous than any other urban center in the hierarchy and was exceptionally expressive of national capacity and sentiment.[240] From the middle of the seventh century onward, and perhaps earlier, each in the succession of capitals had exhibited this characteristic to a marked degree, with Nara finally exceeding many fold, in magnitude of population, area, diversity of functions, and prestige, any other urban center in Japan. It was this variance in scale (rather than simple size) between the *Misato* and the regional centers that inspired the words attributed to the young provincial, Ōtomo Kumagori, which we have inscribed at the beginning of this book:

> Always talking about it and wondering,
> When shall I see the City?

More than a millennium later, Francine Herail could still discern this dissonance between life-styles and perceptions in the capital and in the provinces, "la première imbue de la civilisation et des pratiques chinoises, les secondes admirant le savoir et l'élégance des aristocrates qui entouraient l'empereur, ne refusant pas de soutenir leur existence, mais ne comprenant peut-être pas très bien le sens et la portée des dispositions légales imposées par la cour."[241]

Envoi

We began this study with the preconception of Japan as a realm of secondary urban generation but also with the expectation that the process of urban genesis would prove to have taken a course significantly different from that postulated in the generalized model presented in *The Pivot of the Four Quarters*. To our surprise, the Japanese experience turned out to fit the model reasonably closely in its essentials. The earliest discernible functional center for control of a society beyond the scale of the tribe, and in that sense a creator of effective space, was a locus of power and authority that can properly be characterized as a ceremonial center in the technical sense defined on page 75. If the *Hou-Han Shu* is to be believed — and, whatever its deficiencies in other respects, we deem it worthy of credit in this particular instance — the process of aggregation of control mechanisms in one place had already been initiated by the first century A.D., and it had achieved at least the degree of centralization of a low-level chiefdom by the beginning of the third century. That the process was materially affected by the diffusion of cultural traits from the Asian mainland is beyond dispute, so that there is no call to reconsider our categorization of Japan as a realm of secondary urban generation.

In attempting to explicate the associated processes of centralization of leadership and institutionalization of power to govern by force as well as authority, two courses were open to us. The first was to isolate the characteristics which early Japanese society shared with other societies at apparently similar levels of integration and to assign those functional traits to compartments in an ecumenically encompassing interpretative structure developed on the basis of such perceived commonalities. This has been the method employed, often with remarkable sophistication, by members of the so-called Tōkyō school of Marxist historians. But although it is easily rendered operational, this method suffers from epistemological shortcomings. Because it focuses on the characteristics common to all societies, to the virtual exclusion of their disparities, it does not permit the verification of its own hypotheses (or, more accurately, an approach to verification through cumulative attempts at falsification). Moreover, the ascription of a particular society to a compartment within the interpretative framework automatically transforms it into a symbolic representation of the structure of a generalized society at a specific stage of development, thereby at one and the same time depriving it of its actual evolutionary past and furnishing it with a projected future that it may in fact not survive to experience. The second course, and the one which we adopted, was to allow our themes to develop out of the data under the impulsion of their own intrinsic logic and then to search the relevant literature for conceptual structures whose articulations might illuminate the themes and so reveal the nature of the processes at work in early Japanese society. By this means we believe that we have been able to take the first steps toward explaining by one and the same set of principles not only certain similarities but also some of the differences between the Japanese case and other Archaic/Ancient societies, and toward correlating the initial phases of the urbanization process in Japan with similar beginnings in other parts of the world without suppressing what was specific to the Japanese experience. We have regarded it as our business to render diversity intelligible, not to subsume, disregard, or suppress it; and it is within that framework that we have adduced the models of social differentiation discussed in chapter 1.

Until the end of the Early Tumulus period the twin state-forming processes of centralization and segregation appear to have maintained a rough parity of effect. By the third century A.D. certainly, and by inference up to two centuries earlier, these complementary processes (discussed in chap. 1; summarized on pp. 77-78) had induced the formation of a series of polities that can be safely assigned to southern Japan, even though their precise locations are in dispute. The only one of these proto-states to have been described in detail took the form of a classical-type chiefdom of the sort described on page 72. From a fortified administrative and ceremonial enceinte, the celebrated *Yamatai* of Japanese historiography (neither the orthography nor the vocalization of the actual name is entirely free of doubt), a paramount chieftainess ruled over a score or so of subordinate territories and, with the aid of a corps of officials, collected revenues, supervised market transactions, organized the corvée, and, in a typically patrimonial manner, administered punishments to those who transgressed her directives. To judge from the Chinese accounts of this chieftainess, her ability to

160

draw on privileged force to compel obedience was somewhat limited, but sanctity,
as manifested in her commerce with earthly and heavenly deities, was a more than
adequate functional equivalent — except when it came to the selection of her
successor. Apparently the rules of succession had not at that time been effectively institutionalized, so that it was still possible for the paramountcy to be
disputed. It is probably significant, however, that the claims of sanctified
lineage and, apparently, of sex ultimately triumphed, with the cooperation of
Chinese frontier authority, over an attempt to establish a male succession.

The Chinese provided a description of only one third-century chiefdom in
southern Japan but strongly implied that others existed, as well as a variety of
tribal groups, about which they had no reliable information. This picture of the
Wa territories as occupied by a mosaic of tribal groups at widely differing levels of technological achievement is, generally speaking, supported by the character and distribution of the Late Yayoi archeological assemblages described in
chapter 2. The century and a half following the death of the *Yamatai* chieftainess is an exceedingly obscure period, but what little evidence there is implies
that powerful chiefdoms consolidated their authority in several regions of southern Japan, with one among them, the Yamato confederacy, establishing a hegemony
from a base in the Kinai. This chiefdom is considered by some influential scholars, such as Mizuno Yū, to have provided the first historical (as opposed to
mythological) dynasty to have held sway over Japan south of the Tōhoku. Whether
or not it was related in any way to the older chiefdom with which the Chinese
had had dealings in the third century, is a matter of continuing debate, but its
designation by Mizuno and others as ritual-religious in character shows that it
fell within the same general organizational tradition.

Whether or no the workings of the antithetical processes of centralization
and segregation (or differentiation) discussed in chapter 1 would ultimately have
resulted in the formation of a fully urbanized level of statehood in southern
Japan will never be known, for, just prior to the opening of the fifth century,
this course of development was interrupted by a sequence of events which, though
capable of other interpretations, are probably best construed as a foreign conquest. In the opinion of Gari Ledyard, the invaders were Puyŏ, who incorporated

southern Japan into an imperium that reached from central Korea to the Kinai.
The fifth century is as poorly documented as any in Japanese history, but such
evidence as can be gleaned from the chronicles would seem to imply that the new
masters of Yamato differed from their predecessors, the so-called ritual-religious
sovereigns, in that they relied to a greater extent on military force and less on
sanctity to impose their will on the Wa tribes. But, as was pointed out in chapter 1, it is sanctity that prescribes the acceptable options within a range of
possible societal responses. Without it, there are likely to be variable degrees
of failure to impose the cognized values of higher-order controls as the reference values for lower-order systems, so that lower-order social groups may be
tempted to "promote" (in the technical sense defined on p. 12) their own special-
purpose functions to positions of dominance at higher and more self-serving levels. This is what appears to have happened in fifth-century Yamato, when two
lineages managed to promote their own interests so as virtually to monopolize the
paramountcy, now denoted by the style *Ōkimi*. That the new rulers, in the absence
of the information-verifying sanctity that had pervaded the old ritual-religious
dynasty, failed adequately to imbue social groups functioning as components in
lower-order systems with their own centralist values is to be inferred both from
the chronic indeterminacy of succession that is apparent even in the garbled versions of events preserved in the chronicles and from the importance of the roles
played by members of nonroyal lineages in the succession process.

When, at about the beginning of the sixth century, Mizuno's third dynasty of
Archaic Japan (p. 71 , above) replaced the line of conquest rulers in what Ledyard has characterized as a resurgence of indigenous Wa power, sanctity seems to
have been invoked in support of socially regulative conventions with renewed fer-
vor. Within a few decades it is possible to discern the beginnings of that
emphasis on the special status of the ruling lineage which, by early in the
eighth century, when the great chronicles were compiled, had been codified as
claims to antiquity, continuity, and manifest divinity. Progressively the office
of supreme ruler assumed a ceremonially unique set of functions, so that, as Cornelius Kiley has phrased it, "Sacredness became an incident of the royal office
rather than a precondition for it." Although the Yamato court was able to draw

on a not inconsiderable reserve of military force when necessary, the circumstance that its directives emanated from a sanctified source was, in the long
run, an even more potent factor in the regulation of Japanese society. But sanctity would have been of little avail had there not been strong flows of information capable of disseminating the cognized values of the center through the
lower-order systems of the provinces. These flows derived from a centralization
process that increased in intensity through the sixth and, particularly, the seventh centuries.

In its efforts to control the territories that it had wrested from the conquest dynasty of the fifth century, the Yamato court was constrained to extend
and diversify the linkages between itself and districts hitherto bound only
loosely to the central government as patrimonial-style benefices. This continuing concern to ensure — in the language we have employed in chapter 1 — that
lower-order controls should maintain crucial variables within designated goal
ranges necessitated the repeated activation of highest-order controls, with a
consequent bypassing of intermediate-level institutions, and the development of
powerful linearizing mechanisms (p. 13). At the beginning of the sixth century
many regional nobles still functioned as quasi-autonomous potentates largely outside the Yamato court structure; half a century later virtually all of them had
been subsumed within the national bureaucracy as *kuni no miyatsuko*. The system
of marriage alliances obtaining within the upper echelons of the Yamato court,
despite not infrequent discrepancies between ceremonial status and political
power, similarly tended to strengthen links binding individual lineages to the
court, often to the detriment of those binding lineage to lineage (cf. p. 88).
The management of *miyake* by the court (p. 87) afforded a classic instance of a
linearization mechanism verging, by its permanence, on meddling, as was the payment of taxes by families and groups directly to the central government (pp. 147-
48). The Jingikan provided an equally apt example of linearization in the sphere
of religious administration, for this centrally situated bureau supervised all
officially sponsored shrines and maintained registers of the priesthood and religious corporations, not only in the capital but throughout the kingdom.

These examples are representative of a large class of linearizing mechanisms which were developed during the sixth and seventh centuries to bind the provinces and districts of the kingdom to the center. This type of massive interference by the center in affairs of the periphery, however, inevitably weakened the boundaries between subsystems, leading to a decline in regional autonomy and a consequent simplification of the political structure. But, as Flannery has pointed out, the maintenance of such simplification necessitates more management, which in turn requires the creation of new formal institutions; and the sixth and seventh centuries were indeed a period of institutional innovation. The new institutions arose in two ways. The first was through the elaboration of roles within preexisting institutions, as was exemplified by the formation of a service nobility during the sixth century, an event of considerable importance in that it signified the beginning of a transition from traditional to rational-legal authority (pp. 86 and 100). The newly created communities of *tomo-be* are examples of another institutional form which developed in this way, as the *uji* appears also to have been, though its evolution is very obscure (pp. 92-103). The other way in which what amounted to a new institution might come into being was through the elevation of an already existing institution to a higher position in the control hierarchy. An instructive instance of such an upward translation was afforded by the Soga no Ōmi in the middle of the sixth century, when their function as a sort of fiscal service corps (a major innovation in the Yamato bureaucracy) endowed them with a political power far exceeding that customarily associated with their formal rank. On a more general level, the instruments which raised managerial innovation to the level of thoroughgoing political reconstitution were the great codes of the seventh and early eighth centuries. Beginning with Prince Shōtoku's so-called Constitution, through the Taika Reform Edict to the Taihō and Yōrō Codes, virtually the whole of Japanese secular, and a good deal of religious, institutional life was reorganized to a greater or lesser degree (p. 91). Chapter 3 of the present work is essentially an exposition of the manner in which the capital city was reorganized in conformity with these codes, from the comprehensive injunction "to regulate the *Misato*" down to the appointment of ward headmen and the assignment of building lots within residential blocks.

It was from about the middle of the sixth century that the palace-capitals

of Yamato had begun to develop into something more than the seats of tribal con-
federacies. At that time, increasing societal differentiation and specialization
combined with the forging of linkages between subsystems and higher-order controls to generate voluminous information flows, which were invariably transmitted
through, and as often as not generated within, the administrative complex centered on the ruler's palace. In either case the processed messages were impreg-
nated with the norms and values of the Yamato court. And, as the scale of Yamato
society broadened (p. 95), so the capital, the primary node in the communications network, not only expanded in order to cope with the augmented quantity of
information generated by the interactions of already existing agencies but also
became institutionally more complex as a response to the need to process an
increasingly diverse range of information more rapidly. Thus far the Japanese
ceremonial and administrative center — at least proto-, if not fully, urban in
its role as a focus of societal control, as a creator of effective space — could
be matched both functionally, and to no inconsiderable degree structurally, in
most other realms of secondary urban generation and, indeed, in those where the
process was primary. But during the seventh century the built form of the emergent Japanese city, consisting basically of a governmental and ritual complex
surrounded by a ragged selvedge of plebeian dwellings and workshops, was forced
into a rigid framework adopted from continental urban design. Whereas the analogues of the Japanese city in this phase of its development in, say, the Maya,
Khmer, Chinese, or Yoruba territories continued to elaborate indigenous traditions of urban organization, disposing volume and space in their own culturally
distinctive symbolic patterns, the Japanese city had imposed on it an orthogonal
lattice of foreign provenance, which was also consonant with a much later phase
of urban evolution. Specifically, a Japanese urban form that would not have been
egregiously out of place in the Spring-and-Autumn period of Chinese history was
transformed by imperial fiat into a reduced replica of a T'ang metropolis of a
thousand years later. Within this ritually defined framework, society continued
to develop in its own distinctively Japanese fashion, but the built form of the
capital would henceforth be based on a canonical design shared at one time or
another with regions as far distant as western Asia.

This, in outline, is the framework within which we have sought to elicit the origins of the Japanese urban tradition. We do not claim to have documented all its manifold complexities; in our opinion, that is not at present a feasible undertaking, partly because of a relative paucity of relevant archeological investigation, partly because the textual sources have not been adequately eluci- dated for the purposes of the urbanist, partly because of the prevailing fluidity of opinion about the early history of Japan, and, finally, because we do not yet possess a comprehensive and sufficiently analytical theory of urban genesis. Our interpretation is not offered as a definitive statement; rather, it is in the nature of an extended conjecture, a hypothesis which can be tested against new evidence as it becomes available and which can provide a context for evaluating the implications of such evidence. It is to be anticipated that a decade hence it will be possible to explicate an enhanced understanding of social change in early Japan in terms of a more powerful theory of urban genesis. Until that time, we are advancing what is no more than a provisional interpretation which appears to us to be consonant with currently developing thrusts in both the specific study of ancient Japanese society and the comparative investigation of urban origins. It would be contrary to the nature and spirit of the historical enterprise to suppose that the new formulation will verify our inferences in all their details, but that it will pronounce on their usefulness, or otherwise, as an intermediate stage in the explanatory process is assured.

Notes and References

CHAPTER 1: THE NATURE OF THE INQUIRY

1. The term "city" in this volume is used generically to denote any urban form and carries none of the ancillary connotations of size, status, or origin implicit in contemporary everyday American or English usage.

2. Cf. G. P. Chapman, "The Object of geographical analysis," an unpublished paper presented to the Commission on Quantitative Methods of the International Geographical Union (Budapest, 1971). We have not seen this paper, but Chapman's definition of a "first-order object of study" is reported by Brian T. Robson in *Urban growth: An approach* (London, 1973), p. 4, as "an object which can be specified in terms of its morphology, taxonomy, composition, physiology, ecology, chorology and chronology; an object, in other words, which has shape, which is composed of a set of identifiable elements determining its internal functioning, which can be related to other objects defined at a similar scale and having relationships with it at the next-higher scale level, and which varies both over space and time."

3. Robson, *Urban growth*, p. 6. Robson is one of the few writers on recent and contemporary urbanism to have faced squarely the problem of defining the idea, as well as the substantive form, of the city. Another is David Harvey in *Social justice and the city* (Baltimore, 1973), esp. pp. 302–14.

4. In this sense "urbanization" can be said to subsume three analytically separable conceptions, each appropriate to a particular category of questions and each characterized by its own peculiar difficulties of definition and measurement: (1) the behavioral conception, which views urbanization as an adjustment of personal conduct, as a transformation of attitudes and values experienced by individuals over time. (2) The structural conception, which focuses attention on the patterned activities of whole populations, generally in situations where subgroups from mainly agricultural communities are being absorbed into larger, more complex, nonagricultural societies. It follows that this conception of urbanization tends to concentrate on the differential ordering of occupations or industries within a specified territory. (3) The demographic conception, which, while also focusing attention primarily on aggregate groupings within defined spaces, largely ignores both individual behavior and occupational structure and concerns itself almost exclusively with the process of population concentration. Consequently, this conception recognizes only two significant variables, population and space. On this theme see E. E. Lampard, "Historical aspects of urbanization," in Philip M. Hauser and Leo F. Schnore, eds., *The Study of urbanization* (New York, 1965), pp. 519–20; Lampard, "Urbanization and social change: On broadening the scope and relevance of urban history," in Oscar Handlin and John Burchard, eds., *The Historian and the city* (Cambridge, Mass., 1963), pp. 225–47; H. Tisdale, "The Process of urbanization," *Social Forces* 20 (1942): 311–16; J. P.

Gibbs, "Measures of urbanization," *Social Forces* 45 (1966): 170-77; John Friedmann, "Two concepts of urbanization: A comment," *Urban Affairs* 1, no. 4 (1966): 79-84. It should be noted, however, that for some sociologists, notable among whom are Kingsley Davis and his collaborators, urbanization denotes not a *rate of change* in the proportion of urban dwellers to total population but rather that proportion itself; cf. Kingsley Davis and Hilda Hertz Golden, "Urbanization and the development of pre-industrial areas," *Economic Development and Cultural Change* 3 (1954): 6-24.

5. Cf. Robert Redfield, *The Primitive world and its transformations* (Ithaca, N.Y., 1953), p. 53, and *Peasant society and culture* (Chicago, 1956), passim; Eric R. Wolf, *Peasants* (Englewood Cliffs, N.J., 1966), pp. 9-10.

6. The notion of an urbanized society developed in this paragraph is structurally similar to, though considerably broader in application than, the idea of an urban field as proposed by J. Friedmann and J. Miller in "The Urban field," *Journal of the American Institute of Planners* 31 (1965): 312-20, and developed by B. J. L. Berry, "Metropolitan Area redefinition: A re-evaluation of concept and statistical practice," *Working Paper* 29 (Washington, D.C.: U.S. Bureau of the Census, 1968).

7. The concept of levels of sociocultural complexity comprising "a framework of functionally interconnected institutions forming the structural core of a distinctive set of social systems" was proposed by Julian H. Steward in *Theory of culture change* (Urbana, Ill., 1955), and was subsequently applied to the problem of urban genesis by Robert McC. Adams, *The Evolution of urban society* (Chicago, 1966).

8. These levels are discussed in more detail in Paul Wheatley, *The Pivot of the four quarters: A preliminary enquiry into the origins and character of the ancient Chinese city* (Edinburgh and Chicago, 1971), pp. 316-30. The concept of developed village-farming efficiency is owed to Robert J. Braidwood, *The Near East and the foundations for civilization*, The Condon Lectures (Eugene, Ore., 1952), p. 41, and "Levels in prehistory," in Sol Tax, ed., *Evolution of man: Mind, culture, and society* (Chicago, 1960), p. 149.

9. Some of the language of this and the following half-dozen paragraphs has been borrowed from an earlier paper entitled "Urban genesis in continental South East Asia," in Ralph Smith and William Watson, eds., *Early Southeast Asia* (in press).

10. H. M. Blalock and A. B. Blalock, "Toward a clarification of system analysis in the social sciences," *Philosophy of Science* 26 (1959): 84-88.

11. J. Klir and M. Valach, *Cybernetic modelling* (London, 1967).

12. Talcott Parsons and Edward Shils, eds., *Toward a general theory of action* (Cambridge, Mass., 1952), pp. 4, 39, 56, and 101.

13. In this connection one is reminded of R. F. Murphey's thesis that the acculturative situation is not only empirically the condition of, but is also

structurally necessary to, virtually all human societies; see his "Social change and acculturation," *Transactions of the New York Academy of Sciences* ser. 2 22 (1963-64): 845-54.

14. It was presumably this type of diffusion that Bronislaw Malinowski had in mind when he wrote that, "Diffusion . . . is not an act, but a process closely akin in its working to the evolutionary process. For evolution deals above all with the influence of any type of 'origins'; and origins do not differ fundamentally, whether they occur by invention or by diffusion" (*A Scientific theory of culture* [Chapel Hill, N.C., 1944], pp. 14-15). In a similar vein cf. Julian Steward, "Cultural causality and law: A trial formulation of the development of early civilizations," *American Anthropologist* 51 (1951): 4, and *Theory of culture change*, p. 182; L. A. White, "Evolution and diffusion," *Antiquity* 31 (1957): 214-18.

15. This is John Friedmann's highly apposite phrase. Cf. "Cities in social transformation," *Comparative Studies in Society and History* 4 (1961): 92: "A mere area becomes effective 'space' . . . solely through the agency of urban institutions which extend their influences outward, binding the surrounding regions to the central city and introducing to them urban ways of thought and action." The same author has subsequently applied this concept to problems of development in several papers which have been conveniently assembled in a volume entitled *Urbanization, planning, and national development* (Beverly Hills, Cal., 1973).

16. For varying views of what constitutes a state consult, inter alia, J. K. Bluntschli, *The Theory of the state* (London, 1892); Franz Oppenheimer, *The State: Its history and development viewed sociologically* (reprint edition, New York, 1926); Richard Thurnwald, *Die menschliche Gesellschaft* (Berlin and Leipzig, 1935), vol. 4; Otto Gierke, *Natural law and the theory of society* (Boston, 1950); Wilhelm Koppers, "L'Origine de l'état," *VIth International Congress of Anthropological and Ethnological Sciences 1960* (Paris, 1963), vol. 2, pp. 159-68; Morton H. Fried, *The Evolution of political society: An essay in political anthropology* (New York, 1967), chap. 6; Lawrence Krader, *Formation of the state* (Englewood Cliffs, N.J., 1968); and, most recently, Elman R. Service, *Origins of the state and civilization: The process of cultural evolution* (New York, 1975).

17. Wheatley, *The Pivot of the four quarters*, esp. chap. 3.

18. Otis Dudley Duncan and Leo F. Schnore, "Cultural, behavioral, and ecological perspectives in the study of social organization," *American Journal of Sociology* 65 (1959): 132-46; Schnore, "Social morphology and human ecology," 63 (1958): 620-34; and Duncan, "Human ecology and population studies," in Philip M. Hauser and Duncan, eds., *The Study of population* (Chicago, 1959), pp. 678-716. For a contrary view see Sidney M. Wilhelm, "The Concept of the 'ecological complex': A critique," *American Journal of Economics and Sociology* 23 (1964): 241-48. There are compendious evaluations of the contributions of the ecological

school of urban studies in Leonard Reissman, *The Urban process: Cities in industrial societies* (New York, 1964), chap. 5, and Wheatley, "The Concept of urbanism," in Peter J. Ucko, Ruth Tringham, and G. W. Dimbleby, *Man, settlement and urbanism* (London, 1972), pp. 606-8.

19. Emile Durkheim, *De la division du travail social: Etude sur l'organisation des sociétés supérieures* (Paris, 1893).

20. Duncan, "Human ecology and population studies," p. 683.

21. Duncan and Schnore, "Cultural, behavioral, and ecological perspectives," p. 138.

22. The factors most commonly invoked in this connection are trade and/or marketing (the mechanism favored by most geographers and many archeologists); warfare (e.g., Robert L. Carneiro, "A Theory of the origin of the state," *Science* 169 [1970]: 733-38); irrigation (associated principally with the name of Karl A. Wittfogel, *Oriental despotism: A comparative study of total power* [New Haven, 1957], though others, such as Julian H. Steward, ed., *Irrigation civilizations: A comparative study*, Pan American Union Social Science Monograph 1 [Washington, D.C., 1955], have contributed significantly); and, to a lesser extent, religion (e.g., Numa-Denis Fustel de Coulanges, *La Cité antique* [Paris, 1864]). In some other interpretations, population and technology are postulated as dependent variables within the ecological complex rather than simply as factors acting on a variable; see, e.g., T. Cuyler Young, Jr., "Population densities and early Mesopotamian urbanism," in Ucko et al., *Man, settlement and urbanism*, pp. 827-42, and, of course, V. Gordon Childe, "The Urban revolution," *Town Planning Review* 21, no. 1 (1950): 9-16.

23. S. N. Eisenstadt, "Social change, differentiation and evolution," *American Sociological Review* 29 (1964): 375-86.

24. For discussion of the functional subsystems of society (which are indeed those of every interaction group of any kind) see pp. 145-54.

25. G. C. Homans and D. M. Schneider, *Marriage, authority, and final causes: A study of unilateral cross-cousin marriage* (Glencoe, Ill., 1955). In this connection we must quote, as others have before us, R. K. Merton: "like the Christian theologians devoted to the argument from design, [the functional analyst] might be cozened by a Ben Franklin who demonstrated that God clearly 'wants us to tipple, because He has made the joints of the arm just the right length to carry a glass to the mouth, without falling short of or overshooting the mark: "Let us adore, then, glass in hand, this benevolent wisdom; let us adore and drink" ' " (*Social theory and social structure: Toward the codification of theory and research*, rev. ed. [Glencoe, Ill., 1957], p. 38).

26. Kent V. Flannery, "The Cultural evolution of civilizations," *Annual Review of Ecology and Systematics* 3 (1972): 399-426.

27. J. G. Miller, "Living systems: Basic concepts," *Behavioral Scientist* 10, pt. 3 (1965): 193-257.

28. Flannery, "The Cultural evolution of civilizations," p. 409.

29. James K. Feibleman, "Theory of integrative levels," *British Journal for the Philosophy of Science* 5 (1954): 61. Or, phrased differently, the output of a higher-order control constitutes the reference value of a lower-order control. Or, stated in yet a third way, a regulatory mechanism does not establish its own output reference values but adopts those of a higher-order regulatory mechanism.

30. Ibid.

31. L. B. Slobodkin, "Toward a predictive theory of evolution," in Richard O. Lewontin, ed., *Population biology and evolution* (Syracuse, N.Y., 1968), pp. 187-205.

32. Flannery, "The Cultural evolution of civilizations," p. 413.

33. Roy A. Rappaport, "Sanctity and adaptation." Paper prepared for the Wenner-Gren Symposium, "The Moral and Esthetic Structure of Human Adaptation" (mimeographed, 1969).

34. Cited from Rappaport, ibid., p. 26.

35. Cited from Rappaport, ibid., p. 24.

36. Flannery, "The Cultural evolution of civilizations," p. 420.

37. Ibid., p. 412.

38. Richard L. Meier, *A Communications theory of urban growth* (Cambridge, Mass., 1962).

39. Wheatley, *The Pivot of the four quarters*, pp. 302-5, 318-20.

40. This was particularly true of two of the more thoughtful reviews, namely, one by David Harvey in *Annals of the Association of American Geographers* 62, no. 3 (1972): 509-13, and a review article by Alan R. H. Baker, "Wheatley as symbol," *Area* 5, no. 2 (1973): 101-4.

41. Roy A. Rappaport, "The Sacred in human evolution," *Annual Review of Ecology and Systematics* 2 (1971): 23-44.

42. Ibid., p. 25.

43. In this and the next paragraph we are relying on Rappaport, ibid., and to a large extent employing his terminology. For a fuller discussion of this conceptualization of sacredness as a function of intrinsic truthfulness see Rappaport, "Ritual, sanctity and cybernetics," *American Anthropologist* 73 (1971): 59-75.

44. Rappaport, "The Sacred in human evolution," p. 32.

45. Ibid., p. 35.

46. Ibid.

47. This is the term used by Rappaport, ibid., p. 33, and defined by him in "Aspects of man's influence upon island ecosystems: Alteration and control," in F. R. Fosberg, ed., *Man's place in the island ecosystem* (Honolulu, 1963), p. 159: "The cognized environment may be seen as the class composed of the sum of the phenomena ordered into meaningful categories by a population." Cf. also Flannery, "The Cultural evolution of civilizations," p. 409.

48. Rappaport, "The Sacred in human evolution," p. 36.

49. Wheatley, *The Pivot*, p. 305.

CHAPTER 2: THE RISE OF THE CEREMONIAL CENTER

1. Yin-Te Index, no. 41.

2. Yin-Te Index, no. 33. Simple references to unspecified parts of the Japanese archipelago also occur in the *Shan-Hai Ching* 山海經 of Former Han date but unknown authorship (Chung-Fa Index, no. 9), in the *Lun Heng* 論衡 compiled by Wang Ch'ung 王充 in A.D. 82/83 (Chung-Fa Index, no. 1), and in the official history of the Former Han dynasty (*Han Shu* 漢書), which was begun by Pan Piao 班彪, carried forward by his son Pan Ku 班固, and completed by the latter's sister Pan Chao 班昭 in about A.D. 100 (Yin-Te Index, no. 36).

3. E.g., Naitō Torajirō 内藤虎次郎, *Shina shigaku shi* 支那史學史 (Tōkyō, 1949), pp. 184-85; John Young, *The Location of Yamatai: A case study in Japanese historiography 720-1945*, the Johns Hopkins University Studies in Historical and Political Science, ser. 75, no. 2 (Baltimore, 1958), p. 31.

4. The sources of Fan Yeh's additional information relating to the *·Jwiɐ̞ can only be matters for speculation. Extensive sections of his history were based on the *Tung-kuan Han-chi* 東觀漢記, voluminous in its original Later Han form but now surviving only in fragments. However, none of the existing fragments contains a single reference to the *·Jwiɐ̞, and neither is there extant mention of a *chüan* dealing with the so-called Eastern Barbarians. Perhaps a source of Japanese materials more likely to have been exploited by Fan Yeh was the now lost *Hsü Han-Shu* 續漢書 by Hsieh Ch'eng 謝承, a work which Fan Yeh did in fact use as a basis for his chapters on administrative geography. He may also have used any or all of a dozen or so other histories of the Later Han now known only by name but ascribed to the second, third, or fourth centuries.

5. The extant quotations are reproduced conveniently in Wada Sei and Ishihara Michihiro 和田清 石原通博, *Gishi Wajinden, Gokansho Waden, Sōsho Wakokuden, Zuisho Wakokuden* 魏志倭人伝, 後漢書倭伝, 宋書倭国伝, 隋書倭国伝, (Tōkyō, 1951), p. 91; and in Hashimoto Masukichi 橋本増吉, *Tōyōshijō yori mitaru Nihon jōkoshi kenkyū* 東洋史上より見たる日本上古史研究 (Tōkyō, 1932), p. 9.

6. The relevant passages in the Chinese histories have been rendered into German by André Wedemeyer, *Japanische Frühgeschichte: Untersuchungen zur Chronologie und Territorialverfassung von Altjapan bis zum 5. Jahrh. n. Chr.* (Tōkyō, 1930), pp. 169-231, and into English by Ryūsaku Tsunoda and L. Carrington Goodrich, *Japan in the Chinese dynastic histories: Later Han through Ming dynasties* (South Pasadena, 1951). The texts have been collected and annotated by Wada (cited in n. 5) and, more recently, by Ōta Akira 太田亮, *Kan, Kan shiseki ni arawaretaru Nikkan kodaishi shiryō* 漢, 韓史籍に顯はれたる日韓古代資料, 4th ed. (Tōkyō, 1944).

7. References to the Chinese standard histories (*cheng shih* 正史) are to the *Po-na Pen Erh-shih-ssǔ Shih* 百衲本二十四史 editions.

8. Modern Standard Chinese *wei, wo*. In this chapter Chinese names and terms occurring in early texts are transcribed according to Bernhard Karlgren's reconstructions of the sound system of the literary language current in north-central China during the sixth century A.D. (though Karlgren himself believed his reconstructed phonology to be that of Ch'ang-an); see his *Compendium of phonetics in Ancient and Archaic Chinese* (Stockholm, 1954), and "Grammata Serica recensa," *Bulletin of the Museum of Far Eastern Antiquities* 22 (1957): 1-332. See also Chou Tsu-mo 周祖謨, "*Ch'ieh-Yün*-te hsing-chih ho t'a-te yin-hsi chi-ch'u" 切韵的性質和它的音系基礎, in Chou Tsu-mo, *Wen-hsüeh Chi* 問學集 (Pei-ching, 1966), pp. 434-73.

9. The *Hou-Han Shu* reads simply: "All together, there are more than one hundred *kuo*" 凡百餘國. The brief passage in the *Ti-li Chih* 地理志-section of the earlier *Han Shu*, after mentioning the "**·Jwiẹ* people" 倭人, notes that "they are divided into upwards of one hundred *kuo*" 分為百餘國.

10. Chüan 116, fol. 1v.

11. Chüan 116, fol. 4r.

12. Cf., for example, the *Kuang-Chou Chi* 廣州記 (not later than the fifth century) as cited in the *So-Yin* 索隱, Commentary on the *Shih Chi*, chüan 113, or the fifth-century *Nan-Yüeh Chih* 南越志, as preserved fragmentarily in the *T'ai-p'ing Huan-yü Chi* 太平寰宇記, chüan 170.

13. See the several extant versions of the report of Chinese envoys to **B'iu-nậm* 扶南 in about A.D. 245 that derive from a work variously entitled *Fu-nan Chi* 扶南記, *Fu-nan I-wu Chih* 扶南異物志, *K'ang-shih Wai-kuo Chuan* 康氏外國傳, etc.; the bibliography and substance are discussed in Wheatley, *The Golden Khersonese* (Kuala Lumpur, 1961), pp. 14-25 and 114-15.

14. The Commentary to the *Hou-Han Shu* (chüan 115, fol. 12v) adds a note to the effect that the contemporary (i.e., fifth-century) vocalization of this name was **Ia-muâ-t'uậi* 邪摩堆. See also *Sui Shu* 隋書, chüan 81, fol. 13r: "The seat of government (都) is **Ia-mjiẹ-tuậi* 邪靡堆: it is what in the *Wei Chih* was called **Ia-ma-d'ậi*." **D'ậi* is Karlgren's reconstruction of the sound of 臺 in north-central China in about A.D. 600, but Gari Ledyard has established that the third-century reading was close to **d'əg*. Subsequently the Chinese -ə- became a standard transcriptional rendering of Japanese -ö- (Ledyard, "Galloping along with the horseriders: Looking for the founders of Japan," *Journal of Japanese Studies* 1, no. 2 [1975]: 230, n. 27).

15. The Chinese perceived these communities of **γân* 韓 as divided into three main groups: the **Ma-γân* (馬韓: Korean = Ma-Han), consisting of 54 *kuo* in the southwest of the peninsula; the **B'iän-γân* (弁韓: Korean = Pyŏn-Han), of 12 *kuo* on the south coast; and the **ǐiĕn-γân* (辰韓: Korean = Chin-Han), also of 12 *kuo*, in the southeast. See *Hou-Han Shu*, chüan 115, fols. 10v-12r.

16. The *Hou-Han Shu* also noted that **Ḭa-ma-dʻ$\hat{a}$i* was 12,000 *li* 里 from the Chinese commandery of **Lǎk-lâng* 樂浪 in north Korea and 7,000 *li* from **Kǝu-ḭa-γân* 狗邪韓 in southeast Korea. For what it is worth, a *li* in Han times was slightly in excess of a quarter of a mile, and, according to John C. Ferguson, a *chʻih* 尺 was equivalent to 0.231 meter; see his "Chinese foot measure," *Monumenta Serica* 6 (1941): 357-82. See also Wolfram Eberhard, "Bemerkungen zu statistischen Angaben der Han-Zeit," *Tʻoung Pao* 36 (1940): 1-25; Ishida Mikinosuke 石田幹之助, "Gishi Wajinden ni tsuite," *Nihon Rekishi*, 魏志倭人伝について 日本歴史 2, no. 3 (1947): 14-25. Needless to say, estimates of distances of this magnitude in early Chinese texts seldom afford more than a vague impression of the relative locations involved.

17. For the history of **Ḭa-ma-dʻ$\hat{a}$i* scholarship, in which there has often been no small degree of casuistry, see Young, *The Location of Yamatai*, passim, and note 35, below. The most thorough, though now badly dated, discussion of the substantive aspects of the problem in a European language is still Wedemeyer, *Japanische Frühgeschichte*, pt. 1, chap. 8.

18. Japanese Kunu. Cf. p. 25, below.

19. In Han historical writing **dʻ$\hat{a}$i-pḭu* signified broadly a person of noble rank. In his translations from the *Chʻien-Han Shu*, Homer H. Dubs usually rendered the term as "grandee" (*The History of the Former Han dynasty*, 3 vols. [Baltimore and London, 1938-55], passim). Cf. also *Chʻien-Han Shu*, chüan 19A, fols. 5r,v and 15r.

20. Arch. Jap. *Pimiko* and Mod. Jap. *Himiko* have become the usual readings of the characters in the name of this ruler, which are said to represent a word signifying "a high-born woman" or "princess" (*pime/pimë* [= a laudatory title for women] < *pi* = sun + *me* = woman). However, **pimiko* is anachronistic in the third century A.D., having been contrived in later times solely on the basis of the *Wei Chih* account. Moreover, Arch. Jap. *-ko* is elsewhere transcribed into Ancient Chinese with *-k-*, which would seem to imply that the Chinese spirant χ was being used to render a different sound. Some scholars consider that **pimiha* would be a more acceptable restoration. See Nagata Natsuki, "Gishi Wajinden yakuon no onka ni tsuite," *Kobe Gaidai Ronsō*, vol. 13, pt. 3 (1962); Roy Andrew Miller, *The Japanese language* (Chicago, 1967), pp. 22-23; Ledyard, "Horseriders," p. 222, n. 13.

The consonant *p*, corresponding to the *ha-gyō* of Modern Japanese, preserved its Archaic vocalization as [p] until early in the Heian period. In the present work, apart from a few instances such as this, where a proper appreciation of a Chinese transcription demands an accurate orthography, no attempt has been made to render the Archaic phonology. We have, for instance, usually written Yamato rather than the strictly accurate Yamatö; Amaterasu Ōmikami rather than Amaterasu Opo Mikami; Takama no hara rather than Takama nö para; and Izanami no Mikoto rather than Izanami nö Mikötö.

On shamanism generally see Mircea Eliade, *Le Chamanisme et les techniques archaïques de l'extase* (Paris, 1951); and, on North Asian (including Northeast Asian) manifestations in particular, see Hans Findeisen, *Schamanentum, dargestellt am Beispiel der Besessenheitspriester nordeurasiatischer Völker* (Stuttgart, 1957). Cf. also Ichirō Hori [*sic*], *Folk religion in Japan: Continuity and change* (Chicago, 1968), chap. 5: "Japanese shamanism."

21. The seat of this commandery, which was established toward the end of the Later Han period, was in the neighborhood of present-day Seoul.

22. See p. 22, above.

23. A group of *γân tribes (cf. n. 15, above) occupying the southeastern extremity of the Korean peninsula.

24. The text reads 其 北 岸, literally, "its north coast," that is, the coast to the north of that which had already been passed.

25. The characters for this name have been used to denote the island of Tsushima, situated almost exactly in the middle of Korea Strait, ever since the Japanese became familiar with the *Wei Chih*. Of this name Miller has written: "There is a good possibility that what today we write as the Middle [Ancient] Chinese form *tuậi* was in fact at the time of the compilation of the *Wei chih* one of a set of forms which in that period still ended in an early -*s*, soon lost, and that the *Wei chih* transcription was intended to represent something on the order of **tus-ma*, for Old Japanese *tusima*, modern Tsushima" (Miller, *The Japanese language*, p. 23).

26. The context within which this "large country" is mentioned would in any case imply that it was the island of Iki 壹岐, lying to the southeast of Tsushima in the Korea Strait; but the Meiji historian Naka Michiyo 那珂通世 suggested that the phrase should be amended to read as a transcription of the name Iki itself, namely, **Iĕt-k'jię* Country 一支國, a form that does in fact occur in the *Liang Shu* 梁書, chüan 54, fol. 25v: "Gaikō shaku-shi," in *Naka Michiyo isho* 外交繹史 那珂通世遺書 (Tōkyō, 1916), vol. 2, p. 304.

27. Identified by Naka Michiyo and others as Matsura in the district of that name in Chikuzen province in northern Kyūshū ("Gaikō shaku-shi," p. 306). Kishimoto Fumiaki 岸元史明 is almost alone in proposing a location farther to the west, in the neighborhood of Matsuoka (*Heian-kyō chishi* 平安京地誌 [Tōkyō, 1974], p. 14 and map on p. 17).

28. Identified by Naka Michiyo and others as Ito 伊都 in the district of the same name in Chikuzen province in northern Kyūshū ("Gaikō shaku-shi," p. 306). In the ancient Japanese chronicle *Nihon Shoki* (Iwanami ed., pp. 324-25; see note 116, this chapter) it is related that the ancestor of the Agatanushi of Ito presented Emperor Chūai with jewels, swords, and mirrors, signifying his recognition of the imperial authority. Chūai Tennō probably reigned during the first half of the fourth century.

29. Identified by Naka Michiyo as the ancient (district of) Na (Na no Agata

儺縣), mentioned in the *Nihon Shoki* under the reign of Chūai Tennō and assigned to the vicinity of Hakata in the district of Naka ("Gaikō," p. 308). But note that, in the *Hou-Han Shu*, *Nuo was located on the extreme southern fringe of the *·Jwię territories, whereas here it is situated well to the north of the Great *·Jwię heartland of *Ia-ma-·įėt/d'ậi. This contradiction between the two texts has not been resolved.

30. From this stage of the itinerary onward, scholarly opinion on the location of toponyms is divided, primarily between those who regard the list as relating to southern Honshū and those who consider it as passing through Kyūshū, but also secondarily among a wide range of views as to possible locations within the respective regions. The matter is discussed briefly below.

31. The *Ia-ma-·įėt of the *Wei Chih*, the seat of a female ruler, is clearly the *Ia-ma-d'ậi mentioned in the *Hou-Han Shu* as the place where the shamaness, *Pįėt-mjię-χuo, held court. Evidently in one of the texts one of the graphs 臺 and 壹 has been substituted for the other, but on the Chinese record alone it is not possible to decide which is the correct reading. The Commentary on the *Hou-Han Shu*, in which the form *Ia-muậ-t'uậi occurs, cannot, of course, be regarded as an independent source (see n. 14, above).

32. The list of dependent territories (*kuo*) is as follows:

*Się-ma 斯馬	*χuo-·įэp 呼邑
*I-pɒk-k'jię 已百支	*γwa-nuo-suo-nuo 華奴蘇奴
*·I-ia 伊邪	*Kjwęi 鬼
*Tuo-k'jię 都支	*Jwię-nguo 為吾
*Mjię-nuo 彌奴	*Kjwęi-nuo 鬼奴
*χậu-kuo-tuo 好古都	*Ia-ma 邪馬
*Pįэu-χuo 不呼	*Kįung-ʑięn 躬臣
*Tsʻuo[?]-nuo 姐奴	*Pa-lji 巴刺
*Tuậi-suo 對蘇	*Kʻjię-iwi 支惟
*Suo-nuo 蘇奴	*·Uo-nuo 烏奴
	*Nuo 奴

The identification of these toponyms has occasioned a great deal of speculation by Japanese scholars, but nothing approaching a consensus has been achieved. Again the primary division is between those who advocate a Honshū locale and those who prefer to locate the names in Kyūshū, but again there is no agreement as to the precise territories involved. See, for instance, the comments of Tsunoda and Goodrich, *Japan in the Chinese dynastic histories*, p. 18, n. 24; Maki Kenji 牧健二, *Nihon no genshi kokka* 日本の原始國家 (Tōkyō, 1968), passim. In any case, the reliability of a toponymic list such as this one, compiled mainly at second or third hand (though the observations of embassies to the *·Jwię in 240 and 247 were incorporated into the Wei account) and across a formidable language barrier, must be regarded as suspect until a great deal more is known about the channels of transmission of Chinese historical information during the third and fourth centuries A.D. The name *Jwię-nguo 為吾, for instance, looks suspiciously like a slightly modified rendering of the *·Jwię-nuo that we have earlier construed as the *Nuo [kuo] of *·Jwię (p. 23), and it is not impossible that *·I-ịa 伊邪 was a clerkly mislection of the *·I-tuo 伊都 described in an earlier passage. Speculations of this type are encouraged by the inclusion in the list of the *Nuo territory previously accorded separate treatment. Perhaps such skepticism is misplaced in the present instance, but prudence would seem to require that the list be subjected to particularly critical scrutiny before attempts are made to restore the original toponyms. Nevertheless, it must be admitted that *Się-ma and *Ịa-ma bear a seductively close resemblance to, respectively, Jap. shima = island and yama = mountain.

33. This is presumably the *Kiu-nuo 拘奴 which figured in the Hou-Han Shu (pp. 20-24, above) as a kuo situated a thousand li across the sea to the east of *Ịa-ma-d'ậi. Cf. note 52, below.

34. In both the Hou-Han Shu and the Wei Chih the schedule of distances was in fact carried far beyond *Kậu-nuo, presumably along the Ryūkyū chain and possibly into Southeast Asia sensu stricto, to whose remote forests were assigned such ethnic entities as the pigmies 侏儒, the Country of the Naked Men 裸國, and the Land of the Black-toothed People 黑齒國. Although these images may have had their bases in a vague knowledge of Negritoes, other primitive peoples, and betel-chewing (which stains teeth black), they figured in Chinese literature as quasi-mythological and cannot be made to yield useful locational data. Despite explicit statements in both the Hou-Han Shu and the Wei Chih that at least some of the groups were situated at a year's voyage to the southeast of *Ịa-ma-·ịĕt/d'ậi, most students of early Japan have located them in the Ryūkyū chain and neighboring islands.

35. The best summary of these discussions prior to 1945 in a European language is that by John Young in The Location of Yamatai (see note 3, this chapter). Since that time, numerous volumes and articles dealing with the topic have appeared. The following are a selection of books on this theme that have been published during the past decade (all with Tōkyō imprimaturs unless otherwise indicated): Harada Dairoku 原田大六, Yamataikoku ronsō 邪馬台國論爭 (1967); Miyazaki Kōhei 宮崎康平, Maboroshi no Yamataikoku まぼろしの邪馬台國 (1967); Niizuma Toshihisa 新妻利久, Yamato Yamataikoku やまと邪馬台國 (1967); Yasumoto Biten 安本美典, Yamataikoku e no michi 邪馬台國への道 (1967); Maki Kenji 牧健二, Nihon no genshi kokka 日本の原始国家 (1968); Yamaguchi Osamu 山口修, Futatsu no Yamataikoku ふたつの邪馬台国 (Kyōto, 1968); Yasumoto Biten 安本美典, Jimmu Tōsen: suribukengakuteki apurōchiio 神武東遷: 数理文獻學的アプローチ (1968); Mishina Akihide (Shōei), ed., 三品彰英, Yamataikoku kenkyū sōran 邪馬台国研究總覽 (1970); Okubo Izumi 久保泉, Yamataikoku no shozai to yakue 邪馬台国の所在とゆくえ (1970); Tomiku

177

Takashi 富來隆, *Himiko* 卑弥呼(1970); Furuta Takehiko 古田武彦, *"Yamatai-koku" wa nakatta* 邪馬台国はなかった(1971); Higo Kazuo 肥後和男, *Yamatai-koku wa Yamato de aru* 邪馬台国は大和である(1971); Hayashi Tomojirō 林屋友次郎, *Nihon kodai kokka ron* 日本古代国家論(1972); Saeki Arikiyo 佐伯有清, *Kenkyūshi: Yamataikoku* 研究史邪馬台国(1972); Saeki Arikiyo 佐伯有清, *Kenkyūshi: Sengo no Yamataikoku* 研究史戦後の邪馬台国(1972); Tōma Seita 藤間生大, *Yamataikoku no tankyū* 邪馬台国の探究(1972); Yamao Yukihisa 山尾幸久, *Gishi Wajinden* 魏志倭人伝(1972); Yasumoto Biten 安本美典, *Himiko no nazo* 卑弥呼の謎(1972); Furuta Takehiko 古田武彦, *Ushinawareta Kyūshū Ōchō: Tennōka izen no kodaishi* 失われた九州王朝 ─ 天皇家以前の古代史(1973); Takeshi Gan 立石巌, *Yamataikoku shinkō* 邪馬台国新考(1973); Gotō Takeshi 後藤毅, *Yamataikoku to Ki-Ki no denshō* 邪馬臺国と記紀の伝承(1974); Murayama Yoshio 村山義男, *Yamataikoku to kin-in* 邪馬台国と金印(1974); Tanaka Takashi 田中卓, *Nihon Kokka seiritsu no kenkyū* 日本国家成立の研究(1974); Yoshida Osamu 吉田修, *Yamataikoku no shūen to fukkatsu* 邪馬台国の終馬と復活(1974).

36. On this point see Hashimoto Masukichi, *Tōyōshijō yori mitaru Nihon jōkoshi kenkyū*, pp. 26-46 (see note 5, above).

37. See note 16, above, In any case we can be reasonably sure that all *Wei Chih* distances in *li* either originated with Chinese envoys or were Chinese conversions; for as late as Sui times it was asserted that the *·Jwiẹ "are not familiar with the *li* as a unit of measurement but estimate distances in terms of days' [travel]" 不知里数但計以日(*Sui Shu* 隋書, chüan 81, vol. 13r).

38. Cf. note 27.

39. For a detailed discussion of the possibilities of manipulating these directions and distances see Young, *The Location of Yamatai*, chap. 2.

40. What is in principle a somewhat similar style of argument relating to the schedule of toponyms has been formulated by Maki Kenji around the difference in meaning between 至 and 到 (*Nihon no genshi kokka*, pp. 48-53).

41. Okubo Izumi 久保泉, *Yamataikoku no shozai to yakue* 邪馬台国の所在とゆくえ(Tōkyō, 1970), p. 231. See also Harada Dairoku 原田大六, *Yamataikoku ronsō* 邪馬台国論争(Tōkyō, 1967), pp. 355-65, esp. figs. 84-89.

42. The significance of this change from 戸 to 家 in the unit of enumeration is not readily apparent.

43. A minor textual difference between the *Hou-Han Shu* and the *Wei Chih* is that, whereas the former refers to these people simply as *·Jwiẹ, the *Wei Chih* describes them under the rubric of the *·Jwiẹ people 倭人.·

44. The enhanced command over strategic resources enjoyed by the "important persons" (大人) of *·Jwiẹ included easier access to women. Whereas the 大人 were described as each having four or five wives, the lower orders (下戸) had to be content with two or three each.

45. Some scholars have seen in certain actions of the Sun Goddess as

related in early Japanese chronicles (see pp. 64-65) the lineaments of a shaman-istic performance. These same scholars have also sometimes postulated that the sun deity was originally a male god, served by shamanesses, who eventually came to assume the gender of his servants. See, e.g., Saigō Nobutsuna西 郷 信 綱, *Kojiki*古 事 記(Tōkyō, 1947), pp. 31-32.

Others before us have noted certain structural similarities between the role of Pimiko, as described by the Chinese annalists in the third century A.D., and the role of priestesses of the Noro cult in various parts of the Ryūkyū archipel-ago in later times. Under the old kingdom usually referred to in Western writ-ings as Loo Choo (Liu Ch'iu琉 球), the Noro constituted a veritable female the-ocracy, whose influence at court at the beginning of the sixteenth century was ensured by the fact that the leading priestess ranked above the official queen. Succession at that time was reserved to females of a specified agnatic lineage (cf. p. 36 on the succession from Pimiko to Iyö [Töyö]). As late as 1952, on Amami Ōshima, there still existed a male functionary known as the *tejiri* who was not of the Noro lineage but who represented the village in dealing with the priestess. As described by Douglas G. Haring, this functionary raised money from the villagers to support the Noro cult, superintended collective labor on its behalf, and generally acted as a business agent; see Haring, "The Noro cult of Amami Ōshima: Divine priestesses of the Ryūkyū Islands," *Sociologus* 3, no. 1 (1953): 108-21. Cf. also R. S. Spencer, "The Noro, or priestesses of Loo Choo," *Transactions of the Asiatic Society of Japan* 2d ser. 8 (1931): 94-112; Clarence J. Glacken, *The Great Loochoo: A study of Okinawan village life* (Berkeley and Los Angeles, 1955), pp. 286-90.

46. Contrast the phrasing of the *Hou-Han Shu*, p. 23 , above.

47. Described on p. 23 , above.

48. This is a difficult phrase to interpret and has been ignored by the majority of commentators on the *Wei Chih*. Wedemeyer (*Japanische Frühgeschichte*, p. 181, n. 434), apparently attaching significance to the phonetic rather than the radical of the character 邸, translated the substantive[s] as "Grund-Kammern oder Grundstücks-Kammern" and added, "Hier müssen den mitteljapanischen Miyake . . . entsprechende Einrichtungen gemeint sein." Tsunoda and Goodrich rendered the whole phrase as "There are granaries" (*Japan in the Chinese dynastic histo-ries*, p. 12). Presumably they, like Wedemeyer, were influenced by certain ref-erences to such storage facilities (*miyake*屯 倉), sometimes in connection with army provisions, in the *Nihon Shoki*; see, e.g., William George Aston's transla-tion of the *Nihon Shoki* (first published in 1896, reprinted in 1924 and 1972), vol. 1, pp. 178, 214, 282, and vol. 2, pp. 8, 13, 17, 27, 28, 32, 60, 78, 79, 136 (see note 116, below, for Aston publication data). The dictionaries define *ti* 邸 as, originally, the lodgings provided for Chou princes when they rendered homage at the capital and, subsequently, by synecdoche, as the capital itself. Here it has been interpreted as projecting the former meaning to denote a struc-

ture designed to accommodate conclaves of subordinate chiefs summoned to *Ia-ma-
·$i\overset{\smile}{e}t$/$d^{\prime}\hat{q}i$ by the paramount ruler, but it could possibly also have been read in an
adjectival sense as denoting the council chambers proper to the chief settlement
of the chiefdom. Moreover, we think that Wedemeyer may have been on the right
track when he wrote of a "Grundstücks-Kammern." By choosing the particular graph
that they did, the compilers of the *Wei Chih* may well have been attempting to
convey the idea of the roofed pit known in older Japanese literature as *muro*
(室 or 窖). In the *Kojiki* and the *Nihon Shoki* the term is used both for the
pit dwellings of the Ezo and for a much larger semisubterranean hall capable of
holding at least 160 persons that was constructed for one of Jimmu Tennō's more
nefarious schemes (*Kojiki*, book 2, chap. 51, 9-15; Chamberlain's translation, pp.
141-42; Philippi's translation, pp. 171-72; *Nihon Shoki*, vol. 1, pp. 202-3;
Aston's translation, vol. 1, pp. 123-24). (For extended comments on the nature
of the *Kojiki* see note 112, below.) Moreover, just such a pit, discovered on the
Early Yayoi archeological site at Karako, was interpreted by its excavators as a
meeting hall. This, I suspect, is the sort of structure that the Chinese authors
were attempting to represent. *Ko* 閤 denoted specifically a small side door but
here was certainly used for *ko* 閤 (= council chamber or government office), with
which it was interchangeable.

For alternative interpretations of 郎 閤 see Nishikawa Kōji 西川幸治,
Toshi no shisō 都市の思想(Tōkyō, 1973), p. 58, who draws liberally on the
work of Ō Koku'i 王国維, "Teikakukō"郎閤考Kanda Kiichirō 神田喜一郎 *Nihon
Shoki kokun kōshō*日本書紀古訓攷証, a volume which we have not been able to
consult; Yamao Hisao 山尾幸久, "Seiji kenryoku no hassei"政治権力の発生,
in *Iwanami Kōza Nihon Rekishi, 1: Genshi oyobi kodai*岩波講座日本歴史原始お
よび古代(Tōkyō, 1975).

49. Great *·*$Jwi\rlap{\raise1.5ex\hbox{}}{e}$ = *Ia-ma-$i\overset{\smile}{e}t$/$d^{\prime}\hat{q}i$; cf. p. 22 , above. Incidentally, this
is the only occasion on which Great *·*$Jwi\rlap{e}{}$ is mentioned in the *Wei Chih*, and the
reference would be unclear to a reader unfamiliar with the account in the *Hou-
Han Shu*.

50. In the section on the "Eastern Barbarians" in the *Wei Chih* it is
reported that the *$\gamma\hat{a}n$ (Han 韓), the *$\chi u\hat{a}t$ (Yeh 濊), and the *·*$Jwi\rlap{e}{}$ used iron
from Pyŏn-chin as a medium of exchange in their markets "in the same way as money
was used in China"用鐵|如中國|用錢(chüan 30, fols. 23r,v). However, it is
debatable whether the *·*$Jwi\rlap{e}{}$ (Wa) referred to here were located in the Japanese
islands or were members of other groups dwelling in south Korea (cf. chap. 3,
p. 81).

51. This is Edward H. Schafer's felicitous rendering of the term in his
The Vermilion bird: T'ang images of the south (Berkeley and Los Angeles, 1967),
p. 7.

52. The orthographies of this name used in the *Wei Chih* and the *Hou-Han Shu*
differ slightly, but the graphic forms of the characters are so similar (狗 and

拘 , respectively) that one cannot but be a scribal error for the other. In
spite of the graphic error, the Ancient vocalizations of the two characters were
close, and, given the fact that in both texts this *kuo* is the only one specified
as not subject to the authority of *Pi̯et-mji̯ę-χuo, there can be little doubt that
we are dealing with one territory rather than two. Almost invariably on the testimony of the *Wei Chih* rather than the *Hou-Han Shu*, *Kǝu-nuo* has been equated
with a variety of localities, ranging from eastern Honshū to southern Kyūshū.
For a conspectus of historical interpretations of this name see Young, *The Location of Yamatai*, passim, but esp. pp. 99-100 and 107-9.

53.   Traces of such a sexual opposition are apparently still discernible in
the Sakhalin Ainu distinction between mountains (the abode of male deities) and
shore zone (the preserve of female deities) (see Emiko Ohnuki-Tierney, "Spatial
concepts of the Ainu of the northwest coast of southern Sakhalin," *American
Anthropologist* 74, no. 3 [1972]: 426-57), but they are more fully recorded for
Indochina, where they are sometimes taken to preserve archetyped remembrances of
a transformation from matriarchy to patriarchy; see Louis Malleret, "Traditions
légendaires des Cambodgiens de Cochinchine relevant d'une interprétation ethno-
sociologique," *Institut Indochinois pour l'Etude de l'Homme, Bulletins et Travaux*
4, fasc. 1 and 2 (1942): 169-80; Eveline Porée-Maspero, *Etude sur les rites
agraires des Cambodgiens* (Paris, 1962), vol. 1, pp. 137-42; François Martini, "De
la signification de 'Ba' et 'Me' affixés aux noms de monuments khmèrs," *Bulletin
de l'Ecole Française d'Extrême-Orient* 44 (1947-50): 201-9.   The mythical opposition of a Men's Hill (*Wozaka* 男 坡) and a Women's Hill (*Mezaka* 女 坡), each the
post of an army of appropriate gender, as mentioned in the *Nihon Shoki* (vol. 1,
pp. 198-99; Aston trans., vol. 1, p. 119) is especially close to certain of the
myths collected by Porée-Maspero (ref. above).   Paired male and female shrines
exist in Japan even today, as exemplified, for instance, by the "male" Asuka
Niimasu shrine and its "female" counterpart, some five kilometers away.

54.   Rendered in Japanese as, respectively, *ikima, mimasho, mimagushi*, and
nakato.   By some scholars these terms have been traced to the names of persons or
gods supposedly associated with the early Yamato court (see, for example, Naitō
Torajirō 内藤虎次郎, *Dokushi sōroku* 讀史叢録 [Tōkyō, 1929], pp. 38-42), but
others have sought to refute the argument (e.g., Hashimoto, *Nihon Jōkoshi Kenkyū*,
p. 138).   The frequent identification of *nuo-kai-tiei* with the clan name Naka-
tōmi (allegedly from *naka torimoti* = [those who] have charge of the middle, or
naka tu omi = chieftain of the middle) has not been adequately substantiated.

55.   *Mji̯ę-mji̯ę* suggests itself as a transcription of Jap. *mimi*, a title in
use at latest from the end of the sixth century, when Prince Shōtoku (574-622) as
a youth was styled Tōyö to Mimi nö Mikötö.   Cf. Roy Andrew Miller, *The Japanese
language* (Chicago, 1967), p. 21.   None of the identifications proposed thus far
for *mji̯ę-mji̯ę-nâ-lji* is satisfactory.

56.   *Ta-muo* is usually considered to be a transcription of Japanese *tömö*, a

corporation of persons all with the same hereditary occupation or office.
According to Naka ("Gaikō shaku-shi," p. 303), *pjię-nuo-mៗu-ljię = pinamöri <
pina = "outlying area," "rural" + möri-, deverbal from mör-u = "guard," "defend."
Cf. also Miller, The Japanese language, pp. 20-21.

57. Japanese shimako, according to Yamada Yoshio 山田孝雄, a name 島子
("Kunu Koku Kō 狗奴國考, pt. 4, "Kōkogaku Zasshi 考古學雜誌 12, no. 12
[1922]: 50).

58. Japanese niki, semmoku, and hekkuho. Niki (1) < inaki 稲置 = an imperial granary in a province and, hence, its custodian, or (2) < nushi 主 = chief or
lord; see Hashimoto, Nihon, p. 135; Yamada, "Kunu . . . ," vol. 12, no. 11, p.
50. The other two terms are thought to have derived from personal names.

59. Anc. Japanese *piko, an honorary affix to names of males in ancient
times; Mod. Jap. = hiko. Cf. pp. 93-94, below.

60. For Max Weber's original conceptualization of patrimonial domain see
his Wirtschaft und Gesellschaft (Tübingen, 1924), vol. 2, pp. 679-752, which are
chaps. 12 and 13 of vol. 3 of the English translation edited by Guenther Roth and
Claus Wittich, Economy and society: An outline of interpretive sociology (New
York, 1968). There is an admirable expository discussion of Weber's political
sociology, including the notion of patrimonialism, in Reinhard Bendix, Max Weber:
An Intellectual portrait (New York, 1962), pt. 3.

61. Jap. Nashonmi.

62. Among the gifts that were sealed in boxes and dispatched to *Pĭět-mjię-
χuo in the care of Nashonmi were valuable textiles, gold, jade, red beads, and —
what will prove of significance in subsequent sections of this work — two swords
刀 , each 5 ch'ih (between 3 and 4 feet) in length, and 100 bronze mirrors (銅
鏡).

63. Jap. Isegi Yazaku. Naitō Torajirō has suggested a connection with
Isaga, the name of a clan in Izumo that worshiped a deity known as Isaga no
Mikoto, the son of its ancestral god; see Dokushi sōroku, pp. 45-46.

64. See Jack Goody, ed., Succession to high office, Cambridge Papers in
Social Anthropology 4 (Cambridge, Eng., 1966), Introduction.

65. Jap. Iyö; but most Japanese scholars have considered this form to be a
mislection for *D'ậi-ịwo 臺與 , Jap. Töyö, allegedly derived from Töyö no Kuni,
a toponym in Kyūshū. Cf., inter alia, Iijima Tadao 飯島忠夫, Nihon jōkoshi
ron 日本上古史論 (Tōkyō, 1947), p. 82.

66. William Gowland, "The Dolmens and burial mounds in Japan," Archaeologia
55 (1897): 439-524; Henry [Heinrich Philipp] von Siebold, Notes on Japanese
archaeology with especial reference to the Stone Age (Yokohama, 1879); Edward S.
Morse, "Shell mounds of Ōmori," Memoirs of the Science Department, University of
Tōkyō (Tōkyō, 1879); Ernest Mason (later Sir Ernest) Satow, Ancient sepulchral
mounds in Kauzuke with 14 illustrations (1880); Romyn Hitchcock, The Ancient
burial mounds of Japan, Report of the Smithsonian Institution (Washington, 1891).

67. There is a succinct account of the achievements and limitations of Meiji archeology in Young, *The Location of Yamatai*, chap. 6.

68. See, for example, Tomioka Kenzō 富岡謙藏, "Futatabi Nihon shutsudo no Shina kokyō ni tsuite," *Kokyō no Kenkyū* 再び日本出土の支那古鏡に就いて古鏡の研究 (Kyōtō, 1920), p. 338; Umehara Sueji 梅原末治, "Genka no Nihon kōkogaku," *Jinbun* 人文 1, no. 2 (1947): 47. Ishida Eiichirō 石田英一郎 has pointed out that it was not so much the actual archeological excavation, or indeed the factual reporting of it, that was suppressed under the Meiji but rather the drawing of inferences from the data if they could be construed as impugning the sanctity of the imperial family. This was most likely to happen when an author attempted to reconcile archeological with literary evidence, as in the case of Professor Tsuda Sōkichi 津田左右吉, who, together with his publisher, Iwanami Shigeo, was brought to trial in 1940 on the charge of having violated "the spirit of clarification of the national polity" (*Nihon bunka ron* 日本文化論 [Tōkyō, 1968]; English translation by Teruko Kachi under the title *Japanese culture: A Study of origins and characteristics* [Tōkyō and Honolulu, 1974], p. 27). A similar situation had arisen earlier, in 1892, when Kume Kunitake had been dismissed from the Tōkyō Imperial University because antigovernment interests had expressed approval of a paper he had written allegedly denigrating Shintō ("Shintō wa saiten no kosoku," *Shigakkai Zasshi* 3, nos. 33-35 [1892]: 1-15; 25-40; 12-24). Again in the same university, in 1911, Kida Teikichi was dismissed because, in a textbook written for schoolteachers, he had perversely accorded equal treatment to the Northern and the Southern courts that competed for control of Japan in the fourteenth century (Miura Kaneyuki, *Nihonshi no Kenkyū* 日本史の研究 [Tōykō, 1930], pp. 406-9).

69. Nihon Kōkogaku Kyōkaihen 日本考古学協会編, *Toro* 登呂 (Tōkyō, 1954).

70. A generalized ecosystem is one in which there exists a great variety of species, so that the energy produced by the system is distributed among a large number of different species, each of which is necessarily represented by only a small number of individuals. A specialized ecosystem is one in which a relatively small number of species is represented by a large number of individuals.

71. The horticultural component in the *·*Jwię* farming system was emphasized in both the *Hou-Han Shu*, chüan 115, fol. 12v, and the *Wei Chih*, chüan 30, fol. 25v, where it was recorded that vegetables 菜 were grown throughout the year. In both accounts dry-field grains (禾) were mentioned side by side with padi (稻). That hunting continued to play a subordinate, though by no means insignificant, role in the Yayoi economy is attested both by the stone, bone, bronze, and very occasionally iron arrowheads that have come to light on archeological sites and by the hunting scenes scratched on pottery or depicted in relief on bronze bells. One of twelve panels on a bell traditionally associated with Kagawa Island, for example, shows a hunter and five trained dogs closing in on a wild boar, while another panel depicts an archer stalking a deer. A second

source of dietary protein was fishing. Stone and clay net-sinkers have come to
light in numerous excavations, bone fishhooks and remains of both fresh-water and
marine species figured prominently at the Urigo shell mound in Toyohashi city,
and sections of scoop nets were recovered at Chitane on Sado Island.

72. The houses excavated at Toro in Shizuoka were moated dwellings, roughly
oval in plan, and mostly facing south toward their fields. A house of this type,
reconstructed on the site, has been described by J. E. Kidder, Jr., as follows:

> A reconstructed dwelling, though not built over an ancient pit, has
> four massive uprights across which lie heavy beams, and to these are
> leaned dozens of slender poles; thatch is thickly overlaid to form the
> walls. Overhead is the additional roof member, still familiar today,
> that acts as both a ventilator and sun protector. The doorway has its
> own small cover. [*Japan before Buddhism*, rev. ed. (New York, 1966), p.
> 97 and pl. 34.]

Yayoi dwellings that have been excavated have usually covered an area of the
order of 24 ft. x 21 ft.

73. Murakawa Yukio 村川行弘, *Ege no Yama* 会下山, cited in Wajima
Seiichi 和島誠一, ed., *Nihon no kōkogaku*, vol. 3: *Yayoi jidai* 日本の考古
學：弥生時代 (Tōkyō, 1966).

74. The proponents of this point of view are presumably envisaging the sort
of transformation reported by Ralph Linton and Abram Kardiner when the Tanala of
Madagascar, who were already growing dry padi in a swidden system, adopted techniques of wet-padi cultivation from their Betsileo neighbors. Linton was able to
document the following sequence of changes in the structure of Tanala society:
the gradual emergence of a group of landowners; the disruption of the joint family, endogamy, and self-sufficiency; the establishment of permanent settlements;
modifications in the patterns of warfare; the attachment of an economic value to
slaves and a formulation of ransom procedures; and the institutionalization of
kingship. See Linton's work, "The Change from dry to wet rice cultivation in
Tanala-Betsileo," in Abram Kardiner, ed., *The Individual and his society* (New
York, 1939); reprinted in T. M. Newcomb and E. L. Hartley, eds., *Readings in
social psychology* (New York, 1952), pp. 222-31.

75. Yanagita Kunio 柳田國男 propounds this point of view with great vigor
in his *Kaijō no michi* 海上の道, which comprises part of volume 1 of his works,
collected under the title *Teihon Yanagita Kunio shū* 定本柳田國男集 (Tōkyō,
1968). The problem of the origins of Japanese culture has also been discussed
from a variety of different points of view by, among others, Ishida Eiichiro,
Japanese culture: A Study of origins and characteristics (Honolulu, 1974), chap.
3; Ōno Susumu 大野晋, *Nihongo no kigen* 日本語の起源 (Tōkyō, 1960); Matsumoto
Nobuhiro 松本信廣, *Nihon shinwa no kenkyū* 日本神話の研究 (Kamakura, 1944),
and *Nihon no shinwa* 日本の神話 (Tōkyō, 1959); Hattori Shirō 服部四郎,
Nihongo no keitō 日本語の系統 (Tōkyō, 1959), and "The Relationship of Japanese
to the Ryukyu, Korean, and Altaic languages," *Transactions of the Asiatic Society*

of Japan 3d ser. 5 (1948): 101-33. The aspects of the problem relating specifically to padi farming are discussed by Kenjiro Ichikawa [*sic*: Jap. order Ichikawa
Kenjirō], "The Genealogy of the paddy-field culture in ancient Japan," *Proceedings of the International Association of Historians of Asia: Second Biennial Conference, October 1962* (Tʻaipei, 1962), pp. 259-67. This author distinguishes
between broadcast sowing of padi in seasonal swamps, a practice which he thinks
reached northern Kyūshū from southeast China by way of south Korea, and irrigated
cultivation with bunded fields and feeder canals, a technique which he derives
from north China by way of north Korea. Cf. also Yawata Ichiro, "Prehistoric
evidence for Japanese cultural origins," in Robert J. Smith and Richard K.
Beardsley, *Japanese culture: Its development and characteristics* (Chicago, 1962),
pp. 7-10. Cf. also Hamada Hideo浜田秀男, "Nihon ine no keitō"日本稲の系
統 in Kanaseki Takeo金関丈夫et al., eds., *Nihon minzoku to Nampōbunka*日本民
族と南方文化(Tōkyō, 1968), pp. 325-74; Andō Hirotarō安藤廣太郎, *Nihon
kodai inasaku-shi zakkō*日本古代稲作史雜考(Tōkyō, 1951), and *Nihon kodai
inasaku-shi kenkyū*日本古代稲作史研究(Tōkyō, 1959).

    76. Egami Namio江上波夫, *The Beginnings of Japanese art* (New York and
Tokyo, 1973), pp. 32-33. This book is a translation of *Nihon bijutsu no tanjō*
日本美術の誕(Tōkyō, 1969).

    77. Watanabe Yoshimichi渡部義通has cited the legend in which Izanami no
Mikoto and Izanagi no Mikoto competed to induce births and deaths and which, in
the *Kojiki*, ends with the statement "This is why a thousand people inevitably die
every day while fifteen hundred are born" — an etiological recognition of an
increase in population numbers accompanying the diffusion of wet-padi farming
during the second and third centuries A.D. (*Kojiki kōwa*古事記講話[Tōkyō, 1936],
p. 52).

    78. There is a note in the *Nihon Shoki* (vol. 1, pp. 378-79) to the effect
that Korean textile workers were brought to Japan in the thirty-seventh year of
Ōjin Tennō, whose adjusted dates fall within the second half of the fourth century (the text actually specifies Wu 呉 China as the provenance of these immigrants, but the context implies that they were Korean, or possibly Chinese
already living in that country).

    79. In connection with the remarks in this section, it is interesting to
note that the *Nihon Shoki* reports that, during the reign of Suinin Tennō, whose
adjusted dates (see note 114 to this chapter) would place him in the second half
of the third century, a Korean envoy to the Yamato court presented, among other
items, a sword, a spear, and a mirror (*Nihon Shoki*, vol. 1, pp. 260-61; Aston
trans., vol. 1, p. 169). According to this same source, in the second half of
the fourth century the ancestor of the Agata-nushi of Ito presented *yasaka*
(almost certainly *magatama*) jewels, mirrors, and swords to Chūai Tennō, saying:

> As to these things which thy servant dares to offer, mayst thou govern
> the universe with subtlety tortuous as the curvings of the *yasaka*

jewels; may thy glance survey mountain, stream and sea-plain bright as
the mirror of white copper; mayst thou, wielding this ten-span sword,
maintain peace in the Empire. [Aston trans., vol. 1, p. 221.]

80. *Kojiki*, book 1, chap. 3, line 3: 渟 in the phrase "*jeweled* spear" is
usually considered to be a phonetic rendering of *nu* 瓊 (an ancient word for jew-
el), which is in fact used as an epithet in precisely this context in the *Nihon
Shoki*, vol. 1, pp. 80-81; Aston trans., vol. 1, pp. 10-12.

81. *Nihon Shoki*, vol. 1, pp. 318-19; Aston trans., vol. 1, pp. 215-16.

82. Cited in Kidder, *Japan before Buddhism*, p. 116.

83. Egami has suggested that the depiction of specific subjects within regularly arranged panels on some bells may have connoted some form of agricultural
calendar, so that

> the turtles and snakes could symbolize early spring, when those crea-
> tures come to life after their hibernation; the spade dance could rep-
> resent some celebration prior to embarking on the cultivation of the
> paddy fields; the mortars could suggest the autumn harvest and rites
> celebrating the new rice; the dragonflies and water birds could repre-
> sent, respectively, early autumn and late autumn, when birds of passage
> arrive in Japan; and the hunting scenes could symbolize winter. [*The
> Beginnings of Japanese art*, pp. 136-37.]

All of which would seem to imply that the *dōtaku* were used in seasonal rituals
and observances.

84. Jean Buhot, *Histoire des arts du Japon* (Paris, 1949), vol. 1, pp. 33-
34. This interpretation of the function of the bells is approved by Kidder,
Japan before Buddhism, p. 121. W. G. Aston (*Nihongi*, vol. 1, pp. 11-12, n. 1
[see note 116, below]) observed phalli spaced along the road from Utsonomiya to
Nikko in 1871, and other nineteenth-century references to phallic cults and symbols in Japan are not rare. After 1868, however, the Meiji government did its
best to suppress such cults and, it might be argued, perhaps removed most of
those that, on Buhot's hypothesis, might once have been associated with *dōtaku*.
See also D. Richie and K. Ito, *The Erotic gods: Phallicism in Japan* (Tōkyō,
1967).

85. For an informative exposition of the typologies of bronze mirrors in
early Japan and of their symbolic significance see Umehara Sueji, "Ancient mirrors and their relationship to early Japanese culture," *Acta Asiatica: Bulletin
of the Institute of Eastern Culture*, no. 4 (1963), pp. 70-79 (translated by Money
L. Hickman).

86. A splendid example of a mirror bearing this style of geometric relief
was recovered during excavations at the Oagata site in Kashiwara machi, Naka-
kawachi county, Ōsaka. It is now in the Tōkyō National Museum.

87. The circumstances of the alleged discovery of the seal are described by
Nakayama Heijiro 中山乎次郎, "Kan no Wa no Na no Kokuō in no shussho wa Na no
Kokuō no funbo ni arazarubeshi," *Kōkogaku Zasshi* 漢委奴國王印の出所は奴國王
の墳墓に非らざるべし,考古學雜誌 5, no. 2 (1914): 1-19, and "Kan no Wa no

Na no Kokuō in no shutsudo jōtai yori mitaru Kan Gi jidai no Wa no kuni no dōsei
ni tsuite," *Kōkogaku Zasshi*漢委奴國王印出土狀態より見たる漢魏時代の倭
國の動靜に就て　考古學雜誌5, no. 2 (1914): 19-42. Cf. the bibliography of
the Shigashima seal in Iwai Hirosato岩井大慧, *Shina shisho ni arawaretaru
Nihon*支那史書に現はれたる日本vol. 17, Nihon Rekishi, Iwanami Kōza series
(Tōkyō, 1935), pp. 74-78.

88. Saku Tatsuo 佐久達雄, *Nihon kodai shakaishi*日本古代社会史(Tōkyō,
1933), p. 116; Murayama Yoshio林山義男, *Yamataikoku to kin-in*邪馬台国と金印
(Tōkyō, 1974), passim.

89. Kidder, *Japan before Buddhism*, p. 107. There is a succinct summary of
the problems involved in the interpretation of archeological evidence relating to
Yayoi burial practices in Erika Kaneko, "Japan: A review of Yayoi burial practices," *Asian Perspectives* 9 (1966): 1-26.

90. This is not to discount the overlap between the two types of burial
that occurs on a very high proportion of sites. However, at Tennōzan, in southeast Yamaguchi prefecture, jar burials were discovered above cist graves. The
customary lack of funerary furniture in cist graves speaks to the same point.

91. Egami, *Nihon bijutsu no tanjō*, p. 60; *The Beginnings of Japanese art*,
p. 37. Egami first propounded his interpretation of the Tumulus culture in 1948
at a symposium on the formation of the Japanese state. A report of the symposium
was carried by *Minzokugaku Kenkyū*民族学研究 vol. 13, no. 3 (1949) under the
title "Nihon minzoku: bunka no genryū to Nihon kokka no keisei"日本民族文化の源
流と日本国家の形成 and subsequently published in book form under the title
*Nihon minzoku no kigen*日本民族の起源(Tōkyō, 1958). See also Egami, *Kiba minzoku kokka: Nihon kodaishi e no apurōchi*騎馬民族国家日本古代史へのアプロ
ーチ(Tōkyō, 1950; 24th printing, 1973). In 1964 Egami developed his theory in
greater detail and replied to certain criticisms of his earlier version; see the
symposium report entitled *Nihon kokka no kigen*日本國家の起源(Tōkyō, 1966),
and Egami's monograph *Nihon ni okeru minzoku no keisei to kokka no kigen*日本にお
ける民族の形成と国家の起源(Tōkyō, 1967). See also chap. 3, note 2, of
the present work.

92. The trichotomous view of the Tumulus period is based on a postulated
evolutional sequence in which the fifth century is regarded as the apogee of
tomb-building activity and the periods before and after as, respectively, eras of
development and decline. The two-phase view is essentially committed to a break
in cultural continuity between the Early and Late periods (see pp. 79-80, below).

93. A comma- or claw-shaped form probably deriving from the use of claw
necklaces in earlier times.

94. The hoe-shaped jasper bracelets are imitations of a type that resulted
originally from cutting vertically through the shell of a conch known as *tenguni-
shi* (天狗螺).

95. It must be admitted that many of the attributions foisted on to tumuli

by officials of the Imperial Household Agency are less than scientifically attested. The complex near Sakai, for instance, has been ascribed to Nintoku (and as such has become a datum for tumulus chronology) solely on the ground that it is the largest surviving *kofun* and ancient texts assert that Nintoku received the most elaborate burial of any of the early rulers; see Mori Kōichi 森浩一, *Kofun bunka shōkō* 古墳文化小考 (Tōkyō, 1974), p. 115.

96. A classic example of a *zempō-kōen* tomb from the Early Tumulus is that of Chausuyama at Sakurai in Nara prefecture. The overall length is 207 meters, the diameter of the circular mound 110 meters, and the width of the front end of the projection 61 meters. In this instance the projection is almost rectangular and is not nearly so high as the circular head. The whole structure was originally enclosed by a moat.

97. Kidder, *Japan before Buddhism*, p. 150; Mizuo Hiroshi, "Patterns of kofun culture," *Japan Quarterly* 16, no. 1 (1969): 71–77.

98. Suenaga Masao 末永雅雄, *Nihon no kofun* 日本の古墳, English title *Old tombs from the air* (Tōkyō, 1955), pp. 3 and 13. Buhot (*Histoire des arts du Japon*, vol. 1, p. 270) has suggested that the form owed something to the Chinese symbolism of the gourd. Egami (*The Beginnings of Japanese art*, p. 143) suspects that it represents an indigenous adaptation of the Chinese opposition of *yin* 陰 and *yang* 陽. Saitō Tadashi 齋藤忠 has calculated that no less than 1,087 large *zempō-kōen* type tombs were raised by chiefs in imitation of those built by the paramount rulers; see *Nihon zenshi*, vol. 1: *genshi* 日本全史：原始 (Tōkyō, 1958).

99. Cited in John Whitney Hall, *Government and local power in Japan 500–1700: A study based on Bizen province* (Princeton, N.J., 1966), p. 32. For estimates of the labor required to build comparable monuments in various other parts of the world see Wheatley, *The Pivot of the four quarters: A preliminary enquiry into the origins and character of the ancient Chinese city* (Edinburgh and Chicago, 1971), p. 258. In the middle of the seventh century, nearly three centuries after the period with which we are here concerned, Kōtoku Tennō, noting that "the poverty of our people is absolute owing to the construction of tombs" (*Nihon Shoki*, vol. 2, pp. 292–93; Aston trans., vol. 2, p. 218), restricted the size of tumuli, for persons of the rank of princes and above, to what could be raised by 1,000 laborers in seven days, namely, a structure 9 fathoms square and 5 fathoms high. Tumuli of progressively smaller size were prescribed for lower-ranking officials.

100. There are discussions of some of the issues involved in extrapolating from monumentality to sociopolitical organization in David Kaplan, "Men, monuments, and political systems," *Southwestern Journal of Anthropology* 19, no. 1 (1963): 397–410, and Charles J. Erasmus, "Monument building: Some field experiments," ibid. 21, no. 4 (1965): 277–301. Cf. also Angel Palerm, "The Agricultural basis of urban civilization in Mesoamerica," in *Irrigation civilizations:*

A comparative study. A symposium on method and result in cross-cultural regularities, Social Science Monographs no. 1, Social Science Section, Department of Cultural Affairs of the Pan American Union (Washington, D.C., 1955), pp. 28-42.

101. Ikebe Mahari池邊真榛, *Kogoshūi shinchū*古語拾遺新註(Tōkyō, 1943); English translation, by Genchi Katō and Hikoshirō Hoshino [*sic*], *Kogoshūi: Gleanings from ancient stories* (Tōkyō, 1925).

102. Masamune Atsuo正宗敦夫, ed., *Engi Shiki* 延喜式 (Tōkyō, 1929); "Engi Shiki" 延喜式 in Kuroita Katsumi黒板勝美, ed., *Shintei zōho kokushi taikei*新訂増補國史大系(Tōkyō, 1932), vol. 2; Miyagi Eishō宮城榮昌, *Engi Shiki no kenkyū*延喜式の研究, 2 vols. (Tōkyō, 1955-57); Kaneko Takeo金子武雄, *Engi shiki norito-kō*延喜式祝詞講(Tōkyō, 1951). See also Donald L. Philippi, *Norito: A new translation of the ancient Japanese ritual prayers* (Tōkyō, 1959) (N.B.: the 26 *norito*, or sacred rituals, make up bk. 8 of the *Engi Shiki*). Felicia Gressit Bock has translated the first four books of the *Engi Shiki* into English under the title *Engi-shiki: Procedures of the Engi Era* (Tōkyō, 1970).

103. Takeda Yūkichi武田祐吉, *Man'yōshū zenchūshaku*萬葉集全註譯14 vols. (Tōkyō, 1956-57); text and annotated English translation, with lexical and grammatical notes, by J. L. Pierson, Jr., *The Manyôsû*, 22 vols. (Leiden, 1929-63).

104. It is evident that records of some sort had been transmitted orally by different lineages long before they were written down, and it was these that were incorporated in the first reported literary achievement of the Japanese. This was the *Kujiki*舊事記(*Record of Old Matters*), supposedly compiled in A.D. 620 under the auspices of Prince Shōtoku. In the *Nihon Shoki* (which is discussed later in the present work), under the twenty-eighth year of Suiko Tennō, it is written:

> In this year the Crown Prince (*Kōtaishi*皇太子, i.e., Shōtoku Taishi 聖德太子) and the Great Imperial Chieftain (*Shima no Ō-omi*山鳥大臣, i.e., Soga Umako蘇我馬子) together collated the records of the Sovereigns (*Tennō*天皇), the country, the Imperial Chieftains (*Omi*臣), the Divine Chieftains (*Muraji*連), the Court Chieftains (*Tomo no miya-tsuko*伴造), the Local Chieftains (*Kuni no miyatsuko*國造), the various hereditary corporations (*be*部), and the common people.
> [*Nihon Shoki*, vol. 2, p. 203; Aston trans., vol. 2, p. 148.]

Most of the record compiled in this way was destroyed by fire in 645, and the remnant that allegedly survived, which came to be known as the *Kokuki* (國記: *National Annals*), has long since been lost. The extant work that bears the title *Kujiki* (which is also called the *Kuji Hongi*舊事本記and the *Sendai Kuji Hongi* 先代舊事本記), and which pretends to preserve the *Kokuki*, is a later forgery, probably from the ninth century. Except for a few mythological passages and a list of local governors, it contains nothing not also included in the *Kojiki* or the *Nihon Shoki*.

105. A recent rendering of this passage in a less exalted idiom is incorporated in Donald L. Philippi's translation of the *Kojiki* (Tōkyō, 1968), p. 41.

106. Motoori Norinaga (1730-1801), the greatest of all traditional *Kojiki* scholars, believed that Yasumaro wrote to the dictation of a court retainer (*toneri*舎人) who, on the command of Emperor Temmu, had committed the relevant historical narrative and genealogies to memory. In more recent times this interpretation has been disputed, chiefly on the grounds of internal evidence of compilation from a plurality of written documents and the prevalence of written records at the Yamato court in the seventh century. For an evaluation of the exegetical labors of Motoori see Matsumoto Shigeru, *Motoori Norinaga, 1730-1801* (Cambridge, Mass., 1970).

107. Also read as *Saki nö yö nö puru götö*.

108. Also known, significantly, as *Sumera Mikötö nö Pi Tsugi*, or Imperial Sun-Lineage.

109. See Tsuda Sōkichi 津田左右吉, *Kojiki oyobi Nihon Shoki no shin ken-kyū* 古事記及び日本書紀の新研究 (Tōkyō, 1919), pp. 94-97. Reprinted in vol. 29 of *Tsuda Sōkichi zenshū* 津田左右吉全集 (Tōkyō, 1963-66). Honorifics were reincorporated in the imperial styles on the accession of the twenty-seventh emperor.

110. Shen Yüeh 沈約 *Sung Shu* 宋書, presented to the throne in 488 in response to an imperial order of 487. The material relating to Japan (the *·Jwiə country 倭國) is included in chüan 97, fols. 23v-25r. A closely parallel passage also occurs in the *Nan Shih* 南史, compiled privately by Li Yen-shou 李延壽 in 659.

111. The customary identifications of the imperial names are as follows:

1. *Tsân 讚 (who sent an envoy to the Chinese court in the second year of Yüan-chia 元嘉 = 425) either (*a*) < *saza* in [Opo] Saza[ki] [大]鷦[鷯] , the name of Nintoku Tennō, the sixteenth emperor (cf. Naka Michiyo, "Gaikō shaku-shi," in *Naka Michiyo isho* 4 [Tōkyō, 1915]: 548-50); or (*b*), perhaps more probably, < *za* in [I]za [Po Wakë] [去]来[穂別], the name of Richū Tennō, the seventeenth emperor (cf. Iijima Tadao 飯島忠夫, *Nihon jōkoshi ron* 日本上古史論 [Tōkyō, 1947], p. 86).

A less likely interpretation would derive the Chinese *tsân (= praise) from Jap. *pomu* = (to praise) in Pomuda Wakë nö Mikötö 品陀和氣命, the personal name of Ōjin Tennō, who probably reigned during the second half of the fourth century A.D.

2. *T̯iěn 珍 (who sent tribute to the Chinese court when he succeeded his elder brother on the throne). This graph is roughly synonymous with 瑞 , the first character in Midu Pa Wakë 瑞齒別, the name of Hanzei Tennō, whose full name is Tadipi nö Midu Pa Wakë nö Mikötö (see Iijima, *Nihon jōkoshi ron*, p. 86]. Hanzei Tennō was in fact a uterine brother of Richū Tennō (*Nihon Shoki*, vol. 1,

pp. 430-31; Aston trans., vol. 1, p. 310). As this was the first recorded instance of sovereignty devolving on a brother rather than a son, it would appear to confirm the identification of *Tsân in paragraph 1b, above, as Richū Tennō.

3. *Tsiei 濟 (who sent tribute to the Chinese court in the twentieth year of Yüan-chia = 443) < Wo Asaduma Wakugo nö Sukune [nö Mikötö] 雄朝津間稚子宿禰, a name of Ingyō Tennō. It has been suggested that *tsiei (= to cross a stream) may have been an attempt to render something of the sound and sense of 津 (= a ford); see Iijima, Nihon jōkoshi ron, p. 86.

4. *χiəng 興 (who was confirmed as ruler of *·Jwię 倭國王 by the Chinese emperor in the sixth year of Ta-ming 大明 = 462). This graph is roughly synonymous with 秀, a homonym of 穗 in Anapo [nö Mikötö] 穴穗, the name of Ankō Tennō; see Iijima, Nihon jōkoshi ron, p. 86.

5. *Miu 武 (who sent an envoy to the Chinese court on his accession to the throne of *·Jwię in the second year of the Sheng-ming period of Shun-ti's reign 順帝昇明 = 478) < the last character in Opo Patuse nö Waka Take [nö Mikötö] 大泊瀨幼武, the name of Yūryaku Tennō; see Iijima, Nihon, p. 86.

Not all the above identifications are phonetically or semantically convincing, but together they leave a powerful cumulative impression of reasonableness. The play upon graphic, as well as semantic and phonological, connotations in these renderings of Japanese names would seem to imply that, by the fourth century, some mode of written communication had already been established between the *·Jwię and the Chinese court. On this point see Mori Kōichi, Kofun bunka shōkō, pp. 82 ff., who has adduced an impressive body of evidence for the early use of Chinese script in Japan, including some 300 examples of archeological remains inscribed with Chinese characters, reliably dated from the first century A.D. onwards.

A recent tentative suggestion that the list of rulers may have included only kings descended from Kazuraki royal consorts (a proposition deriving from the possibility that in the fifth century the Kazuraki lineage, undoubtedly possessed of strong ties to the mainland, may have handled Yamato foreign relations) has not yet been worked through; see Gari Ledyard, "Galloping along with the horse-riders: Looking for the founders of Japan," Journal of Japanese Studies 1, no. 2 (1975): 251, n. 92.

112. Since 1822 the standard edition of the text of the Kojiki has been Motoori Norinaga's 本居宣長 Kojikiden 古事記傳, in 44 volumes and furnished with prolegomena, indexes, and other scholarly apparatus. Tachibana no Moribe's 橘守部 Nankojikiden 難古事記傳 provides a still valuable critique of Motoori's commentary. Modern Kojiki studies, which view the compilation essentially as an instrument of political legitimation, can be said to have begun with the publication in 1913 of a paper by Tsuda Sōkichi 津田左右吉. That, and other papers by Tsuda on the Kojiki and allied topics, are now conveniently accessible in Nihon koten no kenkyū 日本古典の研究, 2 vols. (Tōkyō, 1948-50); see also

the same author's *Nihon jōdaishi no kenkyū*日本上代史の研究(Tōkyō, 1947).
There is a recent annotated version of the *Kojiki* by Inoue Shunji, published by
Nihon Shūji Kyōiku Renmei in Fukuoka in 1958, with a revised edition in 1966.
The earliest rendering into a European language was that by Basil Hall Chamberlain, "'Ko-ji-ki' (古事記) or 'Records of ancient matters,'" *Transactions of
the Asiatic Society of Japan*, supplement to vol. 10 (Yokohama, 1882; reprinted
1906). A more recent translation is by Donald L. Philippi, *Kojiki* (Tokyo, 1968),
a work which is furnished with a most useful introduction to the text and copious
explicatory notes; on pages 30-33 there is a succinct statement of the manuscript
traditions and historical scholarship relating to the *Kojiki*. The translation
itself is based on the variorum edition published by Heibonsha in 1956-58 as vol.
7 of the *Kojiki taisei*古事記大成, edited by Hisamatsu Sen'ichi久松潜et
al. in 8 books (Tōkyō). This is also the edition utilized by the authors of the
present work. Cf. also the French translation of Masumi and Maryse Shibata, *Le
Kojiki (Chronique des choses anciennes): Introduction, traduction intégrale et
notes* (Paris, 1969). Critical articles and annual bibliographies of *Kojiki* studies are included in the *Kojiki Nempō*古事記年報, published by the learned
society called *Kojiki Gakkai*古事記学会since 1953. The *Kojiki* myths are subjected to particularly close scrutiny in Takeda Yūkichi武田祐吉, *Kojiki
setsuwa-gun no kenkyū*古事記説話群の研究(Tōkyō, 1954).

113. For example, a certain amount of information about Korea during the
period between Ōjin, the fifteenth emperor, and Keitai, the twenty-fifth, was
derived from the so-called *Kudara ki*百濟記, a Paekche chronicle probably composed before the end of the sixth century A.D. (dated by means of linguistic
analysis by Kinoshita Reiji木下礼仁, "*Nihon Shoki* ni mieru Kudara shiryō no
shiryōteki kachi ni tsuite"日本書紀に見える百濟史料の史料的價値について
て, *Chōsen Gakuhō*朝鮮學報no. 21/22 [1961], pp. 673-723). More specifically,
the *Wei Chih* itself (cf. pp. 24 ff., above) is quoted verbatim four times in the
Nihon Shoki, under the thirty-ninth, fortieth, forty-third, and sixty-sixth years
of Jingu Kōgu. In addition, the chronicle is by no means free of Chinese ideas,
literary devices, and sentiments, the opposition of *yin* and *yang* being especially
prominent. On one occasion a speech attributed by the *Sui Shu* 隋書to the
Emperor Kao-tsu高祖was put into the mouth of Yūryaku Tennō, who had died 125
years before Kao-tsu's decease in 604. The text of the following decree, attributed to Sujin Tennō (*Nihon Shoki*, vol. 1, pp. 248-49), illustrates just how Chinese certain passages in the *Nihon Shoki* might be:

> Ever since we received the Celestial Dignity and undertook the guardi-
> anship of the ancestral shrines, Our light has been subject to obscura-
> tion, and Our influence has been wanting in placidity. Consequently
> there has been disaccord in the action of the male and female princi-
> ples of nature, heat and cold have mixed their due order, epidemic
> disease has been rife, and calamities have befallen the people. But
> now in order to be absolved from Our offences and to rectify Our errors,
> we have reverently worshipped the Gods of Heaven and Earth. We have

also dispensed Our instructions and thus pacified the savage tribes, and by force of arms have chastised those who refused submission. In this way authority has been maintained. . . . [Aston trans., vol. 1, p. 160.]

114. Naka Michiyo那珂通世, "Nihon jōko nendai kō," *Bun* 文 , vol. 1, nos. 8 and 9 (1888); and "Jōsei nengikō," *Shigaku Zasshi* 上世年紀考 史學雜誌 8 (1897): no. 8, pp. 29-60; no. 9, pp. 50-76; no. 10, pp. 57-81; no. 12, pp. 48-73; Suga Masatomo 菅政友, "Kojiki nenkiko," *Shigaku Zasshi* 古事記年紀考 史學雜誌 2, no. 17 (1891): 39-55. The problem of correcting the dates furnished by the *Nihon Shoki*, as Naka conceived it, is essentially as follows. The chronology is affirmed in terms of a sexagenary calendrical cycle based on the Chinese notion of ten "heavenly stems"天干(Japanese *jikkan*) articulating with twelve "earthly branches"地支(Jap. *jūni-shi*). Naka believed that the compilers of the *Nihon Shoki* had in mind an early version of a formulation that was known as the Shin'i theory讖緯説and which was in fact eventually adopted by the court. According to this formulation, substantial change was likely to occur every sixty years, when the stem辛and the branch酉combined in the Shin'yu year, and climactic change every 1,260 years. It was allegedly during Prince Shōtoku's聖德regency that calendrical computations were first undertaken, but the only Shin'yu year during that period was 601. Therefore, argued Naka, this was the datum year for the calculation of the dates in the *Nihon Shoki*. Moreover, glosses in one manuscript of the *Kojiki* also fixed the *hōnen*崩年(or year of an emperor's death) for fifteen of the rulers in its list by means of the sexagenary cycle. The difficulty lay in determining to which particular cycle the *hōnen* pertained. Fortunately, the references in the *Sung Shu* 宋書 to emperors between numbers sixteen and twenty-one (cf. note 111, above) provided another datum from which to calculate the *hōnen* of any emperor after the sixteenth. Thus, the cyclical year戊寅, when, according to the *Kojiki*, Sujin Tennō died, was deduced to be 258, and Chūai Tennō's death in the year壬戌was shown to have occurred in 362. In the absence of any *hōnen* date for emperors earlier than the tenth, Naka was forced into an arbitrary allocation of thirty years to each reign. This brought the accession of Jimmu Tennō to about the middle of the first century B.C. Subsequent scholars have adjusted Naka's calculations from time to time, notably Hoshino Hisashi 星野恒("Nihon kokugō kō," *Shigaku Zasshi*日本國號考 史學雜誌 3, no. 30 [1892]: 16-36, and no. 31 [1892]: 23-59; "Nihon kokugo hokō"日本國號補考, ibid. 10, no. 11 [1899]: 17-38), who proposed that the year 362 in Naka's interpretation should be amended to 302, with preceding *hōnen* dates adjusted accordingly; but in various modified forms Naka's revisions of the *Nihon Shoki* chronology have been adopted by the vast majority of historians of Japan. It is interesting to note, though, that, in undertaking to revise the *Nihon Shoki* chronology, Naka felt constrained to explain that "It would be against the wish of the emperor who was responsible for the compilation of the

Nihon Shoki if the errors were to remain uncorrected" ("Gaikō shaku-shi," in *Naka Michiyo isho* [Tōkyō, 1916], p. 2).

115. One example must suffice for many. Ichimura Kisaburō 市村其三郎 has shown how the compilers of the *Nihon Shoki* selectively recorded and modified the circumstances surrounding the succession dispute that followed the death of Tenji Tennō in 671 in order to demonstrate the continuity and invincibility of imperial authority (*Himerareta Kodai Nihon* 秘められた古代日本, 3d ed. [Ōsaka, 1953], p. 41).

116. For long the standard edition of the *Nihon Shoki* has been the variorum *Shoki Shūkai* 書紀集解, a Confucian-style interpretation, completed by Kawamura Hidene 河村秀根 in 1785, in which the text proper is printed in large black type, the "Original Commentary" in smaller type, and the editor's explicatory notes in still smaller characters. An earlier Shintōist interpretation, entitled *Nihon Shoki Tsūshō* 日本書紀通証, prepared in 1747 by Tanigawa Kotosuga 谷川士清, has not on the whole commanded comparable esteem among scholars. The present authors have relied principally on the Iwanami Shoten edition of the text, with annotations by Sakamoto Tarō 坂本太郎, Ienaga Saburō 家永三郎, Inoue Mitsusada 井上光貞, and Ōno Susumu 大野晋: *Nihon koten bungaku taikei* 日本古典文學大系, vols. 67-68 (in our book designated as volumes 1 and 2 of the *Nihon Shoki*) (Tōkyō, 1965-67). References in the present work are to the volumes (not the so-called "books") and cumulative pagination of this edition. The English translation by William George Aston, although first published as long ago as 1896, is still the only one of its kind: *Nihongi: Chronicles of Japan from the earliest times to A.D. 697*, Transactions and Proceedings of the Japan Society, London, supplement 1, 2 vols. (London, 1896); one-volume reprint (London, 1924); Tuttle paperback edition (Rutland, Vt. and Tōkyō, 1972). Combined references to the Sakamoto edition and the Aston translation will hereafter be cited as *Nihon Shoki* and Aston trans.

117. On Japanese mythology generally see Matsumura Takeo 松村武雄, *Nihon shinwa no kenkyū* 日本神話の研究, 4 vols. (Tōkyō, 1954-58), and, for the etiological aspects, Ōbayashi Taryō 大林太郎, *Nihon shinwa no kigen* 日本神話の起源 (Tōkyō, 1961).

118. Cf. the Land of the Luxuriant Reed Plains and the Bursting Rice Ears (*Töyö Ashi Para nö Mizu Po nö Kuni* 豐葦原水穗國) of the *Kojiki*, bk. 1, chap. 38, line 7 (Chamberlain's trans., p. 107; Philippi's trans., p. 137); *Nihon Shoki*, vol. 1, p. 147; Aston trans., vol. 1, p. 77.

119. Tsuda, *Nihon koten no kenkyū*, vol. 1, pp. 537-38; Matsumura, *Nihon shinwa no kenkyū*, vol. 3, pp. 521-30.

120. Among the more opprobrious of Susa no wo no Mikoto's carryings-on was the breaking-down of the bunds between Amaterasu's padi fields, the turning-out of Heavenly piebald colts to wallow in them, the filling-in of irrigation channels, and the opening of irrigation sluices (*Kojiki*, book 1, chap. 16; Chamber-

lain's trans., pp. 52-53; Philippi's trans., p. 79; *Nihon Shoki*, vol. 1, pp. 111-
13; Aston trans., vol. 1, p. 40). This is one of many examples of the inability
of the chroniclers to comprehend a world without rice. Incidentally, the first,
third, and fourth of these actions figure among the eight heavenly sins as specified in the *norito* for the "Great Exorcism of the Last Day of the Sixth Month"
(Philippi, *Norito*, pp. 45-49).

121. The *Izumo fudoki* is the sole example to survive intact and in its
original form of a genre of general topographical writings modeled to a large
extent on a Chinese tradition that became popular during the period of the Six
Dynasties. The oldest copy extant, which is certainly earlier than the beginning
of the seventeenth century, has been preserved in the library of the Hosokawa
family. It has recently served as a basis for a definitive critical edition of
the text by Kato Yoshinari 加藤義成, *Izumo no kuni fudoki sankyū* 出雲国風土
記参究 (Tōkyō, 1962). For a critical evaluation, bibliography, notes, and English translation see Michiko Yamaguchi Aoki, *Izumo fudoki* (Tōkyō, 1971).

122. The diversity of the myths contained within the Yamato corpus stems not
only from discrepancies between the *Kojiki* and *Nihon Shoki* versions but also from
the alternative accounts that constitute such a valuable element in the structure
of the *Nihon Shoki* itself. These alternative versions tend to present more and
fuller accounts of Izumo than does the main text.

123. "Realm of Darkness," in one or other of its phrasings, was the term
used in the corpus of Yamato myths to denote territories outside the sphere of
authority of the central government. Assignment to that realm therefore signified loss of power. Aoki (*Izumo fudoki*, p. 51) writes, "In depicting Izumo as
the Realm of Darkness, the Yamato court meant to designate, or perhaps magically
to effect, the powerlessness of a recalcitrant people."

124. At a structurally more fundamental level this myth can be interpreted
as the triumph of a divine kingship sustained by the seasonal rites of a basically agricultural society over a possibly pre-farming community whose religious
beliefs focused on a chthonic god or gods. It has been pointed out that the myth
also reproduces the general character of events consequent on the Taika Reform of
646, when local rulers (*kuni no miyatsuko* 國造) were deprived of political
power but permitted to retain their religious functions. See Philippi, *Kojiki*,
p. 412; Matsumura Takeo 松村武雄, *Nihon shinwa no kenkyū* 日本神話の研究
(Tōkyō, 1954-58), vol. 3, pp. 485-89.

125. *Nihon Shoki*, vol. 1, pp. 122-23; Aston trans., vol. 1, p. 53. The
Izumo fudoki refers to the high quality of the iron produced in the district of
Nita 爾以多 (Aoki's trans., p. 135; map, p. 40). For the archeological evidence
bearing on this point see Yamamoto Kiyoshi 山本清, "Iseki no shimesu kodai
Izumo no yōsō" 遺跡の示す古代出雲の様相, in Hiraizumi Kiyoshi, ed., 平泉
澄 *Izumo no kuni fudoki no kenkyū* 出雲国風土記の研究 (Shimane, 1953).

126. The styles of all the early rulers whom we shall mention in this sec-

tion are doubly anachronistic. The Chinese-style title *Tennō* 天皇 (in ancient times read as *Sumera Mikoto*: Heavenly Emperor) was not adopted by Japanese monarchs until early in the seventh century. Jimmu 神武 (Divine Valor) is one of a set of posthumous names foisted on previous rulers during the reign of Kammu (782–806). Gari Ledyard is certainly correct in advocating the abandonment by historians of both "the ludicrous use of the word 'emperor'" in this context and the posthumously bestowed names; see his "Galloping along with the horseriders: Looking for the founders of Japan," *Journal of Japanese Studies* 1, no. 2 (1975): 218–19, n. 5.

127. *Nihon Shoki*, vol. 1, pp. 188–89; Aston's trans., vol. 1, p. 110. In a speech that is wholly Chinese in sentiment, Jimmu Tennō goes on to refer to the eastern land that is the goal of his travels as "without doubt suitable for the extension of the Heavenly task [i.e., the further development of imperial power]," and he adds, "It is unequivocally the center of the world."

128. *Nihon Shoki*, vol. 1, pp. 212–13; Aston trans., vol. 1, p. 131. Both the *Kojiki* (book 2, chaps. 96–97; Chamberlain trans., pp. 237–38; Philippi trans. pp. 266–69) and the *Nihon Shoki* (vol. 1, p. 342; Aston trans., vol. 1, pp. 236 ff.) include an account of a revolt by two older half-brothers of the young Homuda, destined eventually to be Emperor Ōjin, while his mother, the Empress Jingu, was in Anato (= the ancient name of Nagato). The rebellion was suppressed largely by the efforts of Takeshiuchi no Sukune 武内宿禰, but some scholars have been impressed by the similarities in detail between this second conquest of Yamato by armies from Kyūshū and the progress of Jimmu Tennō along the same route. The question they have raised is whether a relatively recent, though only vaguely remembered, eastward migration to Yamato no Kuni could have been fathered on to Jimmu Tennō, already selected as the first emperor and therefore likely to be associated by the mythologizing process with almost any event of major significance. The matter has not been resolved, though it assumes fundamental importance in the theories of Egami Namio and Gari Ledyard (see pp. 79–85, below). It may also be worth noting that, in the myth, Jimmu Tennō achieved his conquest of Yamato only with the help of a distant kinsman who had preceded him thither. What importance should be attached to the fact that the expedition set out from Himuka [= Hyūga] no Kuni in what was one of the technologically least advanced parts of Kyūshū in Yayoi times is debatable. It is not impossible that the compilers of the chronicles should have regarded the Sun-Facing Country as the appropriate place of origin for the first of their emperors. On the other hand, in later times a substantial number of tumulus burials on the Sadowara plain attest to a very real degree of cultural development (even though the *Nihon Shoki* depicts the whole of southeast Kyūshū as a realm of barbarous tribes). If, as some scholars have suggested, the migration that inspired the legend took place as late as the Tumulus period, there would be no difficulty in accepting the homeland of the conquerors as Hyūga.

For the idea that Empress Jingu, who was depicted in the *Nihon Shoki* as possessing the powers of a shamaness, was a legendry ruler, modeled on the Pimiko
of the Chinese accounts, and that Takeshiuchi no Sukune was the male medium who
interpreted her utterances (see p. 23 , above), see Okamoto Kenji岡本堅次,
*Jingu Kōgō*神功皇后(Tōkyō, 1959), pp. 145-68.

129. *Kojiki*, book 1, chap. 18, line 4; Chamberlain's trans., pp. 59-60;
Philippi's trans., p. 87; *Nihon Shoki*, vol. 1, pp. 102-3; Aston trans., vol. 1,
pp. 32-33. The individual crops and the particular parts of the body from which
they were produced (e.g., eyes, rice; ears, millet; nose, beans; and so forth),
at least in the *Kojiki* version, constitute so many plays upon words — but upon
Korean rather than Japanese words. This circumstance must surely point to a
Korean provenance for the myth.

130. *Nihon Shoki*, vol. 1, p. 275; Aston trans., vol. 1, p. 183. See also
vol. 1, pp. 392-93; Aston trans., vol. 1, pp. 281 and 282, where it is recorded
with wholly spurious exactitude that the excavation of an irrigation canal in
Konku utilized the water of the Ishikaha River to bring more than 40,000 [Chi-
nese] *ch'ing*頃of padi land under cultivation. Not only was the unit of measurement Chinese, but the magnitude of the enterprise was also modeled exactly on
the results achieved by the excavation of the Cheng Kuo郑国canal in Ch'in秦
times, as recorded in Ssŭ-ma Ch'ien's *Shih Chi* (司馬遷 史記), chüan 29.

131. *Nihon Shoki*, vol. 1, p. 249; Aston trans., vol. 1, p. 161.

132. *Nihon Shoki*, vol. 1, pp. 248-49; Aston trans., vol. 1, pp. 160-61.
The two taxes mentioned were imposts, respectively, on game and skins and on textile fabrics.

133. *Nihon Shoki*, vol. 1, pp. 296-97; Aston trans., vol. 1, p. 200.

134. *Nihon Shoki*, vol. 1, pp. 316-17; Aston trans., vol. 1, p. 214; *Kōjiki*
uses the term屯家in book 2, chap. 78, line 7; (Chamberlain, p. 205; Philippi,
p. 231).

135. *Nihon Shoki*, vol. 1, p. 241; Aston trans., vol. 1, p. 154.

136. *Nihon Shoki*, vol. 1, pp. 214-15; Aston trans., vol. 1, p. 133.

137. *Nihon Shoki*, vol. 1, p. 271; Aston trans., vol. 1, p. 178.

138. *Nihon Shoki*, vol. 1, pp. 318-19; Aston trans., vol. 1, p. 215.

139. 邊土未清餘妖尚梗: *Nihon Shoki*, vol. 1, pp. 212-13; Aston
trans., vol. 1, p. 131.

140. This is the usual orthography, but in the account of Jimmu Tennō's
muro, mentioned above, the Tsuchi gumo are rendered semiphonetically as土雲.

141. Mimana seems to have been the fifth-century name for a group of tribes
that during the third century A.D. had been known as Pyŏn-Han弁韓(Ch. *B'ian-
ɣan*; cf. p. 22 , above, and n. 15, this chapter).

142. Modern T'ung-kou通溝. Hot'ae, also known as Kwanggaet'o廣開土,
reigned over Koguryŏ高句麗in north Korea from 391 to 412. The inscription, of
more than 1,500 characters, affords a summary of the events that took place dur-

ing the reign of this king. The stele on which it is carved was erected in 414 in Hot'ae's memory by his grandson, who succeeded him on the throne. *Shōhin*, no. 100, is devoted to reproductions of the inscription. See also Umehara Sueji and Fujita Ryōsaku 梅原末治 藤田亮策 *Chōsen Kobunka Sōkan* 朝鮮古文化綜鑑 (Kyōtō, 1959), vol. 4; Ikeuchi Hiroshi and Umehara Sueji 池内宏 梅原末治 *Tsūkō* 通溝 (Tōkyō, 1940); Saeki Arikiyo 佐伯有清, *Kōkaitoō hi* 廣開土王碑 (Tōkyō, 1974).

According to the *Nihon Shoki*, citing the *Kudara ki*, Empress Jingu mounted a large-scale expedition into central Korea (*Nihon Shoki*, vol. 1, pp. 330-61; Aston trans., vol. 1, pp. 224-53), perhaps in defense of Mimana, but it is uncertain whether or not this legend-encrusted tale should be related to the events recorded on the Hot'ae stele. Fujiki Kunihiko and Inoue Mitsusada (eds., 藤本 邦 井上光貞, *Seijishi* 政治史 [Tōkyō, 1965], pp. 31-33) have attributed this Korean campaign to Ōjin Tennō, whose adjusted dates fall within the second half of the fourth century. See also Ueda Masaaki 上田正昭, *Nihon Kodai kokka ron-kyū* 日本古代国家論究 (Tōkyō, 1968), pp. 119-33. For Ledyard's radical reinterpretation of events on the Korean peninsula during the third and fourth centuries see chapter 3, pp. 83 ff., below. In particular, not only is the alleged invasion of the Korean peninsula by Wa armies there castigated as distortion of fact, but Empress Jingu herself is categorized as an invention conjured up to bring the concocted Yamato genealogy into accord with the *Wei Chih* account of Pimiko.

For the history of Mimana see Suematsu Yasukazu 末松保和, *Mimana Kōbōshi* 任那興亡史 (Tōkyō, 1949); Kobayashi Yukio 小林行雄, "Jingu Ōjin ki no jidai" 神功応神紀の時代 *Chōsen Gakuhō* 朝鮮學報, no. 36 (1965), pp. 25-48; Inoue Mitsusada 井上光貞 "Jingu Kōgō to Chōsen no kiroku" 神功皇后と朝鮮の記録 in vol. 1 of *Nihon no rekishi* 日本の歴史 (Tōkyō, 1965). Wedemeyer's comments on the foundation and development of Mimana in *Japanische Fruhgeschichte* (pp. 119-38) are still useful.

For the *Kudara ki* see Mishina Akihide (Shōei) 三品彰英, "Kudara ki, Kudara shinsen, Kudara hongi no tsuite" 百濟記,百濟新撰,百濟本記について *Chōsen Gakuhō* 朝鮮學報, no. 24 (1962), pp. 1-19; reprinted in the same author's book, *Nihon Shoki Chōsen kankei kiji kōshō* 日本書記朝鮮關係記事考證 (Tōkyō, 1962), vol. 1.

143. The formula favored by the *Kojiki* runs differently: [An emperor's personal name] resided in (坐) the ——— Palace (宮) at ———. In the case of Emperor Ōjin, for example, it reads: Homuda Wake no Mikoto resided in the Akira Palace at Karushima 品陀和氣命坐輕嶋之明宮·

144. The list furnished by the *Kojiki* not only differs significantly in its schedule of palaces and locations but also provides variant graphs for the same names, e.g., Izakaha 伊邪河, Mitsukaki 水垣. It is interesting to note that Jimmu and Ōjin, both allegedly invaders of Yamato territory from the west, were

each credited with several palaces, whose names and locations were recorded in phrases quite different from the formula employed for the rest of the emperors.

145. E.g., the Palace of Takaya高屋in Hyūga日向 (*Nihon Shoki*, vol. 1, pp. 290-91; Aston trans., vol. 1, p. 195); the Palace of Kehi笥飯in Tsunuga 角鹿 (*Nihon Shoki*, vol. 1, pp. 322-33; Aston trans., vol. 1, p. 218).

146. *Nihon Shoki*, vol. 1, pp. 238-89; Aston trans., vol. 1, pp. 151-52. Cf. also *Kojiki*, book 2, chap. 65; Chamberlain, p. 175; Philippi, pp. 201-2, where a different story is told, but one which still implies that Emperor Sujin was responsible for a reorganization of shrine administration. In the *Kogoshūi*, a formal statement of the claims of the Imbe lineage to ritual office (cf. p. 59, above), Sujin's unease was attributed to his sharing the same roof as the Mirror sacred to Amaterasu Omikami and the divine Herb-quelling Sword, but the outcome was the same as that related in the *Nihon Shoki*; see Genchi Katō and Hikoshirō Hoshino, *Kogoshūi*, pp. 36-37.

147. For the differentiation of secular from sacral power in ancient Mesopotamia see Thorkild Jacobsen, "Primitive democracy in ancient Mesopotamia," *Journal of Near Eastern Studies* 2, no. 3 (1943): 159-72, and "Early political development in Mesopotamia," *Zeitschrift für Assyriologie und Vorderasiatische Archäologie* n.s. 18 (1957): 91-140; Robert McC. Adams, *The Evolution of urban society: Early Mesopotamia and Prehispanic Mexico* (Chicago, 1966), chap. 4. In particular, Igor M. Diakonoff has postulated an analogous clash of interests in Lagash toward the end of the Ur-Nanshe dynasty in "Some remarks on the reforms of Urukagina," *Revue d'Assyriologie* 52 (1958): 12. In Mesoamerica, Paul Kirchhof has construed the legendary conflict between the gods Quetzalcóatl and Tezcatlipoca as an expression of tension between emerging militaristic cults and an established theocratic leadership ("Quetzalcoatl, Huemac, y el fin de Tule," *Cuadernos Americanos* 14 [1955]: 163-96). It is also possible that a reorganization of the government undertaken by the Inca shortly before the Spanish Conquest may have reflected a desire on the part of those grasping for secular power to extend the sphere of their control (Paul Kirchhoff, "The Social and political organization of the Andean peoples," in Julian H. Steward, ed., *Handbook of South American Indians*, bull. 143 of the Bureau of American Ethnology, Smithsonian Institution, vol. 2: *The Andean civilizations* [Washington, D.C., 1949], p. 308). For a somewhat similar situation apparently obtaining in the Yoruba state of Oyọ during the eighteenth century see Wheatley, "The Significance of traditional Yoruba urbanism," *Comparative Studies in Society and History* 12, no. 4 (1970): 410-11. There is a general discussion of this phase of social evolution in Wheatley, *The Pivot*, pp. 311-16.

148. Kuroita Katsumi黒板勝美, *Kōtei kokushi no kenkyū*更訂國史の研究 (Tōkyō, 1931), vol. 2A, pp. 29-93. An influential adaptation of Kuroita's thesis in English was published by Robert Karl Reischauer, *Early Japanese history (c. 40 B.C. - A.D. 1167)*, 2 vols. (Princeton, 1937). Cf. also Ishii Ryōsuke,

Tennō (Tōkyō, 1950). It is essentially the Kuroita style of interpretation that is invoked by Yazaki Takeo矢崎武夫in the earlier chapters of his standard work on the evolution of the Japanese city, *Nihon toshi no hatten katei*日本都市の発展過程(Tōkyō, 1962); English translation by David L. Swain under the title *Social change and the city in Japan from earliest times through the Industrial Revolution* (Tōkyō, 1968).

149. Mizuno Yū水野祐, *Zotei Nihon kodai ōchō shiron josetsu*増訂日本古代王朝史論序説 (Tōkyō, 1952; rev. ed., 1954; 3d printing, 1968).

150. Egami Namio, *Kiba minzoku kokka: Nihon kodaishi e no apurōchi* (Tōkyō, 1950) (see n. 91, above). See also Naoki Kōjirō直木孝次郎, "Ōjin ōchōron josetsu"応神王朝論序説, in Naoki, *Nihon kodai no shizuoku to tennō*日本古代の氏族と天皇(Tōkyō, 1969), pp. 173-200. For further remarks on Egami's thesis see below, chap. 3, pp. 82-83.

151. Mizuno's interpretation of early Japanese history is considerably more involved than we have represented it in these pages. In his view (which is derived almost exclusively from literary sources), when the invading Korean chiefs and their followers had reached Kyūshū, Emperor Chūai, the last member of an old indigenous Yamato dynasty, attacked them under the pretense of subjugating the Kumaso熊襲tribes. When the Yamato forces were defeated, the newly united Kyūshū polity, under Nintoku Tennō, transferred its chief ceremonial center from Hyūga, in Kyūshū, to Naniwa, at the eastern end of the Inland Sea. It was this conquering dynasty that, in the fifth century, sought to control not only eastern Japan but also southern Korea.

Mizuno's derivation of the Kyūshū dynasty also breaks with traditional interpretations. He sees Nintoku's line as descending, not from Pimiko of *Yamatai* (or *Yamawi*), but from the male ruler of the neighboring, allegedly Tungusic, chiefdom of Kuna (in the Chinese dynastic histories rendered as *Kₐu-nuo*; see pp. 22-23 and 25, above), which had overcome *Yamatai*, united Kyūshū, and opportunistically extended its authority into Korea to fill the power vacuum created by the fall of the Chinese Wei dynasty in 265. Mizuno also gives his reasons for believing that this Kuna had once formed part of the Na (Chinese *Nuo*; see pp. 23, 25, above) tribal confederacy. When that congeries of tribes had been incorporated into the *Yamatai* polity, the Na chiefs, together with some of their followers, had migrated to eastern Kyūshū, where they had established the ritual center at Hyūga. Toward the end of the third century, according to Mizuno's chronology, the chiefs of Kuna conquered *Yamatai*, and a century later they extended their control eastward to the Kinai. In this way Mizuno is able to account for, among other things, the tumuli scattered over the Sadowara plain in southeast Kyūshū, which appear anomalous in the traditional interpretation.

Our adoption of some of Mizuno's theses must not be held to imply that we espouse his interpretation in its totality. We do believe, however, that he is basing his approach to early Japanese history on correct assumptions and that, generally speaking, his method of interpretation is sound in principle (Mizuno Yū, *Zōtei Nihon kodai ōchō shiron josetsu*; see note 149, above). Moreover, several of his more important conclusions are strongly supported by Ledyard's independent analysis, discussed in chap. 3, pp. 83-85.

152. The fact that a *·*Jwię* tribute-bearing mission was permitted to visit the Chinese court in A.D. 57 implies (1) that similar missions had already been arriving at the border settlements for a sufficient period of time to have established their credentials and (2) that they came from a political entity that the Chinese were prepared to recognize as a genuine *kuo* or territorial organization. Casual groups of tribesmen would not have been permitted to proceed beyond the commandery city of *Lâk-lâng*.

153. Kent V. Flannery, "The Cultural evolution of civilizations," *Annual Review of Ecology and Systematics* 3 (1972): 403. See also Elman R. Service, *Origins of the state and civilization: The process of cultural evolution* (New York, 1975), pp. 15-16 and 151-52.

154. Certain Japanese scholars have seen a significant parallel between the relationship of *Piět-mjię-χuo and her "brother," on the one hand, and that of the Sun Goddess, Amaterasu Ōmikami and her brother Susa no wo no Mikoto, on the other. Some have gone further, postulating a reversal of status when, in the distant past, a female ruler exercising supreme authority was forced to surrender her primacy to a formerly subordinate male whose jurisdiction had previously been restricted to secular affairs. However, this does not accord with the myth of Amaterasu, who in a single persona subsumed the roles of both sorceress and ruler of High Heaven; on this last point see Aoki, *Izumo fudoki*, p. 50. It should be noted also that female chieftains were not unknown to the eighth-century chroniclers; see, inter alia, *Nihon Shoki*, vol. 1, pp. 286-89; Aston trans., vol. 1, pp. 193-94.

155. In the *Nihon Shoki* the first use of corvée labor in the construction of a palace was attributed to the reign of Nintoku Tennō, who may have had some basis in reality (vol. 1, pp. 392-93; Aston trans., vol. 1, p. 280). If so, he probably ruled right at the end of the period we are considering.

156. It is a characteristic of the patrimonial ethic that it tends to transform questions of law and adjudication into questions of administration; cf. Bendix, *Max Weber*, pp. 367-68.

157. The Chinese graphs *kuei* 鬼 (lower/earthly spirit) and *shen* 神 (higher/ heavenly spirit) would appear to be an attempt to render a notion that occurs frequently in the *Kojiki* and *Nihon Shoki* and that is explicated by Motoori as distinguishing those deities who either now dwell in Heaven or at some time descended thence to earth from deities who came into existence in Japan. The parallel Japanese phrase was *amatsu kami kunitsu kami*.

158. Robert N. Bellah, "Religious evolution," *American Sociological Review* 29, no. 3 (1964): 358-73, esp. 361-66.

159. Ibid., p. 363.

160. In addition to Bellah's remarks on this topic (ibid., p. 365), see also Henri Hubert and Marcel Mauss, "Essai sur la nature et la fonction du sacrifice," *L'Année Sociologique* 2 (1897-98): 29-138.

161. And probably elsewhere in Japan as well, but these are the only two regions for which mythologies are available for analysis.

162. Bellah ("Religious evolution," p. 365) sees this lack of structural differentiation within religious collectivities as potentially the most important limitation on Archaic religious organization, not only in Japan but in all other societies at a comparable stage of development.

163. Such information on this topic as can be gleaned from the *Kojiki* and the *Nihon Shoki* merely reflects the architectural features of the Yamato court at the time these records were compiled. Although possibly utilizable for the purpose of illustrating a passage in one of the Chinese texts or an inference from archeological data, it can never be relied on as historical observation.

164. I.e., any of several forms of wholesaling undertaken at government instigation and under governmental control. The term was first given its technical meaning in the works of Karl Polanyi; see, for instance, Polanyi, Conrad M. Arensberg, and Harry W. Pearson, *Trade and market in the early empires* (Glencoe, Ill., 1957).

165. This is the terminology used by Eric R. Wolf, *Peasants* (Englewood Cliffs, N.J., 1966), chap. 1.

166. The changing emphases placed on these approaches by different individuals and schools of history from ancient to recent times have been documented by John Young in *The Location of Yamatai*.

167. *Yamahi*, of which *$\underset{\sim}{I}a$-ma-·$i\breve{e}t$ would be a phonetically adequate transcription, is excluded from the roster of possibilities by the fact that present-day *hi* was vocalized in Archaic Japanese as *pi*. Virtually all Japanese scholars, despite the fact that they have customarily considered the *Wei Chih* more reliable than the *Hou-Han Shu*, have amended *$\underset{\sim}{I}a$-ma-·$i\breve{e}t$ [壹] to read *$\underset{\sim}{I}a$-ma-d'$\hat{q}i$ [臺], presumably influenced by the assumption that the latter form was a transcription of Yamatö. This has often involved those who favored a location in Kyūshū in severe intellectual contortions. An exception to the prevalent restoration of the name as Yamatai is the work of Furuta Takehiko 古田武彦 , "Yamawikoku no ronri to kōdaishiryō" 邪馬壹国の論理と後代史料, *Shoku Nihongi kenkyū* 續日本紀研究 , no. 176 (1974), pp. 1-21, and no. 177 (1975), pp. 26-31.

One etymology of the name Yamatö which, despite its having been accepted by several authorities, can be discounted is Kagami Kanji's 鏡味完二 derivation of the word from a supposed Indonesian *yamatuan*, which, he says, signifies 王 or "person in authority" (*Nihon chimeigaku* 日本地名學 1 [Tōkyō, 1957]: 267-68). The title in question is *yamtuan*, but this is only a popular, and almost certainly a fairly late, variant of *yang di-pertuan* = "supreme lord," "sovereign," which can bear no etymological relationship to *Yamatö*. In volume 2 of his work

(p. 309) Kagami provides a map showing the distribution of the name Yamato in

both modern and, insofar as it can be reconstructed, ancient times.

Incidentally, we would urge that, in future investigations of the location

of *Ia-ma-d'ậi*, three main facets of the problem should be treated separately,

namely: (1) Is *Ia-ma-d'ậi* despite the authority of the *Wei Chih*, the correct

reading? (2) If so, is *Ia-ma-d'ậi* a transcription of Yamatö? (3) If so, was

the *Yamatö of the Chinese texts the same Yamato as that which subsequently

became the cradle of the Japanese state?

168. See pp. 35-36, above.

CHAPTER 3: THE EARLY CAPITALS

1. A good deal of support for such an interpretation can indeed be garnered

from the totally independent reevaluations of available literary evidence under-

taken by Mizuno Yū 水野祐, *Zōtei Nihon kodai ōchō shiron josetsu* 增訂日本古代

王朝史論序説 (Tōkyō, 1952; rev. ed., 1954; 3d printing, 1968).

2. Egami Namio 江上波夫, *Kiba minzoku kokka: Nihon kodaishi e no apurō-

chi* 騎馬民族国家日本古代史へのアプローチ(Tōkyō, 1950; 24th printing,

1973). This author's views are presented in English in "The Formation of the

people and the origin of the state in Japan," *Memoirs of the Tōyō Bunko* 23 (1964):

35-70. A detailed critique of Egami's theory of an invasion by a horse-riding

folk is provided by Gari Ledyard, "Galloping along with the horseriders: Looking

for the founders of Japan," *Journal of Japanese Studies* 1, no. 2 (1975): 217-54.

Cf. also Suzuki Takeo 鈴木武樹, "Kiba minzoku to Yamatai koku," *Dentō to Gen-

dai* 馬民族と邪馬臺國 伝統と現代, no. 26 (1975), pp. 20-33; and, though

with caution, J. H. Kamstra, *Encounter or syncretism: The initial growth of Japa-

nese Buddhism* (Leiden, 1967), pp. 35-40.

3. See esp. pp. 166-70 of *Kiba minzoku kokka*.

4. Arrows with pierced hollow knobs attached to their shafts, as a result

of which they whirred loudly in flight, thereby alarming an enemy. They are men-

tioned in the *Kojiki*, book 23, chap. 13; book 31, chap. 4; and book 131, chap. 2.

5. *Haniwa* took the form of hollow clay cylinders often surmounted by human

or animal figurines, utensils of daily use, or even models of buildings. As many

as 20,000 were spaced around the tomb of Nintoku Tennō. Horses figured promi-

nently among these sculptures, and in their accoutrements they attest to a mas-

tery of equestrian skills. Representations of warriors were usually placed on

the summit, and often toward the front, of a tomb, where their clothing, armor,

and weapons pointed incontrovertibly to a continental provenance.

The origin and development of *haniwa* are still vexed questions. A passage

in the *Nihon Shoki* (vol. 1, pp. 272-75; Aston trans., vol. 1, pp. 178-81) pur-

ports to explain how the erection of such figures was substituted for the immola-

tion of live retainers on the burial of their lord during the reign of Emperor

Suinen, whose adjusted dates fall within the third century A.D. In the passage
here referred to, the emperor was made to categorize the burial of attendants
alive in the precincts of a tumulus grave as an ancient practice, but a brief
remark in the *Kojiki* (book 2, chap. 64, line 10; Chamberlain's trans., p. 174;
Philippi's trans., p. 200, Commentary, pp. 416-18) states unambiguously that the
first occasion on which a "human fence" (*pitö gaki* 人垣) was constructed in
this way was at the interment of Yamato Hiko no Mikoto during the reign of
Emperor Sujin (whose adjusted dates fall within the first half of the third century A.D.). The *Nihon Shoki* version is to be preferred. For a similar practice
ascribed to the time of Yūryaku (second half of the fifth century) see *Harima
Fudoki*, in Takeda Yūkichi 武田祐吉, ed., *Fudoki* 風土記: vol. 97 in *Iwanami
Bunko* (Tōkyō, 1939), pp. 188-89; translated by Philippi, *Kojiki*, p. 417.
Although the author of the *·*Jwiĕ* section of the *Wei Chih* noted that the practice
of "following to burial" (徇葬; Jap. *junshi*) took place on the death of Pimiko
in the middle of the third century A.D. (cf. p. 36, above), and although it was
considered necessary to prohibit such actions in a special provision of the
famous Reform Edict of 646 (*Nihon Shoki*, vol. 2, pp. 294-95; Aston trans., p.
220), the custom has thus far not been verified archeologically (see *Zukai kōkogaku jiten* 図解考古学辞典 [Tōkyō, 1959], p. 449). However, archeology has
thrown doubt on the origin myth propagated in the *Nihon Shoki* by showing that
simple clay cylinders preceded those bearing models by about a century and that,
generally speaking, inanimate objects antedated human beings, the former pertain-
ing mainly to the fifth century or earlier, the latter to the sixth. The theory
that the simpler forms of *haniwa* were originally developed as a means of counter-
ing soil creep on the slopes of the tumuli is contradicted both by the fact that
they were frequently clustered on particular parts of a tomb without relation to
the operation of gravity and by the wide spacing that characterized many of the
earlier examples. Probably Gotō Shuichi's 後藤守一 suggestion that the figures
constituted a symbolic barrier delimiting hallowed space is as reasonable as any;
see his *Nihon kodaishi no kokogakuteki kentō* 日本古代史の考古学的検討
(Tōkyō, 1947), pp. 90-91. It is to be noted that, although the *haniwa* often
reflected foreign influences, the techniques with which they were modeled were
thoroughly indigenous, having evolved directly out of a Yayoi tradition. In
later times their manufacture was considered to have been a prerogative of the
Hajibe, whom Suinin Tennō allegedly designated as caretakers of tombs. On *haniwa*
generally, see R. A. Miller, *Haniwa: The clay sculpture of protohistoric Japan*
(Tōkyō, 1960), an English adaptation of Miki Fumio 三木文雄 *Haniwa* はにわ
(Tōkyō, 1960).

6. For a general overview and discussion of the polity of the T'o-pa Wei
see Wolfram Eberhard, *Das Toba-Reich Nordchinas* (Leiden, 1949). See also Louis
Bazin, "Recherches sur les parlers T'o-pa (5e siècle après J.C.)," *T'oung Pao* 39
(1949-50): 228-329, and Peter A. Boodberg, "The Language of the Toba Wei,"

Harvard Journal of Asiatic Studies 1 (1936): 167-85.

7. See Ch'en Shou 陳壽 *San-Kuo Chih* 三國志 (late third century, A.D.),
chüan 30, with quotations from the approximately contempory *Wei Lüeh* 魏略
appended by P'ei Sung-chih 裴松之 early in the fifth century; R. Sh. Dzharylga-
sinova, "Nekotorye voprosy istochnikovedeniie Koguryŏ," in *Istoriographiya i
istochnikovednie stran zarubezhnogo vostoka*, NAUKA (Moscow, 1967), pp. 57-73; Yi
Tal-hŏn 李達憲 and Mishina Akihide (Shōei) 三品彰英, "Kōkuri, Shiragi no kan-
kei-soshiki no seiritsu katei" 高句麗新羅の官階組織の成立過程, *Chōsen-
kenkyū-nempyo* 朝鮮研究年表 no. 1 (1959), which is a Japanese summary of a
paper in Korean by Kim Ch'ŏljun 金哲埈. An excellent summary of the fortunes
of the Koguryŏ state is incorporated in K. H. J. Gardiner, *The Early history of
Korea: The historical development of the peninsula up to the introduction of Buddhism in the fourth century A.D.*, Centre of Oriental Studies, Oriental Monograph
Series No. 8 (Canberra, 1969), passim.

8. See Imanishi Ryū 今西龍, *Kudara-shi kenkyū* 百濟史研究 (Keijo,
1934); Shiratori Kiyoshi 白鳥清, "Kudara no kigen ni tsuite," *Shigaku* 百濟の
起源について 史學 (December, 1947); Mishina Akihide (Shōei) 三品彰英,
Nihon Shoki Chōsen kankei kiji kōsho 日本書紀朝鮮關係記事考證, vol. 1
(Tōkyō, 1962); Gardiner, *The Early history of Korea*, pp. 43-47.

9. See, for example, Cornelius J. Kiley, "State and dynasty in Archaic
Yamato," *Journal of Asian Studies* 33, no. 1 (1973): 25-49.

10. "Conical clans" was the term proposed by Paul Kirchhoff to denote
extensive common-descent groups, ranked and segmented on genealogical lines,
which bound their members with familial ties while yet distributing wealth,
social standing, and power according to consanguineal proximity to the main line
of descent ("The Principles of clanship in human society," *Davidson Journal of
Anthropology* 1 [1955]: 1-10; reprinted in Morton H. Fried, ed., *Readings in
anthropology* [New York, 1959], vol. 2). There is a splendidly insightful discussion of these social groups, felicitously characterized as "clanship made political," in Marshall D. Sahlins, *Tribesmen* (Englewood Cliffs, N.J., 1968), pp. 24-
26. Raymond Firth categorized such conical groups as *ramages*, a term which has
been widely adopted by British social anthropologists; see Firth's *We, the Tiko-
pia* (London, 1936).

11. Mizuno Yū, *Zōtei Nihon kodai ōchō shiron josetsu*, passim.

12. *Nihon Shoki*, vol. 1, pp. 188-89; Aston trans., vol. 1, pp. 110 ff. Cf.
Uemura Seiji 植村清二, *Jimmu Tennō* 神武天皇 (Tōkyō, 1958).

13. *Nihon Shoki*, vol. 1, p. 342; Aston trans., vol. 1, pp. 236 ff.

14. Naoki Kōjirō 直木孝次郎, "Ōjin ōchōron josetsu" 応神王朝論序
説, in Naoki, *Nihon kodai no shizoku to tennō* 日本古代の氏族と天皇 (Tōkyō,
1969), pp. 173-200.

15. Presumably the metal was obtained in the vicinity of Kimhae, where iron
slag of considerable antiquity has been found (Gardiner, *The Early history of
Korea*, p. 48).

16. Or Karak: Korean 駕洛; Jap. 加羅 .

17. A king of Wa was mentioned in an inscription on a "seven-branched sword" of Korean manufacture, dated A.D. 369, as a ruler with whom the king of Paekche wished to maintain amicable relations; which particular group of Wa was intended is, however, unknown. It is usually considered to refer vaguely to a people somewhere in the more southerly of the Japanese islands, but it is not impossible that the king of Paekche was referring to a group of Wa in the lower Naktong Valley in south Korea. Cf. Egami, *Kiba minzoku kokka*, pp. 190-93; Fukuyama Toshio 福山敏男, "Isonokami Jingū no shichishitō," *Bijutsu Kenkyu* 石上神宮の七支刀 美術研究 158, no. 3 (1950): 8-38.

18. Suematsu Yasukazu 末松保和, *Mimana kōbōshi* 任那興亡史 (Tōkyō, 1949; reprint, Yoshikawa Kōbunkan, 1956); Nishijima Sadao 西嶋定生, "Rokuhasseiki no Higashi Ajia" 六・八世紀の東アジア, *Nihon rekishi: Kodai* 2 日本歴史古代 (Tōkyō, 1962).

19. The designation is attributed to Sujin in the *Kojiki*, book 2, chap. 68, line 7 (Philippi, p. 208), and in the *Hitachi Fudoki* (sub "Asuka no kori" 香島郡) in Takeda, *Fudoki*. In the *Nihon Shoki* (vol. 1, p. 213, and Supplemental Note 3-20, p. 581; Aston trans., vol. 1, p. 133) it is ascribed to Jimmu.

20. Notably Mizuno Yū, *Zōtei Nihon kodai ōchō shiron josetsu* (Tōkyō, 1968).

21. It may be significant, at least for those who regard Sujin as the founder of the Old Dynasty, that the suffix *iri-biko*, which seems to mean something like "entering prince," may have denoted the initiator of a collateral lineage. Cf. Donald L. Philippi, *Kojiki* (Tōkyō, 1968), p. 472.

22. -*na* supposedly signified "tribe" or "lineage." The -*ki* of the personal name is alleged to have denoted "fortification" or "town." It is not without interest that the names of no less than eight of the score or so *·*Jwie* territories listed in the *Wei Chih* (see note 32 to chap. 2) incorporated the suffix -*na*.

23. Egami, *Kiba minzoku kokka* (see note 2, above). Mizuno differs from Egami in that, while regarding Sujin Tennō as the probable founder of the Old Dynasty, he apparently envisages him as ruling in Yamato.

24. This is basically the view of Egami Namio, who seems to envisage a consolidation of Wa power in Mimana before it was ever extended to the archipelago; see his *Kiba minzoku kokka*, pp. 134-98.

25. Ledyard, "Galloping along with the horseriders" (see note 2, above).

26. Mizuno Yū has given reasons for placing Mimaki's death in 318 and that of the last member of the dynasty in 362. The same author also stigmatizes two of the five rulers in the dynastic succession as fabrications of the compilers of the *Nihon Shoki*, in which connection it is surely significant that no death dates (*honen* 崩年) are recorded for them in the *Kojiki*. See *Nihon kodai ōchō*, pp. 99-102 and Table 12.

27. Mizuno, *Nihon kodai ōchō*, passim.

28. "Galloping along with the horseriders," pp. 231 ff.

29. Compiled by Kim Pu-sik in A.D. 1145.

30. Ledyard ("Horseriders," p. 242, n. 59) acknowledges that the germ of this argument was derived from an interpretation of the *Nihon Shoki* incorporated in a paper by Chʻŏn Kwanʻu in *Sin Tongʻa* (December 1972; reprinted as "Mimana mondai ni tsuite," *Han* 2, no. 2 [1973]: 53-84). We have not been able to consult this paper.

31. Incidentally, this interpretation provides a factual basis for the tales of conquest referred to in Yūryaku's memorial to the Chinese emperor in 478 (cf. note 111 to chap. 2).

32. Ledyard also provides an interesting, and almost certainly improved, reinterpretation of the Kwanggaetʻo inscription (see note 142, above), which he suggests is recording not a Wa raid to the north but rather an attempt by insular Puyŏ, together with their Wa subjects, to help their peninsular kinsmen counter Koguryŏ encroachments to the south ("Horseriders," pp. 250-51).

33. Ibid., pp. 243-44 and 251 ff.

34. Ibid., p. 246.

35. Ledyard adduces in support of his reconstructions a certain amount of archeological, ethnological, linguistic, and mythological evidence and suggests where numerous additional parallels might be discovered. One of his more interesting linguistic reconstructions (ibid., pp. 248-49) relates *Kashipara* (橿原, Mod. Jap. Kashiwara), the name of the locality where the Ipare Prince of Divine Yamato (Kamu Yamatö Ipare Biko 神日本磐余彦, 神倭伊波禮毘古), putative progenitor of the Yamato lineage, allegedly established his seat of government (都) (cf. p. 69, above; *Nihon Shoki*, vol. 1, pp. 212-15; Aston trans., vol. 1, pp. 131-33; *Kojiki*, book 2, chap. 52; Philippi, p. 177) to the *Kasŏp* Plain, where the Eastern Puyŏ capital was located (*Samguk Yusa* 三國遺事, thirteenth century A.D., p. 39): Ancient Chinese vocalization of the combination now read *kasŏp* = *ka śi̯ap*; Korean *pŏl* = "plain" is cognate with Archaic Jap. *para*. As Ledyard phrases it, "*Ka śi̯ap para* strongly suggests Jap. Kashi Para." The significance of this equation is considerably enhanced by another of Ledyard's reconstructions (pp. 247-48), namely, the tentative establishment of a philological relationship between the ethnonym Puyŏ 扶餘 and the Japanese toponym *Ipare* 磐餘.

36. In an ingenious interpretation of materials in the *Harima fudoki*, Michiko Y. Aoki has assigned the major role in the process of subjugation to Homuda (Arch. Pomuda) Wake no Mikoto, posthumously styled Ōjin Tennō. According to this theory, Homuda established control over a community of predominantly immigrant Korean padi farmers in the combined Yodo-Yamato delta, a resource base superior both quantitatively and qualitatively to the restricted padi acreage available to the Yamato chiefs in the Nara Basin. After first acquiring membership in the tribal council of the Yamato confederacy by taking a wife from the prominent Kazuraki 葛城 lineage, Homuda ultimately extended his suzerainty over the whole of the Nara Basin (see Aoki, *Ancient myths and early history of Japan:*

A cultural foundation [New York, 1974], chap. 2; this interpretation of Ōjin's role in the conquest is not at all incompatible with Ledyard's reconstruction, discussed above). If this interpretation were to be sustained, it would provide a classic case of Flannery's "promotion" mechanism (discussed on pp. 12-13, above) contributing to the process of segregation by the formation of a new institution. Aoki also infers instances of Homuda subsequently contributing to the process of centralization by intruding his personal power and authority, to a linearizing end, into the lowest levels of administration — by depriving local chieftains of their titles, for instance (see, e.g., Aoki, pp. 42-43). It is doubtful that Aoki's theses will be substantiated in all their ramifications, but her novel approaches to the traditional sources for early Japanese history and the essential rationality of many of her expositions will certainly invite reevaluations of currently received interpretations. In particular, her use of *fudoki* materials (cf. p. 59, above) has drawn attention to a historiographical resource of great potential value.

37. Kiley, "State and dynasty in Archaic Yamato," p. 40; Kasai Wajin 笠井倭人, "Kiki keifu no seiritsu katei ni tsuite," *Shirin* 記紀系譜の成立過程について史林 40, no. 2 (1957): 28-44; Harashima Reiji 原島礼二, *Wa no goō to sono zengo* 倭の五王とその前後 (Tōkyō, 1970).

38. Inoue Mitsusada 井上光貞, "Kodai kokka keisei no shodankai:古代国家形成の諸段階; in Inoue, *Nihon kodai kokka no kenkyū* 日本古代国家の研究 (Tōkyō, 1965), pp. 527-638. See also the same author's *Nihon kokka no kigen* 日本国家の起源 (Tōkyō, 1960).

39. Ledyard ("Horseriders," pp. 250-53) regards the situation as one of competing power groups rather than as a ritually instituted alternation of authority.

40. Max Weber, *The Theory of social and economic organization*, translated from the German by A. M. Henderson and Talcott Parsons (Glencoe, Ill., 1947), pp. 136-38, 329 ff. and 341 ff.; Weber, "Politik als Beruf," *Gesammelte politische Schriften* (Munich, 1921), pp. 396-450.

41. Mizuno Yū, *Zōtei Nihon kodai ōchō shiron josetsu*, pp. 63-107; Kishi Toshio 岸俊男, "Wani uji ni kansuru kisoteki kōsatsu,"ワニ氏に関する基礎的考察, in Kishi, *Nihon kodai seijishi kenkyū* 日本古代政治史研究 (Tōkyō, 1966), pp. 16-89. In Ledyard's view, Keitai Tennō (Wohodo: Arch. J. = Wo Podö) represented a resurgence of native *·Jwię (Wa) power which removed forever the Puyö conquerors ("Horseriders," p. 254). Not unnaturally, the chroniclers of the new dynasty excised from their genealogical records all mention of their prede- cessors as their former rulers. The eighth-century compilers of the *Nihon Shoki* (vol. 2, pp. 8-17; Aston trans., vol. 1, pp. 399-407), though not the authors of the *Kojiki* (book 3, chap. 141; Chamberlain, p. 338; Philippi, p. 383), used the standard model of contemporary Chinese historians to explain the decline of the so-called Middle Dynasty (Mizuno's term); that is, they attributed unutterable

depravities to Buretsu, its terminal representative, on the pattern (and, indeed, replicating some of the crimes) of the legendary last king of the Shang dynasty. Inoue (see note 38, above) interprets this mode of treatment as indicating that, at some period prior to the compilation of the *Nihon Shoki*, Yamato annalists had recognized Buretsu not primarily as an evil ruler but as the last of his line and therefore, by definition, immoral. The terms of reference of the official chroniclers of the *Nihon Shoki* permitted them to accept the logic of this inference but not its reverse. Ledyard goes even farther and designates Buretsu as "completely fictitious" ("Horseriders," p. 254).

42. Liu Hsü 劉昫 , *Chiu T'ang-Shu* 舊唐書(presented to the throne in 945), chüan 199, fol. 14r; Ou-yang Hsiu 歐陽修, Sung Ch'i 宋祁 et al., *Hsin T'ang-Shu* 新唐書(presented to the throne in 1060), chüan 220, fol. 11v.

43. Inoue, "Kodai kokka keisei no shodankai," pp. 591-99; Ueda Masaaki 上田正昭, "Kodai kokka no seiji kōzō" 古代國家の政治構造, in Ueda, *Nihon kōdai kokka seiritsu shi no kenkyū* 日本古代国家成立史の研究(Tōkyō, 1959), pp. 119-219.

44. Inoue Mitsusada 井上光貞, *Taika kaishin* 大化改新(Tōkyō, 1954), p. 122; Michiko Yamaguchi Aoki, *Izumo fudoki* (Tōkyō, 1971), p. 12. An analysis of the references to *kuni no miyatsuko* in the *Nihon Shoki* has led this author to conclude that those bearing the title *atahe* (直 = loyal deputy) were considered more loyal than those awarded other titles, though *omi* 臣 and *muraji* 連 were certainly more prestigious styles.

45. Cf., among other, Hayashiya Tatsusaburō 林屋辰三郎, "Keitai Kimmei chō no nairan no shiteki bunseki" 繼體欽明朝内乱の史的分析, in Hayashiya, *Kodai kokka no kaitai* 古代國家の解體(Tōkyō, 1954), pp. 3-32; Hayashiya, "Futatabi Keitai Kimmei no nairan ni tsuite" ふたたび継体欽明の内乱につ いて, ibid., pp. 33-39; Naoki Kōjirō 直木孝次郎, "Keitai chō dōran to Jimmu densetsu" 継体朝の動乱と神武伝説, in Naoki, *Nihon kodai kokka no kōzō* 日本古代國家の構造(Tōkyō, 1958), pp. 249-68; Tōma Seita 藤間生大, "Iwayuru Keitai Kimmei no nairan no seijiteki kiban: kodai gōzoku ron no hitokoma," *Rekishigaku Kenkyū* いわゆる「継体欽明期の内乱」の政治的基盤─古代豪族論の一齣─歴史學研究239 (1960): 1-12.

46. John Whitney Hall, *Government and local power in Japan, 500-1700: A study based on Bizen province* (Princeton, 1966), p. 46. An anonymous reviewer of this work has queried the degree to which *miyake* (lit. = storehouse) can legitimately be categorized as "land." We believe that it can be accorded that connotation, if not as synonym, at least as synecdoche. In any case, as the reviewer writes, "It is true that rights in *miyake* were so reified that joint sharing in labor pools became impossible and lineages became, accordingly, specialized dependent elements."

47. Namely, Kazuraki no Sotsuhiko 葛城沙至比跪, a Wa chieftain who, late in the fourth century, was either sent by the ruler of Yamato to campaign in

south Korea (this is the version of the chronicles) or, perhaps more probably, was himself a benefice-holder in Mimana; at any rate he exhibited a good deal of independence in his actions. His daughter Iwa no Hime 磐之媛 became Nintoku's principal queen and the ancestress of all subsequent fifth-century Yamato kings. See Inoue Mitsusada 井上光貞, "Teiki kara mita Kazuraki uji" 帝紀からみた葛城氏, in Inoue, *Nihon kodai kokka no kenkyū* 日本古代国家の研究 (Tōkyō, 1965), pp. 29-72; Shida Jun'ichi 志田諄享, *Kodai shizoku no seikaku to densho* 古代氏族の性格と伝承 (Tōkyō, 1971), pp. 69-73. Ledyard ("Horseriders," p. 251) suspects that the Kazuraki were Mimana Wa who secured their status by allying themselves with the conquering Puyŏ, with whom they joined in the conquest of the Kinai. However, their Mimana holdings for long remained the basis of their power.

48. Kiley, "State and dynasty in Archaic Yamato," p. 46.

49. Ralph W. Nicholas, "Segmentary factional political systems," in Marc J. Swartz, Victor W. Turner, and Arthur Tuden, *Political anthropology* (Chicago, 1966), pp. 49-58.

50. Ibid., p. 58.

51. As members of each of the four marriage classes could compete only with other members of their own class, not with those of other classes, they were at any time free to recruit factional allies from these other classes. This meant, in effect, that scions of the primary royal lineage could not expect support from their peers in dynastic disputes but were forced to rely on the assistance of secondary royal lineages or the nobility. For examples of the way in which the system worked out in practice see Kiley, "State and dynasty in Archaic Yamato," pp. 35-48.

52. The Soga received the title *Ō-omi* from Emperor Senka, who reigned from 536 to 540. The role of the Soga no Omi is so well known that in this and the following paragraphs we shall dispense with most documentation. There is a compendious account of the creation of the imperial state system in chapter 2 of John Whitney Hall's *Government and local power in Japan, 500-1700: A study based on Bizen province* (Princeton, 1966).

53. Ueda Masaaki 上田正昭, "Asuka no kyūtei" *Nihon rekishi koza 1: Genshi kodai* (Tōkyō, 1958), pp. 145-47; cited in Hall, *Government and local power in Japan*, pp. 52-53. Cf. also Murao Jirō 村尾次郎, *Ritsuryō zaiseishi no kenkyū* 律令財政史の研究 (Tōkyō, 1961), pp. 35-37. The *shiro* was equivalent to 100 *mou* 畝 (1 *mou* = approximately one-sixth of an acre).

54. As was noted above (p. 84), it is extremely improbable that anything like all these communities consisted of voluntary migrants. The corporate status of many of the early arrivals is amply attested by Bruno Lewin, *Aya und Hata: Bevölkerungsgruppen altjapans kontinentaler Herkunft* (Wiesbaden, 1962). Cf. also Seki Akira 関晃, *Kikajin* 帰化人 (Tōkyō, 1956), though the type of voluntary commitment implied by the term *kikajin* was almost certainly rare among early

migrants to the islands, however commonly it may have been invoked by later gene-
ologists.

Ledyard is inclined to attribute the disappearance of the Wa from the Chinese dynastic histories at this time to the conquest of Mimana, the Wa territory
closest to China, by the Puyŏ ("Horseriders," p. 251, n. 92).

55. John Whitney Hall, *Japan from prehistory to modern times* (New York,
1970), p. 40.

56. This is the year given by the *Nihon Shoki*, vol. 2, pp. 100-101 (Aston
trans., vol. 2, p. 66), but the *Shoku Nihongi* 續日本紀 implies a date of 538.
For a general statement on the introduction of Buddhism into Japan see Anesaki
Masaharu, *History of Japanese religion* (London, 1930), pp. 51-56.

57. *Nihon Shoki*, vol. 2, pp. 180-87; Aston trans., vol. 2, pp. 128-33.
Contemporary scholarship tends to regard this so-called Seventeen-Article Constitution rather as a tribute to Shōtoku's memory than as the work of the prince
himself. But although it was probably not composed until a generation or so
after his death, it is nevertheless believed to convey reasonably accurately the
substance of his ideas. Analysis of the document has shown that the authors,
whoever they were, were not especially discriminating in their choice of sources.
In addition to a Buddhist article (article 2) and the very clear Confucian and
Legalist flavor of the rest, there is evidence of familiarity with the *Shih Ching*
詩經 , the *Li Chi* 禮記, the *Hsiao Ching* 孝經, the *Lun Yü* 論語, the *Tso
Chuan* 左傳, the *Chuang Tzǔ* 莊子, the Han histories, and the *Wen Hsüan* 文選.
And the whole was cast in a mystical framework of cosmic numerology (17 articles
compounded of the magical properties of 8 and 9) and promulgated on a date chosen
for its auspicious position in the sexagenary cycle. It would seem that, at the
opening of the seventh century, Chinese cultural traits were sometimes still valued for their Chinese-ness rather than for their potential applicability to the
Japanese situation.

58. *Nihon Shoki*, vol. 2, pp. 280-83; Aston trans., vol. 2, pp. 206-9. See
also Inoue Mitsusada 井上光貞, "Ritsuryō taisei no seiritsu" 律令体制の成立
in *Nihon rekishi: kodai* 日本歴史古代(Tōkyō, 1962), vol. 3, 1-31; Inoue, *Taika
kaishin* 大化改新(Tōkyō, 1954); Takeda Yūkichi 武田祐吉 ed., *Nihon Shoki* 日本
書紀 (Tōkyō, 1962), vol. 5, pp. 65-67; Seki Akira 関晃 , "Taika kaishin" 大化
改新 *Nihon rekishi: kodai* (Tōkyō, 1962), vol. 2, pp. 209-11; Torao Toshiya 虎尾
後哉 , *Handen shūjuhō no kenkyū* 班田収受法の研究(Tōkyō, 1961), pp. 99-112;
Mayuzumi Hiromichi 黛弘道, "Taika Kaishin sho to ritsuryō to no kankei," *Rekishi Kyoiku* 大化改新詔と律令との関係 歴史教育, 9, no. 5 (1961): 12-17.

59. This was the year in which the Yōrō Codes were drafted; they were not
formally enacted until 757. The relation between the Taihō and Yōrō codes is
obscure, but that it was not a matter of simple revision is attested by the fact
that the Yōrō Codes resembled the first set of (Chinese) K'ai-yüan 開元 Codes
(715) more closely than they did the Taihō Codes; see Ishio Yoshihisa 石尾芳久

*Nihon kodai-hō no kenkyū*日本古代法の研究(Tōkyō, 1959), pp. 112 ff.

60. The congruence between the Japanese and Chinese models was close but never absolute. For instance, not only did the Department of Worship (*Jingikan* 神祇官) take precedence over the Department of State (*Dajōkan*太政官), but the Japanese did not insist that the mandate of Heaven should necessarily be withheld from a ruler without virtue. In Japanese tradition, claims to sovereignty were based on descent alone. In similar fashion, the Japanese never placed such a strong emphasis on talent as a qualification for office as did the Chinese — in theory, at any rate. The Japanese bureaucratic hierarchy was always based primarily on birth. Apart from this ineradicable bias toward the primacy of lineage, the Japanese accepted the basic T'ang principles of government in their essentials.

61. G. Cameron Hurst III, "The structure of the Heian court: Some thoughts on the nature of 'familial authority' in Heian Japan," in John W. Hall and Jeffrey P. Mass, eds., *Medieval Japan: Essays in institutional history* (New Haven, Conn. 1974), p. 40. For more or less conventional interpretations of the kin and territorial bases of *uji* organization see Aruga (Ariga) Kizaemon 有賀喜左衛門, *Nihon kazoku seido to kosaku seido*日本家族制度と小作制度(Tōkyō, 1943), pp. 94-144; Fukuo Takeichirō福尾猛市郎, *Nihon kazoku seido shi*日本家族制度史 (Tōkyō, 1948), pp. 7-34; Hori Ichirō 堀一郎, *Minkan shinkō*民間信仰(Tōkyō, 1951), pp. 119-68; Ōta Ryō太田亮, *Nihon jōdai ni okeru shakaisoshiki no kenkyū* 日本上代に於ける社会組織の研究(Tōkyō, 1929), passim. There is a useful, chronologically arranged bibliography of the *uji* and related topics in Ueda Masaaki上田正昭, *Ronshū Nihon bunka kigen*論集日本文化起源, vol. 2 of *Nihonshi*日本史(Tōkyō, 1971), pp. 573-74.

62. See pp. 35-36, above.

63. *Kojiki*, book 3, chap. 121, line 11:定賜天下之八十友諸氏姓; Philippi, p. 332; Chamberlain, pp. 294-295. Cf. also *Nihon Shoki*, vol. 1, pp. 438-39; Aston trans., vol. 1, pp. 316-17.

64. Cf. pp. 33-34, above.

65. P. 33, above.

66. Ibid.

67. In the *Nihon Shoki* citation of the *Kudara Ki* (vol. 1, pp. 359-61; Aston trans., vol. 1, p. 252) Satsuhiko's exploits are attributed to the sixty-second year of Empress Jingu, i.e., A.D. 262. The adjusted date would fall in the second half of the fourth century, but it is more than doubtful that Jingu had any existence outside the minds of the compilers of the *Nihon Shoki*. On the Kazuraki lineage see Inoue Mitsusada, *Nihon kodai kokka no kenkyū*, chap. 1; Hirano Kunio 平野邦雄, "Nihon kodai ni okeru 'uji' no seiritsu to sono kōzō"日本古代にお ける《氏》の成立とその構造, *Kodaigaku*古代学120, no. 1 (1965): 21-49.

68. Cf. also Azami nö Iri-bime nö Mikötö, Ipokï nö Ire-bime nö Mikötö, Nunakï nö Ire-bime nö Mikötö, Nupata nö Ire-bime nö Mikötö, Putadi nö Ire-bime nö

Mikötö, Takakï nö Ire-bime nö Mikötö, Tö oti nö Ire-bime nö Mikötö, Töyö Sukï
Ire-bime nö Mikötö, and Yasaka nö Ire-bime nö Mikötö, in all of which styles *ire-
bime* probably signified a princess initiating, or adopted into, a collateral
lineage (see Philippi, *Kojiki*, p. 468).

69. Akimoto Kichirō秋本吉郎, *Fudoki* 風土記, vol. 2 of the Iwanami
Shoten's岩波書店*Nihon Koten Bungaku Taikei*日本古典文學大系(Tōkyō, 1958):
"Yamashiro Kuni"山城國, pp. 414-20.

70. See pp. 23 and 25 , above.

71. See note 10, above.

72. An analogous problem has already been largely resolved by conceptualizing Mexican *calpultin* as conical clans. Some scholars formerly regarded these
subgroups as mere kinship units, indicative of a low degree of societal differentiation, while others viewed them as administrative divisions devised by the ruling class to control its subject peoples. In fact the *calpultin* are now seen to
have combined elements of kin, class, and polity (see Eric Wolf, *Sons of the
shaking earth* [Chicago, 1959], pp. 135-36). Incidentally, this is not the only
parallel between precolonial Mexican and early Japanese history. We might also
cite the development in Mexico of the *calpullec* chiefs into a hereditary nobility,
claiming a descent different from that of the mass of the population; the sacral-
izing of that descent by association with the mythical aura of a particular lineage name (the Toltec name in the Mexican case); the exclusiveness of that descent,
reinforced by class endogamy; and attempts by a nobility dependent on tribute to
acquire control over land as such.

73. A possible solution to the enduring problem of the location of *Ⓘa-ma-
d'ậi might be that the resurgent *·Jwiĕ under Keitai reestablished in the Kinai
the hallowed name of an old Kyūshū chiefdom prominent during an earlier phase of
their political development.

74. Mizuno Yū, *Zōtei Nihon kodai ōchō shiron josetsu* (1954 ed.), p. 138.
It has also been claimed, though less convincingly, that *Wake* was added to the
names of Ōjin, Richū, and Hanzei in later times and that the term was not used at
all until the Reign of Empress Jitō at the end of the seventh century. This last
assertion appears to us to be a dubious conclusion.

75. Kirchhoff, "The Principles of clanship," in Fried, *Readings*, p. 268
(see n. 10, this chapter). See also Jonathan Friedman, "Tribes, states, and
transformations," in Maurice Bloch, ed., *Marxist analyses and social anthropology*,
Association of Social Anthropologists Studies no. 3 (London and New York, 1975),
pp. 161-202.

76. Saeki Arikiyo佐伯有清, *Nihon kodai no seiji to shakai*日本古代の
政治と社会(Tōkyō, 1970), pp. 1-87.

77. See p. 33 , above.

78. This incised figure has been reproduced on numerous occasions but as
adequately as anywhere in Saitō Tadashi齋藤忠, *Nihon sōshoku kofun no kenkyū*

日本装飾古墳の研究, vol. 2: *Zuhanpen* 圖版編 (Tōkyō, 1973), fig. 2, p. 275.

79. E.g., *Nihon Shoki*, vol. 1, p. 189; Aston trans., vol. 1, p. 110. We know of the Puyǒ examples only from their mention by Ledyard, "Horseriders," p. 248.

80. The *be* included, in addition to the *tomo*, groups of commoners, mainly peasants, who appear to have been under the direct control of members of the imperial family, and other similarly constituted groups attached to members of the nobility. There can be little doubt that the *be* was an institution borrowed from Korea, perhaps brought into the islands by Puyǒ invaders.

81. Nishijima Sadao 西嶋定生, "Kofun to Yamato seiken," *Okayama Shigaku* 古墳と大和政權　岡山史学 10 (1961): 154-207.

82. Kondō Yoshirō 近藤義郎, "Kofun hassei ni kansuru shomondai" 古墳発生に関する諸問題, in Kondō and Fujisawa Chōji 藤沢長治, eds., *Kofun jidai* 古賁時代, vol. 2 (vol. 5 of *Nihon no Kōkogaku* 日本の考古学 [Tōkyō, 1966]), pp. 356-88.

83. Harashima Reiji 原島礼二, "Yonseiki zengo no shihai kōzō" 四世紀前後の支配構造, in Harashima, *Nihon kodai shakai no kiso kōzō* 日本古代社会の基礎構造 (Tōkyō, 1968), pp. 130-78.

84. Harashima, "Yonseiki zengo no shihai kōzō," pp. 168-69.

85. Ueda Masaaki 上田正昭, *Nihon kodai kokka ronkyū* 日本古代國家論究 (Tōkyō, 1968).

86. See note 80, above.

87. See, among others, Harumi Befu and Edward Norbeck, "Japanese usages of terms of relationship," *Southwestern Journal of Anthropology* 14 (1958): 66-68; Harumi Befu, "Patrilineal descent and personal kindred in Japan," *American Anthropologist* 65 (1963): 1328-41; Keith Brown, "*Dōzoku* and the ideology of descent in rural Japan," ibid. 68 (1966): 1129-51; id., "The Content of dozoku relationships in Japan," *Ethnology* 7 (1968): 113-38.

88. Sahlins, *Tribesmen*, p. 26 (see n. 10, this chapter).

89. John Whitney Hall found that in Bizen province it usually took about four generations for a cadet lineage to effect a complete break with its parent *uji* (signified by the dropping of the name of the stem lineage) and to establish an independent line (*Government and local power in Japan*, p. 37).

90. The full complexity of this sociopolitical patterning has recently been demonstrated with exemplary clarity by Richard J. Miller, *Ancient Japanese nobility: The kabane ranking system* (Berkeley and Los Angeles, 1974).

91. If a generalized model of the sixth- and seventh-century *uji* is required for comparative purposes, then it had better be something akin to Arthur Spiethoff's "real type," which incorporates only structurally and functionally significant components but does so even if they are not universally represented; see Spiethoff, "Pure theory and economic Gestalt theory: Ideal types and real types,"

in F. C. Lane and Jelle C. Riemersma, *Enterprise and secular change* (Homewood, Ill., 1953), pp. 431-63.

92. See note 87, above.

93. See p. 91, above.

94. See *Nihon rekishi daijiten*日本歴史大辞典(Kawade Shobō 河出書房 Tōkyō, 1956), vol. 1, p. 239, *sub* "Ikai"位皆 and vol. 5, pp. 139-42, *sub* "Kan'i" 官位. One important result of Temmu's "rectification" program was the integration into the lower echelons of Japanese society of substantial numbers of immigrant communities who, though often possessed of valued technological skills, hitherto had achieved only an ambivalent status in Yamato society.

95. In any discussion of these antecedents, elucidation of the mythic character of Amaterasu must be a matter of high priority. As the problem cannot be adequately inquired into here, the reader is referred for a beginning to Manabu Waida, "Sacred kingship in early Japan: A historical introduction," *History of Religions* 15, no. 4 (1976): 319-42; Hirohata Sukeo 広畑輔雄, "Kōso-kami Amaterasu no seiritsu," *Minzokugaku Kenkyū*皇祖神アマテラスの成立 民族学研究 40, no. 10 (1975): 191-204; Kakubayashi Fumio角林文雄, "Amaterasu Ōmikami no kigen, Part I," *Shoku Nihongi Kenkyū*天照大神の起源 續日本紀研究, no. 180 (1967), pp. 1-12.

96. Kita Teikichi 喜田貞吉, *Teito* 帝都 (Tōkyō, 1916), pp. 1-22; Yagi Atsuru八木充, *Kodai Nihon no miyako*古代日本の都(Tōkyō, 1974), pp. 201-8. For a pioneer account in English of the migrations of early Japanese capitals, consult R. A. B. Ponsonby Fane, "Ancient capitals and palaces of Japan," *Transactions and Proceedings of the Japan Society (London)* 20 (1922-23): 105-217, though it must be borne in mind that the author is ascribing to the ancient chronicles a veracity totally at variance with that sanctioned by modern scholarship.

97. Yagi Atsuru, *Kodai Nihon no miyako*, pp. 35-42. Yagi appears to believe that state functions *sensu stricto* fell within the purview of the Outer Court, but the instances that he cites from the *Nihon Shoki* (which involved political intrigues, the Kugatachi盟神探湯tests, and the furnishing of hospitality to foreign envoys) afford only ambivalent support for that interpretation. On the contrary, we consider that the Outer Court was concerned primarily, if not exclusively, with provincial matters that fell properly within the control of *uji* chiefs. It has conventionally been inferred from the testimony of the *Nihon Shoki* and the *Kogoshūi* that the Imikura was the earliest of the treasuries to be instituted, followed by the Uchikura during the reign of Richū and the Ōkura at the instigation of Yūryaku (see, e.g., Aston trans., vol. 1, p. 309, note 1, and Yagi, loc. cit.), but it is doubtful whether these chronicles are wholly reliable in this matter.

98. *Nihon Shoki*, vol. 1, pp. 388-89; Aston trans., vol. 1, p. 277. A myth has attached to this palace: Nintoku allegedly refrained from completing the palace so as not to "delay the season of agricultural operations for the sake of

his own personal caprices." "The palace enclosure and buildings," we are told, "were not plastered, the gable rafters and ridgepoles, the posts and pillars, were devoid of ornament; the covering of thatch was not trimmed evenly" (ibid.). Somewhat contradictorily, though, it is related subsequently that the corvée for palace construction was first imposed ten years later (ibid., vol. 1, pp. 392-93; Aston trans., vol. 1, p. 280). The whole sequence smacks of Chinese inspiration, perhaps working on some archetyped recollection of one or another Naniwa palace, in a regnal record that is more than usually permeated by Chinese literary influence, even by the standards of the *Nihon Shoki*.

99. Fujioka Kenjirō藤岡謙二郎, *Toshi bunmei no genryū to keifu*都市文明の源流と系譜(Tōkyō, 1969).

100. *Sui Shu*, chüan 81, fol. 16r:高麗之館上; *Nihon Shoki*, vol. 2, pp. 190-91; Aston trans., vol. 2, p. 136:高麗館の上. In the *Man'yōshū* Naniwa's connection with the sea is a subject of frequent comment; see, e.g., book 6, no. 928, "wave-bright Naniwa"; book 20, no. 4362, "Naniwa of wind-blown reeds," where the author gazes "on the spacious sea"; book 6, no. 1062, "The Palace of Naniwa . . . Stands by the whale-haunted sea"; book 20, no. 4330, "with the ships all trim / At the port of Naniwa."

101. Some scholars have believed that, although the *miya*宮 migrated within the Asuka district, the latter was small enough to be considered itself as a single extended *miyako*都 .

102. Sawamura Jin沢村仁, "Jūkyo no yōsō"住居の様相, in Asano Kiyoshi and Kobayashi Yukio淺野清 小林行雄, eds., *Sekai Kōkogaku Taikei*世界考古学大系 (Tōkyō, 1964), vol. 4, p. 56; J. Edward Kidder, *Early Buddhist Japan* (New York), 1972), p. 62.

103. *Nihon Shoki*, vol. 2, pp. 246-47; vol. 2, pp. 326-27; Aston trans., vol. 2, pp. 179 and 248. In *Nihon Shoki*, vol. 2, pp. 242-43 (Aston trans., vol. 2, p. 176) it is recorded that construction timber was to be assembled from the various provinces, and, accordingly, craftsmen "were levied from Tōtomi遠江in the east (present-day Aichi prefecture) as far as Aki安藝in the west (present-day Hiroshima prefecture)."

104. The arrival in Yamato from Paekche in 588 of two temple carpenters, a metal founder, four potters (probably specifically tile-makers), and a painter was almost certainly connected with the construction of the Asuka-dera (*Nihon Shoki*, vol. 2, pp. 167-69; Aston trans., vol. 2, pp. 117-18). In 590 timber was cut in the hills; in 592 the main hall and cloister were erected; in 593 foundation relics were deposited in the foundation stone of the pagoda; and the temple was completed some three years later. The site was excavated in 1956-57, when the layout was found to be an exact replica of the Korean Ch'ŏnggamni-sa (清岩里寺; Jap. Seiganri-ji). While the Yamato court remained in the neighborhood of Asuka, the Asuka-dera appears to have filled the role of state temple. In ancient literature it was known first as the Hōkō-ji法興寺and later, in the

Nara period, as the Gangō-ji 元興寺. See Nara Kokuritsu Bunkazei Kenkyūjo 奈良国立文化財研究所, *Heijōgū hakkutsu chōsa hōkoku* 平城宮發掘調査報告 (Nara, 1958), passim; Ōoka Minoru 大岡実, *Nara no Tera* 奈良の寺 (Tōkyō, 1965), pp. 14-15 and 22-23; English trans., *Temples of Nara and their art* (New York, 1973), p. 17; Kidder, *Early Buddhist Japan*, pp. 87-90.

105. Kidder, *Early Buddhist Japan*, pp. 94-95.

106. *Nihon Shoki*, vol. 2, pp. 174-75; Aston trans., vol. 2, p. 123. The Shitennō-ji (the Temple of the Four Heavenly Kings), situated in what is today the Tennōji sector of Ōsaka city, was excavated in 1955. See Fujishima Genjirō 藤島亥治郎 et al., *Shitennō-ji* 四天王寺 (Tōkyō, 1967).

107. The Yakushi-ji (Yakushi < Skt. Bhaisajyaguru, the Buddha of Healing) was conceived by Temmu Tennō in 680, when his consort (subsequently the Empress Jitō) fell ill (*Nihon Shoki*, vol. 2, p. 29; Aston trans., vol. 2, p. 348), but it was not completed until near the end of the century. See Fukuyama Toshio and Kuno Takeshi 福山敏男 久野健, *Yakushi-ji* 藥師寺, 2d ed. (Tōkyō, 1963); Machida Kōichi 町田甲一 *Yakushi-ji* 藥師寺 (Tōkyō, 1960); and Tamura Yoshinobu 田村丹澄, *Yakushi-ji* 藥師寺 (Ōsaka, 1965). This Yakushi-ji also incorporated for the first time in Japanese temple design the feature of the paired pagodas, borrowed directly from the Sillan Sach'onwang-sa 四天王寺 but ultimately from the Hwangnyong-sa (皇龍寺 = Jap. Kōryū-ji), also in Silla.

108. Jap. Gunshuri-ji.

109. See Ishida Mosaku 石田茂作, *Hōryū-ji* 法隆寺 (Tōkyō, 1970); Mizuno Seichi 水野清一, *Hōryū-ji* 法隆寺 (Tōkyō, 1965); Murata Jirō and Ueno Teruo 村田治郎 上野照夫, *Hōryū-ji* 法隆寺 (Tōkyō, 1960); Machida Kōichi, "A Historical survey of the controversy as to whether the Hōryū-ji was rebuilt or not," *Acta Asiatica* 15 (1968): 87-115.

110. For 伽藍 < sōgarama 僧伽藍 < Skt. *saṁgharāma*.

111. Tō < sotoba 窣塔婆 < Skt. *stūpa*.

112. In the earliest temples, the Koma *shaku* (尺), which was slightly longer than the Japanese foot (= 1.158 English foot), was the standard unit of measurement; it was apparently introduced from Korea by the craftsmen who worked on the Asuka-dera (see p.216, above). In the construction of the Kawahara-ji a composite unit was employed, and, in the Yakushi-ji, the Kara *shaku* or Chinese foot, which later became the standard unit in Nara Japan.

113. *Nihon Shoki*, vol. 2, p. 279; Aston trans., vol. 2, p. 205. Construction of the new capital had been initiated by Empress Kōgyoku earlier in the same year (*Nihon Shoki*, vol. 2, pp. 260-61; Aston trans., vol. 2, p. 190).

114. Kidder, *Early Buddhist Japan*, p. 74; *Nihon Shoki*, vol. 2, pp. 438-39; Aston trans., vol. 2, p. 344: but see note 119, below.

115. Ōsaka Shiritsu Daigaku 大阪市立大學, Naniwa kyūshi kenkyūkai 難波宮址研究會 (Ōsaka, 1958); Yamane Tokutaro 山根徳太郎, *Naniwa no miya* 難波の宮 (Tōkyō, 1964); "Naniwa no chotei" 難波の朝庭, in Ueda Masaaki 上田

正昭 , ed., *Asuka to Nara* 飛鳥と奈良 (Tōkyō, 1967), pp. 164-67; *Naniwa ōchō* 難波王朝 (Tōkyō, 1969).

116. *Nihon Shoki*, vol. 2, pp. 366-67; Aston trans., vol. 2, p. 285. For investigations of the Ōtsu palace see Higo Kazuo 肥後和男, *Ōtsu kyōshi no ken-kyū* 大津京阯の研究, 2 vols. (1929-31).

117. *Nihon Shoki*, vol. 2, pp. 406-7; Aston trans., vol. 2, p. 320. Whether or not Temmu was influenced by the popular resentment that, according to the *Nihon Shoki*, vol. 2, pp. 366-67 (Aston trans., vol. 2, p. 286), manifested itself in satirical ditties and arson is a moot point, but the fact that the transference of a capital from one point to another within the Yamato area should have occasioned unrest is itself some indication of the degree of centralization exercised by the court.

The transitoriness of the imperial capitals of the Yamato period was a stock theme for poets of later ages. The rise and fall of Ōtsu was rendered as follows by Kakinomoto Hitomaro 柿本人麻呂, usually considered the greatest of the Man'yō poets:

> Since the era of that sage Sovereign [i.e., Jimmu Tennō]
>   At the palace of Kashihara
> Under the hill of Unebi,
> All the Sovereigns born to the Throne,
> Reign after reign, ruled the under-heaven,
> Remaining in Yamato;
> Then the Emperor, a god,
> Forsaking the ancient land,
> Crossed the hills of Nara,
> And, though I know not what he meant,
> Held court at Ōtsu of Sasanami
> In the land of Ōmi,
> Remote place as it was.
>
> But now, though I am told his royal palace towered here,
> And they say here rose its lofty halls,
> Only the spring weeds grow luxuriantly
> And the spring sun is dimmed with mists.
> As I see these ruins of the mighty palace
> My heart is heavy with sorrows!
>
> . . . .
>   [Nippon Gakujutsu Shinkōkai translation, in *The Manyōshū*
>   (New York and London, 1965), p. 27.]

118. *Nihon Shoki*, vol. 2, pp. 280-81; Aston trans., vol. 2, pp. 206-7.

119. Nearly fifty years ago Fujita Masaharu 藤田元春 (*Shakudo sōko* 尺度綜攷 [Tōkyō, 1929]), who had himself conducted excavations at the site of Naniwa, suggested that the city as a whole had been laid out as an orthogonal grid at least as early as the sixth century. He based this belief on two observations: (1) the compound of the Shitennō-ji, allegedly built in 593 on the southern edge of the city, was apparently integrated into a 40-*ken* (間) system of land division; and (2) a similar system obtained in the general area of present-day Senba and Shimanouchi to the northwest of the ancient city. Fujita therefore concluded that the residential sectors, situated between the two areas of 40-*ken* divisions,

had probably conformed to the same grid pattern. Subsequently, Fujioka Kenjirō
(*Toshi bunmei*, pp. 158-60) questioned whether the two sections of the grid that
have been reconstructed (and which he interpreted as parts of an archaic version
of the *jōrisei*) did in fact continue across the terrain occupied by the intervening city. He has, however, made the interesting observation that they closely
resembled the lattice within which was fitted the fourth-century Sillan capital
of Kumsŏng.

What the excavations of Professor Yamane Tokutarō (*Naniwa no miya*, passim)
have established beyond doubt is that the palace-complex of Nagahara Toyosaki was
located to the north of the Yodo River on the site of present-day Ōsaka castle.
Subsequently, Emperor Temmu's palace was raised on the same site, surviving
remains of the two structures being distinguishable only by the sizes of their
pillar sockets. For a recent short account of the early Chinese-style capitals
in Japan see Fujioka, *Toshi bunmei*, pp. 154-83.

120. *Nihon Shoki*, vol. 2, pp. 406-7; Aston trans., vol. 2, p. 320.

121. Cf. Kidder, *Early Buddhist Japan*, p. 64.

122. John W. Hall, "Kyoto as historical background," in Hall and Jeffrey P.
Mass, *Medieval Japan: Essays in institutional history* (New Haven and London,
1974, p. 5.

123. *Nihon Shoki*, vol. 2, pp. 454-55; Aston trans., vol. 2, p. 357.

124. *Nihon Shoki*, vol. 2, pp. 460-61; Aston trans., vol. 2, p. 362. For
the attribution of the idea of a new capital to Temmu Tennō, and for reasons supporting the belief that this emperor was responsible for the overall plan of
Fujiwara, see Kishi Toshio 岸俊男, *Asuka kara Heijō e* 飛鳥から平城へ, in
Tsuboi Kiyotari 坪井清足 and Kishi, eds., *Kodai no Nihon: 5, Kinki*, 古代の日
本：5 近畿 (Tōkyō, 1970).

125. *Nihon Shoki*, vol. 2, pp. 506-7, 511-13, 515-17, 522-23, 524-25, 526-
27; Aston trans., vol. 2, pp. 400, 401, 404, 408, 413, 414, 417.

126. Kudō Yoshiaki 工藤圭章, *Fujiwara-kyū* 藤原宮 (Tōkyō, 1967), p. 27.
Another not unreasonable estimate is 3 km. x 2; see Kojima Shunji 小島俊次,
Nara-ken no kokogaku 奈良県の考古学, vol. 1 of Saitō Tadashi 斎藤忠, ed.,
Kyōdo Kōkogaku Sōsho, 郷土考古学叢書 (Tōkyō, 1965).

127. *Nihon Shoki*, vol. 2, pp. 491-93; Aston trans., vol. 2, pp. 387-88.

128. See Giuseppe Tucci, *The Theory and practice of the maṇḍala* (London,
1961); Alex Wayman, *The Buddhist Tantras* (New York, 1973), chap. 9; Toganoo Shōun
梅尾祥雲, *Mandara no kenkyū* 曼荼羅の研究 (Kōyasan, 1958).

129. Kishi Tetsuo 岸哲男, *Asuka kokyō* 飛鳥古京 (Tōkyō, 1970). See also
Tamura Yoshinaga 田村吉永, *Asuka-kyō Fujiwara-kyō kōshō* 飛鳥京藤原京考証
(Kyōtō, 1965); Ōshima Nobujirō 大島延次郎, *Nihon toshi hattatsushi* 日本都市発
達史 (Tōkyō, 1954), pp. 46-47.

130. We have in mind here not only the highly generalized but apparently
durable models of urban internal structure that are associated with the names of

E. W. Burgess, Homer Hoyt, Chauncy D. Harris, and Edward L. Ullman, but also the pervasive manner in which zonal and sector thinking has influenced studies of urban population densities and bid-rent models of urban land values in general. See Burgess, "The Growth of the city: An introduction to a research project," *Publications of the American Sociological Society* 18 (1924): 85-97, reprinted in Robert E. Park, E. W. Burgess, and R. D. McKenzie, *The City* (Chicago, 1925), pp. 47-62; Hoyt, *The Structure and growth of residential neighborhoods in American cities* (Washington, D.C., 1939); Harris and Ullman, "The Nature of cities," *Annals of the American Academy of Political and Social Science* 242 (1945): 7-17; M. R. Davie, "The pattern of urban growth," in G. P. Murdock, ed., *Studies in the Science of Society* (New Haven, 1937), pp. 133-61, reprinted in G. A. Theodorson, *Studies in human ecology* (New York, 1961); W. Alonso, *Location and land use: Toward a general theory of land rent* (Cambridge, Mass., 1964); L. Wingo, *Transportation and urban land* (Washington, D.C., 1961); R. F. Muth, "The Spatial structure of the housing market," *Papers and Proceedings of the Regional Science Association* 7 (1962): 207-20; Colin Clark, "Urban population densities," *Journal of the Royal Statistical Society* ser. A 114 (1951): 490-96; Brian J. L. Berry, J. W. Simmons, and R. J. Tennant, "Urban population densities: Structure and change," *Geographical Review* 53 (1963): 389-405; B. E. Newling, "The Spatial variation of urban population densities," ibid. 59 (1969): 242-52.

Leo F. Schnore's neoecological interpretation of urban spatial structure is essentially the re-presentation of the Burgess model in the form of a deductive theory (see his "On the spatial structure of cities in the two Americas," in Philip M. Hauser and Leo F. Schnore, *The Study of urbanization* [New York, 1965], pp. 347-98), while the social area analysis popular during the 1950s and early 1960s often turned out to be a means for harmonizing the three classic models of urban spatial structure with which we began this note. See E. Shevky and W. Bell, *Social area analysis: Theory, illustrative application and computational procedures* (Stanford, 1955); M. D. Van Arsdol, S. F. Camilleri, and C. F. Schmid, "The Generality of urban social area indices," *American Sociological Review* 23 (1958): 277-84; D. T. Herbert, "Social area analysis: A British study," *Urban Studies* 4 (1967): 41-60.

131. Wheatley, *The Pivot of the four quarters: A preliminary enquiry into the origins and character of the ancient Chinese city* (Edinburgh and Chicago, 1971), chap. 1.

132. Ibid., chap. 2. See also Wheatley, "Archaeology and the Chinese city," *World Archaeology* 2, no. 2 (1970): 171-72 (several paragraphs of this paper have been partially reproduced in the present section); Miyazaki Ichisada宮崎市定, "Shina jōkaku no kigen isetsu," *Rekishi to Chiri*支那城廓の起源異說 歷史と地理32 (1933): 3.

133. Marcel Granet, *Chinese civilization* (New York, 1958), p. 250 (translation of *La Civilisation chinoise*, 2d ed. [Paris, 1948]).

134. Chüan 12, fol. 14, of the 1886 edition. A nucleus of what was later
to be constituted as the *Chou Li* seems to have been in existence in some form
late in the Chou era, for it was among the works most actively suppressed by Shih
Huang-ti in 213 B.C. In the middle of the second century B.C. a copy in archaic
script, which had somehow escaped the proscription, was presented to the imperial
library, where, about 40 B.C., it came to the notice of Liu Hsiang 劉 向.
Unfortunately, the concluding section was missing, and it was as a replacement
for it that Liu Hsiang substituted the *K'ao-kung Chi*.

135. The attribution of a cosmomagical numerology to the design of Han
Ch'ang-an (8 longitudinal avenues, 9 latitudinal ones, 3 palaces, 3 temples, 9
governmental halls [*fu* 麻], 12 gates, 16 bridges, and so forth) must be accounted an attempt of later ages to bring the capital of the prestigious Former Han
dynasty into conformity with the canonical prescription. The primary reason for
the failure to translate this prescription into practice in the first place was
probably that the idea had not been fully formalized by the Confucian scholars of
the time. For excavations on the site of Han Ch'ang-an see Wang Chung-shu 王 仲
殊, "Han Ch'ang-an Ch'eng k'ao-ku kung-tso-ti ch'u-pu shou-huo," *K'ao-ku T'ung-
hsin*漢長安城考古工作的初步收穫 考古通訊, no. 5 (1957), pp. 102-10, and "Han
Ch'ang-an Ch'eng k'ao-ku kung-tso shou-huo hsü-chi," *K'ao-ku T'ung-hsin*漢長安
城考古工作收穫續記考古通訊, no. 4 (1958), pp. 23-32. The restoration of
the ritual structures in the heart of the city has been described by Wang Shih-
jen, "Han Ch'ang-an Ch'eng nan-chiao li-chih-chien-chu (Ta-t'u-men-Ts'un i-chih)
yüan-chuang-ti t'ui-ts'e, *K'ao-ku* 汉长安城南郊礼制建筑(大土门村遗址)原
状的推测考古, no. 9 (1963), pp. 501-15. The morphology of the city is discussed by Ku Yen-wu 顧炎武, *Li-tai ti-wang chai-ching chi*歷代帝王宅京記,
chap. 4: "Han Ch'ang-an ku-ch'eng"漢長安故城. The Ch'in capital that preceded Ch'ang-an on the same site is very imperfectly known, but it appears to
have exhibited a strong longitudinal axiality, and it possibly incorporated a
degree of astral symbolism; see Ssǔ-ma Ch'ien 司馬遷, *Shih Chi* 史記, chüan
6, fol. 23v; Wheatley, *The Pivot*, p. 442. For a cartographic representation (not
a "plan" as such) of the ancient city see Shan-hsi [Shensi] Sheng Po-wu-kuan Pien
陝西省博物館編(principal author Wu Po-lun 武伯綸), *Hsi-an li-shih shu-
lüeh*西安歷史述略(Hsi-an, 1959), between pp. 48 and 49. On Han cities in
general see Ichisada Miyazaki [*sic*], "Les Villes en Chine à l'époque des Han,"
T'oung Pao 48 (1960): 376-92.

136. Ho Ping-ti, "Lo-yang, A.D. 495-534: A Study of physical and socioeconomic planning of a metropolitan area," *Harvard Journal of Asiatic Studies* 26
(1965-66): 52-101. Not until the middle of the 1950s were the literary texts
relating to Northern Wei Lo-yang, which had been receiving a certain amount of
scholarly attention during the earlier decades of this century, supplemented by
reports of an archeological survey. Even then the expedition was exploratory in
purpose, being concerned almost wholly with defining locations and delimiting the

boundaries of the city. See W. C. White, *Tombs of old Lo-yang* (Shanghai, 1934)
and *Tomb tile pictures of ancient China* (Toronto, 1939); Lao Kan 勞幹 , "Pei-
Wei Lo-yang-Ch'eng-t'u-ti fu-yüan," *Kuo-li Chung-yang Yen-chiu-yüan Li-shih Yü-
yen Yen-chiu-so*北魏洛陽城圖的復原 國立中央研究院歷史語言研究所
20A (1948): 229-312; Mori Shikazō森鹿三, "Hokugi rakuyō-jō no kibo ni tsuite,"
*Tōyōshi Kenkyū*北魏洛陽城の規模について 東洋史研究11, pt. 4 (1952):
317-30; Fan Hsiang-yung范祥雍, *Lo-yang Ch'ieh-lan Chi chiao-chu*洛陽伽藍記校注
(Shanghai, 1958); Chou Tsu-mo 周祖謨, *Lo-yang Ch'ieh-lan Chi chiao-shih*洛陽
伽藍記校釋(Peiching, 1963); Kuo Pao-chün 郭寶鈞, "Lo-yang ku-ch'eng k'an-ch'a
chien-pao," *K'ao-ku T'ung-hsün*洛陽古城勘察簡報 考古通訊1 (1955): 9-21;
Yen Wen-ju 閻文儒, "Lo-yang Han-Wei-Sui-T'ang-ch'eng-chih k'an-ch'a chi," *K'ao-
ku Hsüeh-pao*:洛陽漢魏隋唐城址勘察記考古學報9 (1955): 117-36, and "Sui-
T'ang Tun-tu-ch'eng-ti chien-chu chi ch'i-hsing-chih," *Pei-ching Ta-Hsüeh Hsüeh-
pao: Jen-wen K'o-hsüeh*隋唐東都城的建築及其形制 北京大學學報:人文科
學 4 (1956): 81-100.

137. Wei Shou 魏收 , *Wei Shu* 魏書 (presented to the throne in 554), chüan
60, fol. 8r (I-wen reprint of the Palace edition).

138. The precise reasons why the main markets of Lo-yang were located to
the south of the palace in contravention of the canonical prescription are
unspecified, but it may be significant that the Mang Hills 芒山 approached very
close to the northern edge of the administrative precinct, leaving relatively
little space for other activities. What space did exist was used as a military
parade ground.

139. See Ch'en Yin-k'o陳寅恪, *Sui-T'ang chih-tu yüan-yüan lüeh-lun kao*
隋唐制度淵源略論稿(Ch'un-ch'ing, 1944-45); Naba Toshisada那波利貞,
"Shina shuto-keikakushijō yori Kōsatsushitaru Tō no Chōanjō"支那首都計劃史上よ
り考察したる唐の長安城 , in *Kuwabara Hakushi kanreki kinen Tōyōshi Ronsō*
桑原博士還曆記念 東洋史論叢(Kyōtō, 1931), pp. 1203-69.

140. Wei Cheng 魏徵 et al., *Sui Shu* 隋書(presented to the throne in 636),
chüan 1, fols. 17v-18r; Li Yen-shou 李延壽, *Pei Shih* 北史(659), chüan 11,
fols. 12v-13v; Ssu-ma Kuang 司馬光, *Tzŭ-chih T'ung-chien* 資治通鑑(1084)
(Peiching edition, 1956).

141. Ho, "Lo-Yang," p. 53.

142. As the histories laconically record, "Ch'ang-an was [nothing but]
heaps of earth and wasteland" (Ou-yang Hsiu歐陽修 and Sung Ch'i 宋祁, *Hsin
T'ang-Shu* [presented to the throne in 1060], chüan 10; *Tzŭ-chih T'ung-chien*,
chüan 264).

143. Edward H. Schafer has provided references to medieval and later *lit-
térateurs* who labored to recreate the great city from textual materials, including Pi Yüan 畢沅(1730-97), "the most eminent of all connoisseurs of the famous
metropolis" (Schafer, "The Last years of Ch'ang-an," *Oriens Extremus* 10, pt. 2
[1963]: 170-71).

144. Ho, "Lo-yang," p. 53. For reports on the archeological investigations undertaken since 1956 see Hang Te-chou, Lo Chung-ju and T'ien Hsing-nung杭德州雒忠如　田醒農, "T'ang Ch'ang-an-Ch'eng ti-chi ch'u-pu t'an-ts'e," K'ao-ku Hsüeh-pao唐長安城地基初步探測 考古學報, no. 3 (1958), pp. 79-93; Ma te-chih馬得志, "T'ang-tai Ch'ang-an-Ch'eng k'ao-ku chi-lüeh," K'ao-ku唐代長安城考古紀略 考古, no. 11 (1963), pp. 595-611; Wu Po-lun 武伯綸, "T'ang Ch'ang-an chiao-ch'u-ti yen-chiu," Wen Shih唐長安郊區的研究 文史 3 (1963): 157-83; Chung-Kuo K'o-Hsüeh-Yüan K'ao-Ku-Yen-Chiu-So中國科學院考古研究所, ed., T'ang Ch'ang-an Ta-ming-Kung唐長安大明宮(Peiching, 1959); Liu Chih-p'ing and Fu Hsi-nien刘致平　傅熹年, "Lin-te Tien fu-yüan-ti ch'u-pu yen-chiu," K'ao-ku麟德殿復原的初步研究 考古, no. 7 (1963), pp. 385-402.

Other books and papers bearing on the matter discussed in the following paragraphs include Wan Pai完白, T'ang-tai-ti Ch'ang-an唐代的長安(Shanghai, 1954); Lan Meng-po藍孟博, Hsi-an西安(T'aipei, 1957), pp. 55-84; Hiraoka Takeo平岡武夫, Chōan to Rakuyō長安と洛陽(Kyōtō, 1956); Shan-hsi Sheng Po-wu-kuan Pien, Hsi-an li-shih shu-lüeh (full reference in note 135, above), esp. pp. 71-116; Osvald Sirén, "Tch'ang-ngan au temps des Souei et des T'ang," Revue des Arts Asiatiques 4, no. 1 (1927): 40-46, and no. 2 (1927): 98-104; Arthur F. Wright, "Viewpoints on a city," Ventures 5, no. 1 (1965): 15-23, and "Symbolism and function: Reflections on Changan and other great cities," Journal of Asian Studies 24, no. 4 (1965): 667-79; Jaqueline Tyrwhitt, "The City of Ch'ang-an, capital of the T'ang dynasty of China," Town Planning Review 39, no. 1 (1968): 21-37. The earliest account of Ch'ang-an of which any part survives, and that only a single imperfect chapter, was composed very soon after the design of the city had been adopted by the Japanese court, certainly during the first half of the eighth century. It was written by Wei Shu 韋述 and entitled Liang-ching hsin-chi兩京新記. In about 1075 Sung Min-ch'iu宋敏求used this text as a basis for a history of the city, which he called Ch'ang-an chih長安志(most readily accessible in Pi Yüan's畢沅edition, which constitutes ts'e 11-14 of the Ching-hsün-t'ang nien-i chung ts'ung-shu). In twenty books, this work affords a detailed description of public buildings and city boundaries and of the urban topography in general. At much the same time, Liu Ching-yang劉景陽and Lü Ta-fang呂大防were commissioned to prepare a historical map of the city, which they accomplished at a scale (che fa折法) of 2 inches to the mile (see Chao Yen-wei趙彥衛, Yün-lu man-ch'ao雲麓漫鈔[1206], chüan 2, fol. 11r). This map, titled Ch'ang-an t'u-chi長安圖記, in turn provided a basis for the portfolio of plans drawn up about 1330 by the imperial tutor Li Hao-wen李好文 and called Ch'ang-an chih t'u長安志圖. It is noticeable, however, that there are numerous discrepancies between these plans and Sung Min-ch'iu's topographical description. A lively account of Ch'ang-an as seen by a Japanese in the middle of the ninth century has been preserved in the diary of the Buddhist monk Ennin 圓仁 (or Jikaku Daishi慈學大師(793-864]). This work, whose Japanese title is generally read as *Nittō guhō junrei gyōki* 入唐求法巡禮行記, has been translated in its entirety into English by Edwin O. Reischauer, *Ennin's diary: The record of a pilgrimage to China in search of the Law* (New York, 1955).

145. The precise measurements were 18 *li*, 120 *pu* from east to west and 15 *li*, 175 *pu* from north to south, that is, 9,691 meters x 8,192; these are Hiraoka Takeo's calculations ("Tō no Chōan-jō no koto"唐の長安城の事, *Tōyōshi Kenkyū* 東洋史研究 11 [1952]: 333). Eighteen Chinese feet, actually equivalent to 17 1/2 English feet, was the height of the outer wall after it had been rebuilt in 730. The work was completed in nine periods, each of ten days; see *Tzŭ-chih T'ung-chien*, chüan 213, fol. 10v.

146. 955.5m. x 477.75m., or 3,105.4 ft. x 1,552.7 ft.

147. When the old Sui palace complex was renovated by the T'ang conquerors, it was officially styled Kung Ch'eng 宮城 (Palace City) or Ta Nei 大內. After Kao Tsung removed his permanent residence to the Great Luminous Palace 大明宮 in 662, the name of the Kung Ch'eng was changed to Hsi Nei 西內 (Western Interior), and again in 710 to T'ai-Chi Kung 太極宮 (Palace of the Supreme Ultimate); see Hsü Sung 徐松, *T'ang liang-ching ch'eng-fang k'ao* 唐兩京城坊考 (1810: in *Ts'ung-shu Chi-ch'eng* 叢書集成), vol. 1, pp. 2 and 16.

148. Sometimes called the Nan Nei 南內 (Southern Interior), this palace complex began as a group of mansions for the sons of Jui Tsung. Subsequently Hsüan Tsung (847-60) constituted it as a "traveling" or "temporary" palace (行宮) -- that is, as an informal royal residence.

149. For the symbolism and associations of this name see Schafer, "The Last years of Ch'ang-an," p. 141.

150. 882 meters, or 2,866.5 feet square.

151. See note 170, below.

152. This is Hiraoka's estimate, but direct testimony is lacking; see "Tō no Chōan," p. 334.

153. 477.8 feet.

154. The nucleus of this palace was built by T'ai Tsung in 634 on Dragon-Head Plain 龍首原 as a residence for the retired Emperor Kao Tsu and was named Yung-an Kung 永安宮 (Palace of Eternal Security). On the death of Kao-tsu in the following year, it was renamed the Great Luminous Palace (大明宮), which it remained until the razing of the city in 904 (*Tzŭ-chih T'ung-chien*, chüan 194, fol. 7v; *T'ang liang-ching*, vol. 1, p. 17; Hiraoka, *Tō no Chōan*, pp. 342-43), except for a period in the 660s, when, almost imploringly styled the P'eng-lai Palace 蓬萊宮, it directed an ailing emperor's thoughts to the island of the immortals in the eastern sea.

155. Wright, "Symbolism and function," p. 672.

156. This is the *kun* reading adopted in the Iwanami text, but *keishi* is also possible, if not preferable.

157. This rendering was adopted, if not initiated, by Aston in his transla-

tion of the *Nihon Shoki* (Aston, vol. 2, p. 206) and was subsequently followed by, among others, Robert Karl Reischauer, *Early Japanese history (c. 40 B.C. - A.D. 1167)* (Princeton, 1937), vol. 1, p. 147; G. B. Sansom, *A History of Japan to 1334* (Stanford, Cal., 1958), p. 57, and *Japan: A short cultural history*, rev. ed. (New York, 1962), p. 95.

158. *Shoku Nihongi* 續日本紀, vol. 3, p. 63. The first six *kan* of this work have been rendered into English by J. B. Snellen, "Shoku Nihongi: Chronicles of Japan, continued, from 697-791 A.D.," *Transactions of the Asiatic Society of Japan* 2d ser. 11 (1934): 151-239, and 14 (1937): 209-78. The present reference is to pages 218-20 of the 1937 paper. In this chapter, references are to Saeki Ariyoshi's 佐伯有義 edition of the text in two volumes, constituting vols. 3 and 4 of the *Rikkokushi* 六國史, published by Asahi Shimbun 朝日新聞 (Tōkyō, 1940). The passage in question is cast in a totally Chinese mold and is embellished with quotations from *Wen Hsüan* 文選, *Shih Ching* 詩經, *Tso Chuan* 左傳, *Shu Ching* 書經, and *Chin Shu* 晉書. The empress characterized herself as occupying the Purple Palace 紫宮 (a reference to the Tzŭ Wei-yüan 紫微垣, a zone of some 15 degrees radius enclosing the celestial pole and bounded, on Chinese star maps, by two "barriers" of stars) and noted that it was "an act of imperative statecraft to establish the foundations of the palace by calculating the day and by observing the stars . . . after obtaining the date by divination." The imperial edict also noted that the site of Nara was in harmony with the Four 禽 (that is, the four creatures controlling the cardinal compass directions, namely, the Cerulean Dragon in the East, the Red Phoenix in the South, the White Tiger in the West, and the Dark Turtle in the North) and that divination by both turtle plastra and sticks (a form of sortilege) had confirmed the auspiciousness of the proposed site. Interestingly enough, the edict also prescribed that the roads and bridges should be constructed after the autumn harvest had been gathered in, that is, at a time when the corvée would interfere least with farm work. It may be noted in passing that, in ancient China, autumn was the ritually sanctioned season for construction work; see Wheatley, *The Pivot*, pp. 182-83, and David N. Keightley, "Religion and the rise of urbanism," *Journal of the American Oriental Society* 93, no. 4 (1973): 534.

159. *Shoku Nihongi*, vol. 3, p. 69: 戊寅巡幸平城觀其地形; Snellen trans., 1937, p. 228.

160. Ibid., p. 69; Snellen trans., p. 228.

161. Ibid., p. 70; Snellen trans., p. 229.

162. Ibid., p. 78; Snellen trans., p. 240.

163. The ancient city at Kyŏng-ju is now represented only by sections of its wall, long overgrown by vegetation, and by scattered foundation stones from its former palaces. Archeological investigation has been sporadic, so that the lineaments of the Sillan capital are known only by inference from later literary sources. See Helen B. Chapin, "Kyongju, ancient capital of Silla," *Transactions*

of the Korea Branch of the Royal Asiatic Society 33 (1957): 55-72 (a paper originally read before the Korea Branch of the Royal Asiatic Society in 1948 and published in *Asian Horizons* later in the same year).

164. John W. Reps, *The Making of urban America: A history of city planning
in the United States* (Princeton, 1965).

165. R. Shamasastry, *Kauṭilya's Arthaśāstra* (Mysore, 1956), bk. 2, chap. 4.
Modern views as to the date of the *Arthaśāstra* differ widely, but what is perhaps
the best opinion regards it as an immediately pre-Guptan elaboration of an original Mauryan compilation. If this is indeed the case, then the *Arthaśāstra* was
roughly contemporary with the *Chou Li* as we now know it (see p. 117, above).

Ezekiel (the reference is to chap. 48), one of the four major Hebrew proph-
ets, was active during the first half of the sixth century B.C. The work known
by his name was heavily edited during subsequent centuries. On the same topic
see Numbers 35:1-5.

166. Cf. William D. Pattison, *Beginnings of the American rectangular land
survey system, 1784-1800*, University of Chicago Department of Geography Research
Paper no. 50 (Chicago, 1957), passim; Norman J. W. Thrower, *Original survey and
land subdivision: A comparative study of the form and effect of contrasting
cadastral surveys*, Association of American Geographers Monograph no. 4 (Chicago,
1966), chaps. 1 and 2.

167. See note 170, below.

168. See Roland Martin, *L'Urbanisme dans la Grèce antique* (Paris, 1956),
chap. 2: "L'Ecole milésienne et l'urbanisme fonctionnel." The fact that in Hellenistic cities of this type the blocks invariably exhibited regular and constant
proportions, whereas the streets often did not, indicates that the grid was not
regarded as the determinative element in urban design; rather, it was the uniformity of the block dimensions that generated the gridlike regularity of the
total design.

169. Seki Akira and Aoki Kazuo関晃 青木和夫, "Heijō-kyō," *Nihon
Rekishi Kōza*平城京 日本歴史講座(Tōkyō, 1959); Kishiro Shūichi木代修一,
"Heijō-kyō toshi-seikatsu no ichikōsatsu," *Shichō*平城京都市生活の一考察
史潮1, no. 3 (1931): 61-81; and "Heijō-kyō ni okeru kōbō ni tsuite," *Shichō*平城
京に於ける工房に就いて 史潮4, no. 3 (1934): 78-111; Kamei Katsuichirō
亀井勝一郎, ed., *Heijō-kyū*平城宮(Tōkyō, 1963); Nara Kokuritsu Bunkazai Ken-
kyūjo奈良國立文化財研究所, *Heijōgū hakkutsu chōsa hōkoku*平城宮発掘調
査報告(Tenri, 1958-).

170. The *jōri* system had been prescribed by Article 3 of the Taika Reform
Edict for the apportionment of padi land newly reclaimed and therefore under eminent domain (*Nihon Shoki*, vol. 2, pp. 281-83; Aston trans., vol. 2, p. 208). On
relatively level terrain it resulted in a grid of square bunded fields, each subdivided into thirty-six smaller squares (*tsubo* 坪) with sides of 6 *shaku* 尺 (the
standard *shaku* has been 0.994 English foot, 0.303 meter, though the measure has

in fact varied slightly at different periods). Into this framework, individual
padi fields, 1 *tan* 段 in area, were fitted in a variety of ways, including that
specified in the Reform Edict, namely 30 *bu* 歩 in length and 12 in width. The
Edict allowed for "such arrangements as might be convenient in mountainous or
dissected terrain." Whether the *jōrisei* was in operation in some areas before
646 is unknown, but it was certainly imposed over fairly extensive tracts of padi
land subsequently. Within two decades, for instance, it was evident in the layout and surroundings of the Kawahara temple in Asuka (see p. 108, above), and it
apparently dominated the environs of Fujiwara when that city was laid out by
Empress Jitō early in the 690s. The system was especially well developed in
Yamato, but it has left its traces in scattered areas from Sendai in the north
to as far south as southern Kyūshū. It was progressively abandoned as imperial
landholdings gradually disappeared during the Heian period (781-1167). See Iyanaga Teizo 弥永貞三, "Jōrisei no shomondai" 条里制の諸問題, in Mikami Tsugio
and Narasaki Shōichi 三上次男 楢崎彰一, eds., *Nihon no kōkogaku* 日本の考古学
(Tōkyō, 1967), vol. 7, 205-21; Yonekura Jirō 米倉二郎, *Tōa no shuraku* 東亞の
集落 (Tōkyō, 1960), chaps. 3 and 4, and, in summary, "The Development of the
grid-pattern land allotment system in East Asia," *Proceedings of the International
Geographical Union Regional Conference in Japan 1957* (Tōkyō, 1959), pp. 545-49.
In the *handen* (see p. 91, above) contiguous to Nara (namely, the Kyōnan-, Kyō-
hoku-, and Kyōtō-handen = *handen* to the south, north, and east of the capital),
the sections were numbered in the same manner as the *tsubo* within the capital
(see legend to fig. 9); that is, the section nearest the Daidairi (p. 132, below)
was number 1, and its diagonally opposite section was number 31.

171. For purposes of comparison it may be noted that, in accordance with a
plan devised by the New York State Commissioners between 1807 and 1811, Manhattan
Island as far north as 155th Street was platted with a grid of 12 north-south
avenues, each 100 feet wide, and 155 cross streets, each 66 feet wide. The
resulting blocks, with a few exceptions occasioned by the locational intransi-
gence of some preexisting features, were 600 ft. x 200 ft. See "Commissioners'
remarks," in William Bridges, *Map of the city of New York and Island of Manhattan*
(New York, 1811); I. N. Phelps Stokes, *The Iconography of Manhattan Island, 1498-
1909*, 6 vols. (New York, 1915-28).

172. *Nihon Shoki*, vol. 2, pp. 382-483; Aston trans., vol. 2, pp. 301-81.

173. For Max Weber's discussion of these two forms of government see *Wirtschaft und Gesellschaft: Grundriss der verstehenden Soziologie* (Tübingen, 1925),
vol. 3, chaps. 11 and 12. There is a succinct and systematized contrast between
the bureaucratic apparatus and the system of administration under patrimonial
domain in Reinhard Bendix, *Max Weber: An intellectual portrait* (New York, 1962),
pp. 424-25. For an interpretation of the development of the institution of the
Tennō from a point of view different from that espoused in the present work, see
Manabu Waida, "Sacred kingship in early Japan: An historical introduction," *His-

tory of Religions 15, no. 4 (1976): 319-42.

174. For Weber's definition and discussion of the concept of domination (*Herrschaft*) see *Wirtschaft und Gesellschaft*, vol. 3, chap. 10.

175. Apparently a contraction of the Chinese *t'ien-shen ti-ch'i* 天神地祇 ("deities of heaven and gods of earth"). For a discussion of the difficulties involved in devising an adequate translation of this term see Felicia Gressit Bock, *Engi-Shiki: Procedures of the Engi Era, Books I-V* (Sophia University, Tōkyō, 1970), p. 18. In any case, the *Jingikan* was the organ of government which supervised all officially sponsored shrines in the capital and the provinces and maintained registers of the entire priesthood (*hafuribe* 祝部) and of the religious corporations (*kambe* 神戸). It was located physically within the precincts of the sovereign's palace.

176. In this context the term "household" must be understood to imply not the private apartments of the emperor but rather the whole palace complex. Differences in the degrees of intensity of Chinese influence on the various levels of eighth-century Japanese government are shrewdly evaluated by J. I. Crump in "'Borrowed' T'ang titles and offices in the Yōrō Code," *Occasional Papers of the Center for Japanese Studies, University of Michigan* 2 (1952): 35-58.

177. Part of this terrace can still be seen on the site of the ancient city, a short distance west of present-day Nara. A simplified version of the Daigoku-den has been reconstructed with a high degree of exactitude at Heian Jingū in Kyōtō.

178. These were, of course, the rituals subsequently known as Shintō, but this term was not used during the Nara, or even the Heian, period. Despite the Chinese nomenclature and organizational structure that the reforms of the seventh and eighth centuries had imposed on the *Jingikan*, the forms of worship remained very much what they had been in pre-Taika times. The *saishi* 祭祀, or festivals supervised by the *Jingikan*, for instance, bore no resemblance at all to the ceremonies denoted by the same graphs at the court of T'ang China. See Tsuda Sōkichi 津田左右吉, *Jōdai Nihon no shakai oyobi shisō* 上代日本の社會及び思想 (Tōkyō, 1933), p. 559. For a compendious account of early and institutionalized Shintō see Joseph M. Kitagawa, *Religion in Japanese history* (New York, 1966), pp. 11-16 and 30-33.

179. On this point see Hall, "Kyoto as historical background," pp. 13-14.

180. One preexisting feature of the landscape which could not be fully accommodated to the grid was the tomb of Emperor Suinin.

181. The Kōfuku-ji had already been moved twice previously. Founded by Fujiwara Kamatari in 657 near Yamashina in Yamashiro no Kuni, it had been transferred in 673 to a site near Asuka, where it became the Fujiwara clan temple.

182. This temple had originally been founded by Shōtoku Taishi in 617; it was transferred to a new site in 639 and renamed the Kudaranoō-dera. In 678 it received a third name, the Daikandai-ji, and in 745 it was finally called the Daian-ji.

183. The work of removing the Hōkō-ji (or Gangō-ji) from Asuka to Nara began in 716 and was completed two years later, after which the original temple became known as the original or Hon Gangō-ji 本元興寺.

184. That the Daidairi was not complete when first occupied by the court in 710 is evident from the text of an imperial edict promulgated in 711 (Wadō 4.9.4) that was designed to prevent laborers, brought in from the provinces to work on the palace, from absconding (Snellen, *Shoku Nihongi*, trans., 1937, p. 244).

185. Archeological investigation has recovered little of interest on the site of the Saidai-ji, but the early texts refer to it with admiration. See Asano Kiyoshi 浅野清, "Kodaiji-in no hatten" 古代寺院の発展, in Asano and Kobayashi Yukio 小林行雄, eds., *Sekai Kōkogaku Taikei* 世界考古学大系 (Tō-kyō, 1964), vol. 4, p. 39.

186. Jane Jacobs, *The Death and life of great American cities* (New York, 1961), passim, but esp. the Introduction and chap. 19.

187. For a pertinent discussion of "The Grid as generator," see Leslie Martin in Martin and Lionel March, *Urban space and structures* (Cambridge, Eng., 1972), pp. 6-27. See also Christopher Alexander, "A City is not a tree," *Design*, no. 206 (1966), pp. 46-55.

188. A. R. Radcliffe-Brown, "On social structure," *Journal of the Royal Anthropological Institute* 70 (1940): 5.

189. Elizabeth Sato, "The Early development of the *Shōen*," in Hall and Mass, *Medieval Japan*, p. 92, citing Cornelius J. Kiley, "Property and political authority in early medieval Japan" (Ph.D. diss., Harvard University, 1970), pp. 1-10. For a concise statement on the *ritsuryō* system see Inoue Mitsusada 井上光貞, "Ritsuryō taisei no seiritsu" 律令体制の成立, in *Nihon Rekishi -- Kodai* 日本歴史—古代 (1962), vol. 3, pp. 1-31; for a more detailed treatment see Ishimoda Shō 石母田正, *Nihon no kodai kokka* 日本の古代国家 (Tōkyō, 1971), esp. chap. 3. See also Allan L. Miller, "Ritsuryō Japan: The state as liturgical community," *History of Religions* 11 (1971): 98-121.

190. G. Cameron Hurst III, "The Structure of the Heian court: Some thoughts on the nature of 'familial authority' in Heian Japan," in Hall and Mass, *Medieval Japan*, p. 42 (despite the title of this paper, the author is here referring to Heijō). On the Nara aristocracy in general see Iyanaga Teizō 弥永貞三, *Nara jidai no kizoku to nōmin* 奈良時代の貴族と農民 (Tōkyō, 1950).

191. Yazaki Takeo 矢崎武夫, *Nihon toshi no hatten katei* 日本都市の発展 (Tōkyō, 1969), p. 44.

192. Sawada Goichi 沢田吾一, *Narachō jidai minseikeizai no sūteki kenkyū* 奈良朝時代民政經濟の数的研究 (Tōkyō, 1927), pp. 276-83. This work is a pioneer, though extremely detailed, evaluation of the population statistics available for Heijō. Sawada's figure of 200,000, originally proposed with considerable reservation, has been invoked by countless subsequent authors, but almost always without Sawada's qualification that it related to both the city and

its immediate surroundings; see, for example, Yazaki, *Nihon toshi no hatten katei*, p. 49; Hall, "Kyoto as historical background," p. 6.

193. The *Kugyō* were also known by the elegant style of Moon Nobles 月卿 or, more casually, as *Kantachibe* 上達部.

194. The structure of the Heijō bureaucracy, slightly idealized, was set forth in the Yōrō Codes, drafted in 718 (though not enacted until 757), as preserved in the *Ryō no Gige* 令義解. This latter was a commentary on the *ryō*, prepared, on imperial command, by the Udaijin Kiyowara Natsuno 右大臣清原夏野 in 833 and promulgated in the following year. It has been summarized in several English-language works, but more fully than usual in G. B. (later Sir George) Sansom, "Early Japanese law and administration, Part I," *Transactions of the Asiatic Society of Japan* 2d ser. 9 (1932): 67–109. Strictly speaking, it was the ranks of the officials that varied rather than the structures of the several organizations. Court rank 位 was, as prescribed in the codes, closely correlated with the importance of an office 官. For instance, with few exceptions, all principals were styled *kami*, but distinctions in rank were signified in no uncertain manner by the graph selected to convey that term: 卿 for the head of a ministry (*sho* 省); 大夫 for the master of a Household office (*shiki* 職); 頭 for the director of a bureau (*ryō* 寮); 正 for the director of an office (*tsukasa* 司); 君 for the president of the board of censors (*danjō-tai* 弾正臺); 督 for a general of the guard (*efu* 衛府), and 守 for a governor of a province (*kuni* 國). Similarly, the secretaries of a ministry, a Household office, a bureau, a general office, the board of censors, or a province were all styled *jō*, but the graphs used to denote that term were, respectively, 丞 進 允 佑 忠 and 掾.

195. But see pp. 125–26, above.

196. Specifically, the authority of the *Daibu* 大夫 extended to registers of persons and dwellings, the general welfare of "the populace" (that is, the free people possessing family names), the conditions of lands and houses, labor and taxes, distribution as between free and unfree persons, litigation, trade, markets and warehouses, weights and measures, roads and bridges, guards, police, and the registers of monks and nuns. For most of the Nara period this post carried with it the higher grade of the Fifth Rank, so that the incumbent ranked with the vice-minister (Nakatsukasa no Tayu 中務大輔) in the Ministry of Civil Administration (*Jibushō* 治部省); but in 781 (Kōnin 12) it was raised to the Junior Fourth Rank. Sir George Sansom has compared the post to that of the prefect of a capital city in more modern times ("Early Japanese law, Part I," p. 100). During the Heian period it provided an important stepping-stone to prominence in the careers of numerous aspiring bureaucrats, including the Fujiwara regent, Michinaga.

197. Specifically, the director was charged with responsibility for the quality and circulation of money, the quality of goods, the correctness of weights and measures, the fixing of prices, and, in general, the prevention of

wrongdoing. In these capacities he was a close functional equivalent to the
muḥtasib of the Islāmic world. See, for example, G. E. von Grünebaum, *Medieval
Islam: A study in cultural orientation* (Chicago, 1946), pp. 165-66; M. Gaudefroy-
Demombynes, "Un Magistrat musulman: Le mohtasib," *Journal des Savants* (1947), pp.
33-40.

198. *Ryō no gige* 令義解, in *Kokushi taikei* 國史大系, rev. ed. (Tōkyō,
1966), pp. 75-76. There is a succinct account in English of these household
officials in Hurst, "The Structure of the Heian court," pp. 46-54.

199. Hurst (ibid., pp. 47-54), drawing on Ōae Akira, "Heian jidai no keishi
seido," in Okayama Daigaku, *Hōkei Gakkai Zasshi*, vol. 10, no. 3 (1960), which we
have not consulted.

200. Yazaki, *Nihon toshi no hatten katei*, p. 48.

201. Forced labor (*koeki* 雇役) was common during the first half of the
Nara period but tended to be replaced thereafter by peasants who worked for wages
with which they paid their taxes. Such were known as *wako* 和雇. A type of
forced labor which did survive throughout the Nara period was called *jicho* 仕
丁; it took the form of a requirement for one man from every fifty households.
Wako and *jicho* laborers both received 10 *mon* 文 per day, or enough to buy something between 2 and 3 1/2 *go* 勺 (0.76-1.3 U.S. pints) of unhulled rice (Seki and
Aoki, "Heijō-kyō," p. 253; Yazaki, *Nihon toshi no hatten katei*, p. 48). It is
generally accepted that, during the Nara period, approximately one person in ten
was classified as a slave.

202. Kishiro Shūichi 木代修一, "Jōdai toshi seikatsu no tenkai," *Shin
Nihonshi* 上代都市生活の展開　新日本史(Tōkyo, 1953). Nor was the popula-
tion of the capital exclusively Japanese: there was also a leavening of foreigners, many of whom were attracted to the city by the opportunities it afforded for
Buddhist studies. While they were in Nara, these foreigners, visitors and resi-
dents alike, were under the authority of the Buddhism and Aliens Bureau (*Genba-
ryō* 玄蕃寮). The majority of them were Koreans and Chinese, including some
who were to play a prominent part in the development of the faith. Such, for
example, was Chien Chen 鑑真(Jap. Ganjin: 688-763), who established the Ritsu
Sect in Japan. From farther afield came the Indian ascetic Bodhisena (Jap. Bara-
mon Sōjō 婆羅門僧正= the Brāhmaṇ High Priest), who not only taught Sanskrit and
expounded the *Gaṇḍhavyūha* but also in 752 presided over the dedication ceremony
for the enormous statue of Roshana (Vairocana) which Shōmu Tennō installed in the
Tōdai-ji as the protector of government, capital, and state. Other foreigners
known to have resided in Nara at about the same time included a Cham priest, with
the Japanese name of Buttetsu 佛徹, who was responsible for popularizing the
music of his people at the Japanese court (see Paul Demiéville, "La Musique čame
au Japon," in G. van Oest, ed., *Etudes Asiatiques* 1 [Paris, 1925]: 199-226);
another Cham musician, known in Chinese as Shan T'ing 善聽; a Malaysian whose
name was rendered into Japanese as Gun Hōriki 軍法力 and who provided statues of

bodhisattvas for the great hall of the Tōshōdai-ji; two Sogdians (胡), one of
whom achieved renown as a master of the Vinaya and supervised the construction of
the principal edifice in the Tōshōdai-ji complex; and a Persian physician known
in China as Li the Secret Healer李密醫. For further information on these and
other foreigners in Nara see J. Takakusu, "Le Voyage de Kanshin en Orient (742-
754) par Aomi-no Mabito Genkai (779)," *Bulletin de l'Ecole Française d'Extrême-
Orient* 28, nos. 1-4 (1928): 1-41 and 441-72.

203. Kishiro Shūichi 木代修一, "Heijō-kyō ni okeru kōbō ni tsuite,"
Shichō 平城京に於ける工房に就い 史潮 4, no. 3 (1934): 78-111; Yazaki,
Nihon toshi no hatten katei, pp. 48-49. It is recorded that some especially
skilled craftsmen, often of foreign origin, made as much as 60 *mon* a day and,
working under orders from government officials, employed their own assistants
(Seki and Aoki, "Heijō-kyō," pp. 253-57). Not infrequently they were released
wholly or partly from taxation responsibilities.

204. Kishiro Shūichi 木代修一, "Heijō-kyō toshi seikatsu no ichikōsatsu,"
Shichō 平城京都市生活の一考察 史潮 1, no. 3 (1931): 61-81.

205. It must be remembered that Buddhist scriptures were copied not only
for practical purposes but as a means of acquiring merit. It followed that
scribes were employed in this work by the central administration (where official
copying bureaus existed in the imperial palace and in the empress's household),
by temples and monasteries (it has been estimated that nearly half the documents
in the Shōsōin relate to such matters), and by pious individuals who hoped to
supplement their *karma* by financing the production of Buddhist texts, often
superbly illuminated and enclosed in costly cases.

206. Murayama Shūichi 村山修一, *Nihon toshi seikatsu no genryū* 日本都市
生活の源流 (Kyōtō, 1953; republished [*sic*], 1955), p. 3 of the 1955 edition.

207. Kishiro, "Heijō-kyō toshi seikatsu no ichikōsatsu," p. 80.

208. The dominant modes of economic integration are defined, illustrated,
and elaborated in Talcott Parsons and Neil J. Smelser, *Economy and society: A
study in the integration of economic and social theory* (London, 1956); Smelser,
"A Comparative view of exchange systems," *Economic Development and Cultural
Change* 7 (1959): 173-82, and *The Sociology of economic life* (Englewood Cliffs,
N.J., 1963). For a summary and evaluation of two decades of highly relevant discussions that have centered on the implications of the semantic dichotomy between
economics in the substantivist sense of the provision of material goods and in
the formal sense of rationalizing calculation see Scott Cook, "'Structural sub-
stantivism': A critical review of Marshall Sahlins' *Stone Age Economics*," *Comparative Studies in Society and History* 16, no. 3 (1974): 355-79.

209. See, for example, Aoki Kazuo 青木和夫, "Ritsuryō zaisei" 律令財
政 *Iwanami kōza Nihon rekishi* 岩波講座日本歴史, vol. 3, Kodai 古代 III (Tōkyō, 1964), pp. 117-46; Iyanaga Teizō 弥永貞三, "Ritsuryōsei tochi shoyū,"
律令制的土地所有 ibid., pp. 35-78. See also Hans Adalbert Dettmer, *Die*

Steuergesetzgebung der Nara-Zeit (Wiesbaden, 1959), passim. For a detailed discussion of the inspectorate which was developed to ensure the accuracy of provincial statistics see Francine Herail, "Yodo no tsukai 四度使 ou le système des quatre envoyés," *Bulletin de la Maison Franco-Japonaise*, n.s. 8, no. 2 (Paris, 1966), esp. chap. 7: "Les Envoyés à l'époque de Nara."

210. Following are a few representative instances of a centrifugal flow of goods and services outward from the capital, recorded in volume 3 of the *Shoku Nihongi* for the early years of Heijō: the "poor and pitiable" are given a ration of rice (pp. 59, 62; Snellen trans. [1937], pp. 214, 218); clothes and food are bestowed on the aged (pp. 62, 84; Snellen, pp. 217, 246); medicaments are dispatched to districts stricken with disease (pp. 63, 67, 78, 86; Snellen, pp. 218, 224, 239, 248); mothers of triplets are granted rice and cloth (pp. 83, 102; Snellen, pp. 244, 265); districts reporting auspicious happenings are relieved of the corvée (p. 89; Snellen, p. 252); taxes are remitted in times of crop failure and famine (pp. 82, 98, 104; Snellen, pp. 240, 260, 267); and exemption from taxation and corvée is granted for meritorious conduct (pp. 74, 104; Snellen, pp. 235, 267). The granting of tax relief to the distressed was a prerogative of the *Minbushō* (see p. 134, above).

211. *Shoku Nihongi*, vol. 3, p. 86; Snellen, 1937, p. 249. In any case it should be remembered that the Japanese adoption of Buddhism was to a very large extent expediential in intent, designed to achieve certain integrative aims; as Joseph M. Kitagawa has phrased it, "Buddhism was not the salvation of the people but the protection of the state" (*Religion in Japanese history*, p. 35).

212. J. Murdoch, *A History of Japan* (London, 1925), vol. 1, p. 195.

213. Anton Deimel, "Sumerische Tempelwirtschaft zur Zeit Urukaginas und seiner Vorgänger," *Analecta Orientalia* (Rome, 1931), vol. 2. For a discussion of the economic functions and organization of the Tōdai-ji, officially the Great State Temple (*Sōkokubun-ji*; see p. 137, above), see Hiraoka Jōkai 平岡定海, *Tōdai-ji no rekishi* 東大寺の歴史 (Tōkyō, 1961), pp. 128-41. See also Ishida Mosaku 石田茂作, *Tōdai-ji to Kokubun-ji* 東大寺と國分寺 (Tōkyō, 1959).

214. Kidder, *Early Buddhist Japan*, pls. 14 and 15, and p. 199. Other tallies are pictured in Tsuboi Kiyotari 坪井清足, "Heijō kyuseki to hakkutsu chosa" 平城宮跡と発掘調査, in Kishi Toshio 岸俊男 et al., *Tenpyō Nara zeminaru* 天平奈良ゼミナール (Tōkyō, 1973), pp. 114-17.

215. Kidder, *Early Buddhist Japan*, pl. 16, pp. 199-200.

216. Cf. *Man'yōshū* 6, 933-34:

> Our Sovereign has come to dwell
>   At the Palace of wave-bright Naniwa,
> Where he rules his realm
> Eternally as endure the heaven and earth
> And ever long as shine the sun and moon.
> As a daily tribute from Awaji,
> The Land of Imperial Purveyance,
> Nujima's fisher-folk dive for abalone pearls

Deep to the bottom of the sea,
And gather many from amid the ocean rocks,
And carry them in boats rowed abreast,
So rendering service to his Majesty —
What a noble scene to watch!

Envoi

In the calm of morning
The sound of oars is heard —
It must be the boats of Nujima's fisher-folk
From the Land of Imperial Purveyance.

[Nippon Gakujutsu Shinkōkai translation]

217. It is noticeable, however, that the markets of Heijō, fitted into the urban plat between the great seventh and eighth cross-avenues, were relatively farther removed from the palace complex than the main market places of Ch'ang-an were removed from the administrative complex. For the results of recent archeological excavations in the Eastern Market see Satō Kōji 佐藤興治, "Heijō-kyō Higashi no Ichi no hakkutsu chōsa: saikin no Heijō-miya no chōsa kara," *Kōkogaku Zasshi* 平城京東市の発掘調査——最近の平城宮の調査から 考古學雜誌 vol. 61, no. 2 (1975).

218. Notably, when farm products were exchanged in the city for other goods with which to make tax payments.

219. From among numerous instances: in the fifth month of 711, the price of unhulled rice was fixed at one *mon* 文 for 6 *masu* 升 (*Shoku Nihongi*, vol. 3, p. 82; Snellen, 1937, p. 243); and in the eleventh month it was decreed that the maximum interest rate on rice loans was not to exceed 50 per cent.

220. The oldest coins to have survived in Japan are a few Chinese cash of the Han dynasty that have been recovered from Yayoi burial sites. They were clearly in the nature of heirlooms rather than currency. It is difficult to know what importance should be attached to the statement in the *Nihon Shoki*, under a date corresponding to the year 487, that a *koku* 斛 of rice sold for a single piece of silver (*Nihon Shoki*, vol. 1, pp. 524-25; Aston trans., vol. 1, p. 391). At its face value the notice would imply that some sort of silver coinage was in circulation at the time; but in the context of the passage, which is praising the peace and prosperity of a former age, the reference might well have been, as Aston suggested (ibid.), a retrojection of eighth-century practice, perhaps inspired by recollections from Chinese literature.

221. Kidder, *Early Buddhist Japan*, p. 25.

222. *Nihon Shoki*, vol. 2, p. 415; Aston trans., vol. 2, p. 325.

223. Ibid., pp. 457-59; Aston, p. 360.

224. Ibid., pp. 510-11; Aston p. 403.

225. Ibid., pp. 524-25; Aston, p. 414.

226. *Shoku Nihongi*, vol. 3, pp. 5 and 7; Snellen, 1934, pp. 173 and 176.

227. Ibid., pp. 7 and 8; Snellen, 1934, pp. 176 and 177.

228. Ibid., pp. 61–62; Snellen, 1937, p. 217.

229. Ibid., pp. 67 and 68; Snellen, 1937, pp. 224 and 226. It is possible that coins had been minted unofficially prior to 708. Kidder, among others, suggests that that year saw not the first production of an indigenous coinage but rather the beginning of a serious attempt, inspired by the recent discovery of readily accessible copper deposits, to replace barter as the basis of exchange by market transactions (*Early Buddhist Japan*, p. 26).

230. On these topics generally see Kita Shinroku 喜田新六, "Narachō ni okeru senka no kachi to ryūtsū to ni tsuite," *Shigaku Zasshi* 奈良朝に於ける錢貨の價値と流通とに就いて 史學雜誌 44 (1933): 1–58; Hosokawa Kameichi 細川亀市, *Jōdai kahei keizai shi* 上代貨幣經濟史 (Tōkyō, 1934); Delmer M. Brown, *Money economy in Medieval Japan: A study in the use of coins*, Far Eastern Association Monograph no. 1 (New Haven, Conn., 1951), Introduction; Kidder, *Early Buddhist Japan*, chap. 2.

231. The four provinces originally included in the Shi-Kinai 四畿内 were Yamato 大和, Kawachi 河内, Settsu 攝津, and Yamashiro 山城. Izumi 和泉 was added in 716 to form the Go-Kinai.

232. Prior to the promulgation of the supplementary code (*shiki* 式) of 715 the *sato* was denoted by the graph 里; see *Izumo fudoki* (Aoki trans.), p. 81.

233. "Ryō no gige," in Kuroita Katsumi, ed., *Kokushi taikei*, vol. 22, pp. 61–62.

234. To the general scheme outlined here there were two exceptions. The provinces of Tsu and Chikuzen were accorded special treatment on the grounds that the former included Naniwa, the usual port of entry for foreign envoys on their way to the capital, while the chief settlement of the latter, by reason of its proximity to the Korean peninsula, functioned as a military outpost protecting the southwestern approaches from actual piratical raids and from anticipated but unfulfilled Korean attacks. The governors of both these provinces held higher rank than their counterparts in other provinces.

235. Fujioka Kenjirō 藤岡二郎, *Toshi to kōtsūro no rekishi chirigakuteki kenkyū* 都市と交通路の歴史地理学的研究 (Tōkyō, 1960); Asaka Yukio 浅香幸雄, ed., *Nihon no rekish chiri* 日本の歴史地理 (Tōkyō, 1966), pp. 34–42.

236. Kudo, in Asano and Kobayashi, eds., *Sekai Kōkogaku Taikei*, vol. 4, p. 17.

237. Kidder, *Early Buddhist Japan*, p. 50; Kagamiyama Takeshi 鏡山猛, *Kitakyūshū no kodai iseki* 北九州の古代遺跡 (Tōkyō, 1956), pp. 143–96. The prestige of the Dazai-fu was so great that it was often referred to as the Distant Court (*Tō-no-mikado* 遠の朝廷).

238. Cf. Saitō Tadashi 斎藤忠, "Saikin ni okeru tojōshi no kenkyū," *Nihon no Machi* 最近に於ける都城址の研究 日本の町 (Tōkyō, 1958); Yazaki, *Nihon toshi no hatten katei*, p. 52.

239. Sakamoto Tarō 坂本太郎, *Jōdai ekisei no kenkyū* 上代駅制の研究

235

(Tōkyō, 1928), passim. According to the *Engi-Shiki* (延喜式), the main Japanese highway, or *tairo* 大路, in the tenth century, and almost certainly during the two preceding centuries, was the San'indō 山陰道, which ran through the circuit of that name to link the capital to the country's second largest city, Dazai-fu in Kyūshū. The two routes leading east, along the coast (the Tōkaidō) and across the mountains (the Tōsandō), respectively, were classified as secondary roads (*chūro* 中路), and all the rest as lesser roads (*shōro* 小路). Along these roads, at distances appropriate to the difficulty of the route and the availability of water and grazing, post stations were set up to provide couriers traveling on government business with lodging, horses, and the necessities of the journey (see "Ryō no gige," *Kokushi taikei*, p. 274). Aoki suggests that they were also expected to supply food and lodging for troops in times of military mobilization, perhaps in return for certain tax reliefs (*Izumo fudoki*, p. 28). The personnel of a post station normally consisted of several households under the supervision of an *ekichō* 駅長, appointed by and responsible to the governor of the district. According to the Taihō Code, an *ekichō* was supposed to be allocated 2 *chō* of padi land by the central government as a subsidy for the operation of his station ("Ryō no gige," p. 113). Certain of his employees were also exempted from the labor tax.

240. The concept of metropolitan primacy was first proposed by Mark Jefferson, "The Law of the primate city," *Geographical Review* 29, no. 2 (1939): 226-32. See also Arnold S. Linsky, "Some generalizations concerning primate cities," *Annals of the Association of American Geographers* 55, no. 3 (1965): 506-13; Surinder K. Mehta, "Some demographic and economic correlates of primate cities: A case for revaluation," *Demography* 1, no. 2 (1964): 136-47.

241. Francine Herail, "Yodo no tsukai 四度使 ou le système des quatre envoyés," *Bulletin de la Maison Franco-Japonaise* n.s. 8, no. 2 (Paris, 1966): i.

Index

海岳平生苏之癖冢久里

使汝禊帖出来良难美也

俄波和须禊可标郡出